THE FATHERS
OF THE CHURCH

A NEW TRANSLATION

VOLUME 54

THE FATHERS OF THE CHURCH

A NEW TRANSLATION

EDITORIAL BOARD

ROY JOSEPH DEFERRARI
The Catholic University of America
Editorial Director

MSGR. JAMES A. MAGNER
The Catholic University of America

BERNARD M. PEEBLES
The Catholic University of America

MARTIN R. P. MCGUIRE
The Catholic University of America

REV. THOMES HALTON
The Catholic University of America

ROBERT P. RUSSELL, O.S.A.
Villanova University

WILLIAM R. TONGUE
The Catholic University of America

HERMIGILD DRESSLER, O.F.M.
The Catholic University of America

REV. PETER J. RAHILL
The Catholic University of America

SISTER M. JOSEPHINE BRENNAN, I.H.M.
Marywood College

LACTANTIUS
THE MINOR WORKS

Translated by
SISTER MARY FRANCIS McDONALD, O.P.

Mount Saint Mary-on-the-Hudson
Newburgh, New York

THE CATHOLIC UNIVERSITY OF AMERICA PRESS
Washington, D. C. 20017

NIHIL OBSTAT:

REVEREND HARRY A. ECHLE
Censor Librorum

IMPRIMATUR:

✠PATRICK A. O'BOYLE, D.D.
Archbishop of Washington

May 14, 1965

The *nihil obstat* and *imprimatur* are official declarations that a book or pamphlet is free of doctrinal or moral error. No implication is contained therein that those who have granted the *nihil obstat* and the *imprimatur* agree with the content, opinions, or statements expressed.

Library of Congress Catalog Card No.: 64-18669

Copyright © 1965 by
THE CATHOLIC UNIVERSITY OF AMERICA PRESS, INC.
All rights reserved
ISBN 978-0-8132-2826-6 (pbk.)

MAGISTRIS MEIS

CONTENTS

	Page
PREFACE	ix
THE WORKMANSHIP OF GOD	3
THE WRATH OF GOD	59
THE DEATHS OF THE PERSECUTORS	119
THE PHOENIX	207
ATTRIBUTED WORKS	223
INDICES	231
LIST OF VOLUMES PUBLISHED	243

PREFACE

THE MAJOR WRITING of Lucius Caelius (Caecilius) Firmianus, or Lactantius, as he is generally called, is entitled *Divinae institutiones (The Divine Institutes)*. This apology for Christianity, which might be called 'An Introduction to the True Religion,' was directed to the intellectuals, both the pagans and the recent converts to Christianity, of the author's own lifetime, the first years of the fourth century. It is a splendid thesis, a vindication of reason and faith, in spite of the many places where the author betrays looseness of argument and shallowness of thought. The work is characterized chiefly by a profound sense of the moral efficacy of Christianity. It is because of this quality that the work has maintained place and value throughout the ages; the world ever seems to be in need of moral regeneration. The translation of *The Divine Institutes* appeared as Volume 49 of this series.

The present volume contains the other writings of Lactantius: *De opificio Dei (The Workmanship of God); De ira Dei (The Wrath of God); De mortibus persecutorum (The Deaths of the Persecutors);* and the poems attributed to Lactantius, *De ave phoenice (The Phoenix)*, and *De passione Domini (The Passion of the Lord)*. The Phoenix is generally considered among the genuine Lactantian writings, but the Passion poem is quite certainly of a later period, perhaps even of Renaissance times. For this reason, the poem is included here in an appendix, together with a fragmentary piece, *De motibus animi (On the Affections of the Soul)*, a remnant perhaps of a work which bore this title. Each of these lesser writings is preceded by a separate introduction. A general introduction to the life and times of Lactantius is given in Volume 49 of this series.

Just as for the *Institutiones,* the text used for the works translated in this volume is that of S. Brandt and G. Laubmann, *L. Caeli Firmiani Lactantii Opera Omnia, Corpus Scriptorum Ecclesiasticorum Latinorum,* 27 (Vienna 1897). For the *De mortibus persecutorum,* however, special use was made of the best text and general study available to date, that of J. Moreau, *Lactance: De la mort des persécuteurs* in *Sources Chrétiennes* 39 (Paris 1954).

THE WORKMANSHIP OF GOD

(DE OPIFICIO DEI)

INTRODUCTION

HE DE OPIFICIO DEI *(The Workmanship of God)* is the first work of Lactantius to have been preserved for us. It is perhaps his first Christian work, and, as he states himself in the first chapter, his purpose was to provide some philosophical subject matter for the learned, 'the philosophers' of the religion to which he had been recently converted. Written about 304 or 305, in the period immediately after he had had to resign his chair of rhetoric at Bithynia because of the persecution of 303, the work is not at all allusive to the times during which he was living and writing. It is the production of leisure, of an enforced leisure, due without doubt to the rigors of the persecution in that area.

The task which Lactantius set for himself in the work is no slight one. He attempted to vindicate Divine Providence from the attacks of ancient as well as current schools of thought which denounced the possibility of there being any divine work back of the production of man. The demonstration of Lactantius makes clear that the highest endowment of man is his rationality; but it also analyzes the physical equipment of man and shows how the perfect adaptation of the parts of the body to their ends can be due to none other than the Divine Artificer.

Although there are sections in which the naïveté of the author seems amusing to modern readers, the work is of value. It is thoroughly imbued with the teachings of Aristotle, Varro (most of whose works are no longer extant), and Cicero, and provides a strong witness, therefore, to a reliable classical tradition, as well as an indication of the biological and psychological theories that were current in his day. It is of value also from its inherent clearness and from the reverent and aesthetic tone which pervades it.

The introduction, chapters 1 to 4, contrasts man with the beasts and shows that God made man superior by endowing him with reason. There follows in chapters 5 to 15 the treatise proper: a full description of the anatomy and physiology of the human body. Chapters 16 to 19 treat of the psychology of man, the important concepts of the life-principle, soul, mind, sense, etc. In chapter 20, he concludes by promising a more comprehensive exposition of the Christian doctrines against the false philosophies. This, of course, he fulfilled in his writing of the *Divinae institutiones*.

The work is rational in its tone and in its sources, although it is profoundly reverent and devout throughout. As usual, Lactantius does not call on Christian authorities, but he relies on the masters whose pronouncements he had been trained to uphold. The work serves with Augustine's *City of God* as a good source for much of the lost writing of Varro. Fuller accounts on the source material which Lactantius used for this treatise are the following:

Brandt, S. 'Ueber die Quellen von Laktanz' Schrift "De Opificio Dei," ' *Wiener Studien* 13 (1891) 2.255-292.

Pease, A. S. 'Caeli Enarrant,' *Harvard Theological Review* (1941) 163-200.

Rosetti, L. ' "De Opificio Dei" di Lattanzio e le sue fonti,' *Didaskaleion* 6 (1928) 115-200.

THE WORKMANSHIP OF GOD

Chapter 1

HOW LITTLE REST I AM ENJOYING, and that I am also in the most pressing circumstances, you can judge, Demetrianus,[1] from this little book which I have written for you in language that is almost clumsy and appropriate to the mediocre quality of my talent. My purpose was that you might know of my daily pursuits and that I might not fail you as a teacher even now, but this time a teacher of nobler matter and better doctrine. If you showed yourself to be an eager enough pupil in literary pursuits for nothing more than training in language, how much more docile ought you to be to these truths which pertain to life?

And before you I now profess that I am not impeded by the pressure of anything nor by time, but that I am working out something by which the philosophers of our religion, which we cherish, might become better equipped and more informed in the future. For at present, they are ill regarded and openly rebuked because they live in a way other than what befits wise men, and they conceal vices under the covering of a name. From these vices, they should have been healed, or they should have uprooted them at once in order that they might show by their very lives that the blessed and incorrupt name of wisdom is in accord with their precepts. So I refuse no labor whereby I may instruct at one and the same time both

---

[1] Demetrianus, a former pupil of Lactantius, had become a Christian like himself, and evidently one who would appreciate this type of work. A man educated in the philosophical teachings of the times would welcome this treatise on the Providence of God as manifested in the creation and functioning of the human body.

ourselves and others. Nor can I be forgetful of myself, especially at the time when there is very great need of such remembrance and attention, just as you are aware of the need in your own case, so I hope and desire.

It may be that the demands of public service avert you from true and just works, but it cannot be otherwise than that a mind 'conscious to itself of the right'[2] should gaze repeatedly toward heaven. And I am, indeed, glad that everything which is considered as good is turning out well for you. And things will continue this way if there is no change in the state of your mind. I am afraid, though, that little by little customs and delights, as is usual, will break in upon your soul, and, therefore, I warn you, 'repeating, again and again, will I warn you'[3] not to think of those joys of earth as great or true goods. Those joys are not only deceiving because they are questionable, but they are even insidious because they are sweet.

You know how clever that opponent and adversary of ours is, and likewise often violent, just as we see at present! All the things which can entice he holds as snares, and, indeed, as such subtle ones, that they escape from the eyes of the mind so that they cannot be avoided by human foresight. It is the greatest prudence, therefore, to proceed cautiously, step by step, since all along on each side he inhabits the side paths and he secretly places stumbling blocks in our way. And so that prosperity of yours with which you are now concerned, I urge you for your own good to disdain if you can, or, at least, not to regard it of great importance. Remember your true parent, and in what city you have enrolled yourself, and of what order you are. Surely, you understand my meaning. I do not charge you with pride, of which there is not even a suspicion in you, but these things which I say are to be referred to the mind, not to the body, whose every *system*[4] has

---

2 Vergil, *Aeneid* 1.604.
3 *Ibid.* 3.436.
4 This is the first use in this treatise of the word *ratio*. Its classical meaning is 'reckoning,' 'account,' 'consideration,' etc. The word has a

been so set in order that it might serve the soul as its master and be governed by its nod.

For it is a vessel that is made in a certain way and of an earthen material, in which the soul, that is, the real man himself, is contained.[5] It was fashioned not by Prometheus,[6] as the poets tell, but by the supreme establisher and artificer of things, God, whose divine providence and all-perfect power it is possible neither to grasp with our senses nor to expound in words. I shall attempt, nevertheless, since mention has been made of the body and soul, to explain the fashioning of each as far as the meagerness of my intelligence comprehends it.

I think that this task ought to be undertaken especially for this reason, that Marcus Tullius, a man of exceptional ability, when he had attempted to do this in the fourth book of his *Republic*, restricted within narrow limits material which warranted extensive treatment, superficially selecting only the main points. And that there might not be any excuse why he should not have pursued this matter, he himself has testified that neither desire nor care had been lacking on his part.[7] In his book *On Laws*, when he was summarily considering the same matter, he spoke thus: 'Scipio has sufficiently considered this matter, it seems to me, in those books which you have read.'[8] Afterwards, however, in his work *On the Nature of the Gods*, he tried to follow up the same matter more extensively.[9]

But since he did not handle it adequately even there, I will approach this duty and will boldly take upon myself the function of explaining what a most eloquent man has left almost untouched. Perhaps you may criticize me for attempting a

---

variety of meanings for Lactantius. Here it means 'system' or 'systematic arrangement.' At times it means 'evaluation,' 'manner,' 'nature'; often, too, it means the 'construction-plan,' or 'purpose,' etc. Cf. A. Blaise, *Dictionnaire latin-français des auteurs chrétiens* 696.
5 Cf. Cicero, *De republica* 6.24.26.
6 Prometheus, son of Iapetus and Clymene, brother of Epimetheus. He formed men of clay and animated them by fire from heaven.
7 Cicero, *De republica* 4.1.1.
8 *Ibid. De legibus* 1.9.27.
9 *Ibid. De natura deorum* 2.47ff.

discussion on obscure matters since you see men, commonly called philosophers,[10] of such great temerity that they investigate without hesitation those things which God wished to be abstruse and hidden; and that they delve into the nature of things heavenly and earthly which are far removed from us and which cannot be surveyed by the eyes or touched with the hand or perceived by the senses. Nevertheless, they so discuss the nature of all these things that they wish the matters that they bring forth to seem proved and understood. For what reason, then, should anyone think it offensive of us to wish to examine and study the plan or arrangement of our body? For surely this is not obscure because from the very functions of the members and the uses of the several parts we can understand with what great power of Providence each has been made.

Chapter 2

Our Artificer and Parent, God, gave to man sense and rationality that it might be clear from this that we are made by Him, because He Himself is Intelligence, He Himself is Sense and Reason. Although He has not granted that rational faculty to other living things, still He provided in advance how their life might be more secure. He covered them all with natural skins formed from themselves by which they could more easily withstand the force of frosts and cold. Moreover, He has established for the individual kinds each its own protection in repelling external attacks, so that the weaker animals may either oppose the stronger animals with natural weapons, or withdraw from danger by the swiftness of flight, or that the

---

10 Philosophers are 'the wise.' The term is given a special, ironical significance here. Earlier (1.2) it was used to refer to the intelligentsia among the Christians, but in this connotation we must recognize the sarcasm implied.

ones which, at the same time, lack strength and speed may protect themselves by cunning or secure shelters of hiding.[1] And so others of them are suspended in the air by the aid of light feathers or are supported by hoofs or equipped with horns; some have armor in their mouths, teeth, or hooked claws on their feet; none lacks a protection for its own defense.

But if any fall the prey of greater ones, in order, however, that their kind might not utterly perish, either they have been relegated to a region where the stronger kind cannot exist, or they have received an abundant fertility in reproduction so that they might supply food for those beasts which are nourished on their blood, and also so that their very multitude might survive the slaughter brought upon them and be able to preserve their kind.

Man, however, having been granted reason and the power of perception and speech, was made without the gifts of those things bestowed on other animals, because wisdom could make up for what the condition of his nature had denied. God made man naked and unarmed because he could be armed by his abilities and clothed by his reason. How marvelously the very things which are given to brutes and denied to man are ordered unto the beauty of man defies expression. For if He had added to man the teeth of wild beasts, or horns, or claws, or hoofs, or a tail, or hair of varied hues, who does not realize how unsightly an animal he would be? And in the same way, would not dumb animals be unseemly if they were made naked and unarmed? If you take from these the natural clothing of their bodies or the means by which they arm themselves, they can be neither beautiful nor secure. Thus, if you consider utility, they are marvelously equipped, and if beauty, they are wonderfully adorned. Thus is utility marvelously in accord with beauty.[2]

But since God made man an eternal and immortal animal,

---
[1] Cf. Minucius Felix 17.10.
[2] Cf. *Inst.* 2.10 (vol. 49, this series). This notion of the combination of utility and beauty is a strong argument with Lactantius.

He armed him not exteriorly as He did the other animals, but interiorly; and He placed his defense not in his body but in his soul. For it would have been superfluous, since He had bestowed what was greatest on him, to have covered him with bodily defenses, especially since these would mar the beauty of the human body. Wherefore, I often marvel at the folly of those philosophers in the wake of Epicurus who condemn the works of nature that they may show that the world is formed and governed by no providence.[3] They assign the origin of things to inseparable and solid bodies from the chance combinations of which all things come to be and have arisen. I pass by the things pertaining to the world itself with which they find fault; in this they are mad, even to the point of ridicule. I take up now that which pertains to the subject which we have at hand.

Chapter 3

They complain that man is born more weak and frail than other animals. For as soon as the others come forth from the womb, they are able at once to stand erect and move about with delight, and they are at once able to endure the air because they have come forth into the light fortified by natural protections. Man, on the other hand, they claim, is cast forth naked and unarmed as from a shipwreck and is hurled upon the miseries of this life. He is able neither to move himself from the place where he has been put forth, nor to seek the nourishment of milk, nor to bear the brunt of weather. So they say that nature is not the mother of the human race, but a stepmother. She has been very liberal with the dumb beasts, but she has produced man in such a way that needy, and weak,[1] and in want of all aid he can do nothing else but indicate his condition by wailing and weep-

---

[3] Cf. Epicurus, frg. 372 (Usener, p. 250).

[1] Cf. Cicero, *De republica* 3.1.2; Lucretius, *De rerum natura* 5.223-226.

ing, that is 'as one for whom there remains in life only the passage of evils.'[2]

When they say these things, they are believed to be very wise, because each one without consideration is displeased with his own situation. But I contend that they are never so unwise as when they say these things. For considering the condition of things, I understand that nothing ought to be done otherwise. I do not say that nothing could be done otherwise, for God is all powerful, but it is of necessity that that Most Provident Majesty did what was better and more right.

We may, therefore, question those critics of the divine works as to what they think is lacking in man because he is born weaker. Are men for this reason less instructed? Do they advance the less to the full vigor of age? Is their weakness an impediment to their growth or safety, since reason makes up for what is wanting? 'But the training of man,' they say, 'consists of the greatest struggle. Certainly, the condition of beasts is better, because when these have brought forth their young, they have no care except for their own food. And from this it is brought about that, their teats being distended of their own accord, the nourishment of milk is bestowed upon the young and they get this by the force of nature without any trouble to the mothers.'

What about birds? They have a different nature. Do they not undertake the greatest labors in training their young, so that sometimes they seem to have a portion of human intelligence? They build nests of mud, or they make them of twigs and leaves. Even doing without food, they sit upon their eggs; and, since it is not given to them to nourish their young from their own bodies, they bring them food and spend whole days in doing this, and at night they defend, cherish, and protect them. What more can men do for their young except this alone, perhaps, that, when they are grown, they do not drive them away but keep them bound by perpetual relationship

---

[2] Lucretius, *De rerum natura* 5.227.

and bonds of charity? What about the fact that the offspring of birds is much more frail than that of man, since they do not bring forth the animal itself but that which being warmed by the fostering heat of the mother's body becomes the animal? Also, what of the fact that even when it has been animated and is breathing, still, however, without feathers and tender, it lacks the ability, not only of flying, but also of walking? Would not someone be extremely absurd to think that nature had acted badly in the case of birds; in the first place, because they are born twice,[3] and, then, because they are born so weak that they have to be nourished by food obtained through the labor of their parents? But those critics pick out stronger animals and pass by the weaker.

I ask, therefore, those who prefer the condition of beasts to their own, what they would choose if God should give them the opportunity to select. Would they prefer the wisdom of human beings along with their weakness, or the strength of the beasts along with their natures?[4] Surely, they are not so beastlike as not to prefer even much greater weakness than we now have, provided it is human, to that strength that is irrational. Prudent men, of course, desire neither the reason of man with weakness nor the strength of beasts without reason. Why is it necessary—and this is nothing very repugnant or very inconsistent—that either reason or the condition of nature equip each animal? If it is equipped with natural defenses, reason is superfluous. For what will it devise? What will it make? What will it construct? In what will it display that light of genius, since those things which would be the effect of reason nature provides of its own accord? On the other hand, if it is endowed with reason, what will be the need of defenses of the body when, once the reason has been granted, it can fulfill the office of nature? Indeed, this reason has so much power for adorning and protecting man that nothing greater and better could have been given by God. Finally, al-

---
3 Cf. Isidore, *Origines* 12.7.79.
4 Cf. similar references in *Inst.* 5.11 (vol. 49, this series).

though man has a body that is not great, since his strength is slight, and since he is of weak health, nevertheless, because what he has received is greater, he is better equipped and more adorned than the other animals. Although he is born frail and weak, yet he is safe from all the dumb animals. And all those which are born stronger, even though they strongly withstand the force of the elements, are not able, however, to be safe from man. So it is that reason confers more on man than nature does on beasts, since in them neither greatness of strength nor vigor of body can bring it about that they are not suppressed by us or subject to our power.

Can anyone, therefore, when he sees even elephants with their tremendous bulk and strength in the service of man, complain about the Maker of things, God, because he has received only moderate strength, a small body, and not rather consider the divine benefits toward himself as they deserve to be considered? This would be in keeping with an ungrateful, or to put it more accurately, an insane man. Plato, in order to refute these ungrateful people, I believe, 'gave thanks to nature that he was born a man.'[5] How much better and more sound he who realized that the condition of man was better than those who preferred to have been born beasts! But if, perchance, God should change them into the animals whose lot they prefer to their own, they would surely desire to return at once, and with great clamor they would demand their former condition; because strength and vigor of body are not of such great importance that you would want to be without the function of speech, nor the free passage of the birds through the air such a thing that you would want to be in need of hands! The hands are more important than the lightness and use of wings, and the tongue of more value than the strength of a whole body. What madness, then, is it to prefer those things which, if they were given, you would be unwilling to accept.

---

5 Cf. Plutarch, *Life of Marius* 46.

Chapter 4

Then, too, people complain that man is subjected to sicknesses and untimely death.[1] They are incensed, in fact, that they have not been born gods. 'Not at all,' they will say, 'but from this we demonstrate that man was not made with any providence, and it should have been otherwise.' What if I show that this itself, namely, that man could be vexed with sicknesses and his life often be broken off in the midst of its course was provided for with great reason? For since God knew that the animal which He had made would pass of its own accord to death, in order that it might be able to take that very death which is the dissolution of nature, He gave it weakness which comes upon the approach to death for the dissolution of the animal. If it were of such a strength so that sickness and affliction could not come near it, death could not either, because death is a consequence of sickness.

How, then, would he be free from an untimely death for whom a timely one has been settled? They, mind you, would have no man die except when he has completed a hundred years of life. How could there be any reason for them in such great opposition of things? For in order that someone could not die before he was a hundred, he would have to have bestowed on him something of immortal strength, and upon this grant, the condition of death would, of necessity, be excluded. But what sort of thing could this be which would make man strong and impregnable against sicknesses and external assaults? Since he is composed of bones and sinews and flesh and blood, which of these can be so firm as to resist weakness and death? And for man, therefore, to be indissoluble before that time which they think ought to have been established for him, from what material would they fashion a body for him? All things which can be seen and touched are fragile.

---

1 Cf. Lucretius 5.222ff. Perhaps Lactantius used here a work of Seneca, *De immatura morte;* cf. *Inst.* 1.5; 3.12 (vol. 49, this series).

They would have to resort to seeking something from heaven since there is nothing upon earth that is not weak.

Since, then, man was to be so formed by God that he would die at some time, the matter itself demanded that he be made of an earthly and weak body. It is necessary, therefore, that he should receive death at some time or other, since he has a body, because any body is soluble and mortal. They are extremely foolish, then, who complain of untimely death, because the condition of nature makes place for it. Thus it will be a consequence that man is subject also to diseases, for nature does not allow infirmity to be absent from that body which is at some time to be dissolved.

But let us suppose that it could be done just as they wish: that men would be born in such a condition, that no one would be liable to sickness or death except one who, after having gone through his course of life, had come to extreme old age. And do they not see, therefore, what follows if he were thus constituted, that for every other time, in fact, it would be in no way possible to die? But if anyone is kept from food by another, he will die. So the case demands that for a man who cannot die before a fixed day there is no need for the nourishment of foods, since they can be taken away. But if there is no need for food, that one is no longer a man; he becomes a god. Therefore, as I have said above, those who complain about the frailty of man complain most of all about this, that they were not born immortal and eternal. 'No one ought to die unless he is old.' But still mortality is not able to be conjoined with immortality. If one is mortal in old age, he cannot be immortal in youth. Neither is the condition of mortality foreign to him who is at some time to die, nor is there any immortality for one for whom a terminus is decided. So it happens that the exclusion of 'immortality in perpetuity' and the admission of 'mortality in time' establish man in the condition of being mortal for any amount of time.

The necessity, therefore, is an appropriate one from all considerations, and it ought not to have been done otherwise.

This would not have been right. Our opponents do not see the reason of the outcomes, because they erred once in the very keypoints of this discussion. For when divine providence was excluded from human affairs, it necessarily followed that all things came into being of their own accord. From this stage, they hit upon those impacts and chance comings together of minute seeds, because they saw no origin of things. And when they had cast themselves into these straits, then, sheer necessity forced them to think that souls were born with their bodies and were also extinguished with them. They had taken it for granted that nothing was done by a divine mind. And this very point they could not prove in any other way than by showing that there were some things in which the determination of Providence seemed to limp. They found fault, therefore, with those things in which Providence marvelously, even exceptionally, expressed its divinity, namely, those things I have referred to concerning sicknesses and untimely death, although they should have considered, when they were assuming these things, what would be a necessary consequence. Those things which I have mentioned are the consequences: for example, if man were not able to get sick, and if he needed neither shelter nor clothing, why should he fear wind or storm or cold, the power of which lies in the fact that they bring on sickness? It is on that account that he has received wisdom, to fortify his weakness against what might harm it. So it follows of necessity that, since he takes sickness for the sake of retaining his reason, he may accept death, too, always, because he to whom death does not come must, of necessity, be strong. Infirmity has within itself the condition of death. But where there is strength, there can be no place for old age or for death either, which follows old age.

Besides, if death were fixed for one certain time of life, man would become exceedingly presumptuous and divested of all humanity. For nearly all the rights of humanity, by which we are united among ourselves, arise from fear and a consciousness of our frailty. In a word, all the weaker and more fearful animals band together to be protected by number since they cannot be protected by strength; whereas, the stronger ones seek solitude because they trust in their power and strength. If man also in the same way had at hand a strength for warding off dangers and did not need the help of any other, what society would there be? What mutual respect would there be? What order? What plan? What humanity? Or what would be more disgraceful than man? What more savage? What more cruel? But since he is weak, and is not able by himself to live apart from man, he seeks society, so that life in common may be both more attractive and more secure.

You see, then, that all the reason of man is established most especially in this, that he is born naked and frail, that he is attacked by sicknesses, and that he is sentenced to an untimely death. If these should be withdrawn from man, then must his reason and wisdom also be withdrawn. But I am spending too long a time on very evident things, since it is clear that nothing was ever made, or could ever be made, without Providence. And if I wished now to discuss in order all of the works of Providence, this treatise would be endless. So I have planned to speak about the body of man only, and just to such an extent as to show how great is the power of Divine Providence in it, restricting the subject, however, to those matters which are perceptible and clear. The things which have to do with the soul can neither be observed by the eyes nor can they be comprehended. Now we will speak about the vessel of man itself, that which we see.

Chapter 5

When God made animals in the beginning, He did not want to gather them into a ball and mass them into a round shape that they might easily be able both to be moved for walking and to turn themselves in any direction, but from the very highest part of the body He extended the head. Likewise, He lengthened out further some of the members called feet, that, being fixed on the ground, they might with alternate movements conduct the animal wherever his mind directed or wherever the necessity of seeking food called him.[1] From the vessel of the body itself He made four projections, two posterior ones which in all animals are the feet, and two which are near the head and neck which offer various uses to animals. In cattle and wild beasts, they are feet like the hind ones, but in man they are hands which are produced not for walking, but for doing and holding. There is a third class in which the front limbs are neither feet nor hands but wings, on which feathers are arranged in order to furnish a means of flying. Thus, the one formation has several varieties and uses.

And that He might gather together closely the very density of the body, for uniting the small and larger bones, He constructed a sort of keel which we call the spine.[2] He did not wish to form this from one single prolonged bone, lest the animal should not have the faculty of walking and bending itself. From the middle part of it, as it were, He has extended in diverse directions the ribs, which are transverse and flat bones. By these, slightly curved and almost drawn into themselves as in a circle as they are, the inward parts are covered, so that those parts which had to be softer and less strong could be fortified by the surrounding grasp of solid framework. On the top of that construction which we have likened to the keel of a ship, He placed the head, in which there might reside the government of the whole living organism. And there was given to it this name, as, indeed, Varro writes to Cicero, because from here the senses and nerves take their beginning.[3]

---

1 Cf. Isidore, *Origines* 11.1.112.
2 Cf. Plutarch, *Placita philosophorum* 5.17.3.
3 Frg. 38 of Varro's *Libri grammatici* (Wilmanns, p. 170). The wordplay or etymological significance is lost in English. The author connects *caput* (head) with *capio* (take). Cf. Isidore, *Origines* 11.1.25; *De differentiis rerum* 17.50.

The parts which we have said were extended from the body for the purpose of walking, or doing things, or flying, He wished to consist of bones, not too long for rapid motion and not too short for strength; and He wanted them to be in number but a few, and these large ones. Now they are either two, as in man, or four, as in the quadrupeds. But He did not make these bones solid, lest slowness and heaviness would be a hindrance in walking. He made them hollow and full of marrow inside for the preservation of the vigor of the body. Again, He did not fashion them evenly to their extremities, but their top parts He rounded into a ball shape with thicker knots, so that they could be more easily bound with sinews and more surely turned, whence they are called joints.[4] These knots, when made firm and solid, He surrounded with a certain soft covering called cartilage, clearly it seems, that they might bend without any rubbing of one against the other or any awareness of pain.

Still, He did not form these in just one manner. Some He made simple and rounded into an orb, in those joints, at least, in which it was necessary for the limbs to move in all directions. This is the case, for example, in the shoulder, because it is necessary for hands to be moved about and twisted wherever one wishes. Others, however, He made broad, and symmetrical, and rounded on one end. This type is evident in those places where just the limbs have to be bent, as in the knees, in the elbows, and in the hands themselves. For as it was at the same time both exceedingly beautiful of appearance and useful that the hands should move in every direction from that place from which they start, so, surely, if this same thing also happened in the case of the elbows, such a movement would be superfluous and unseemly. Then, the hand, having lost the dignity which it now has through its exceptional mobility, would seem to be like a proboscis, and man would be completely snake-handed. This is a marvelous effect in that

---

[4] *Ibid. Origines* 11.1.87.

immense animal, the elephant. God, who displays His providence and power in a wonderful variety and number of things, since He had not extended the head of that animal so far that it could touch the earth with its mouth, which would have been a horrible and hideous thing, and since He had so armed its very mouth with protruding tusks which would prohibit the exercise of feeding even if the mouth could touch the ground, lengthened out between these tusks from the top of the forehead a soft and flexible limb for grasping and holding things, lest the jutting size of the tusks or the shortness of the neck should impede the method of getting food.

Chapter 6

At this point, I cannot refrain from exposing again the foolishness of Epicurus—for all of Lucretius' ravings are his. When Lucretius was showing that animals were produced, not by some fashioning of a divine mind, but, as he put it, 'fortuitously,' he said that, in the beginning of the world, there had been in existence innumerable other living creatures of wondrous form and size, but that they could not continue because either the power of getting food or the means of coming together and reproducing had failed them.[1] Of course, to make place for those atoms of his, he had to rule out Divine Providence. But when he saw that there is a marvelous system of providence existing within all things that breathe, what emptiness for that scoundrel to say that there had existed strange animals in which this system ceased!

Since, therefore, everything that we see has come about by a plan—for nothing except the plan of Providence can effect this very coming to be—it is manifest that nothing could be generated altogether apart from this plan. It was provided

---

1 Cf. Lucretius 5.834ff.

beforehand in the making of each individual kind to what extent of service for the necessities of life its members would be devoted, and how far the offspring, brought forth from the union of bodies, would preserve, each according to its kind, all living creatures. Now, if it is the case when a skilled architect has planned to construct some great building that he, first of all, considers what the highest part of the finished building will be, and measures in advance what place will be for light weight and where the structure shall be fixed to withstand great weight, what the spaces between columns shall be, what shall be the conduits, outlets, and receptacles for falling water, and where these shall be placed (he sees to these things first, I tell you, in order to begin whatever is necessary for the finished work along with the very foundations), why should anyone think that God, in making the animals, did not provide all that would be necessary for living before He gave the life itself? The life surely could not exist unless there were first the means by which it exists.

Epicurus saw, therefore, in the bodies of animals the skill of a divine plan, but, in order to accomplish what he had rashly taken upon himself before,[2] he added another piece of nonsense in accord with the former. He said that the eyes of the body were not created for seeing or the ears for hearing or the feet for walking, since these parts were formed before there was any use of seeing and hearing and walking, but that the functions of all of these came about from them after they were produced.[3] I am afraid that to refute ridiculous fictions of this sort seems no less foolish, but it is all right to be foolish when dealing with one who is foolish, so that he may not think himself too smart. What do you say, Epicurus? That the eyes were not made to see? Why, then, do they see? 'Afterwards,' he says, 'their use appeared.' For the purpose of seeing, therefore, they were produced, inasmuch as they cannot do anything else but see. Likewise for the other members; their

---

[2] Epicurus, frg. 373.
[3] Cf. Lucretius 4.822ff.

very use shows for what purpose they have been produced. It is certain that this use could have no existence unless all the members were made in so ordered a way, so providently that they could have a use.

What if you say that birds were not made to fly, wild beasts were not made to rage, nor fishes to swim, nor men to be wise, when it is apparent that living creatures serve that nature and function toward which each one was produced? But, of course, he who has lost the very essence of truth must ever be in error. And if all things come to be, not by Providence, but by the chance comings together of atoms, why does it never happen by chance that those principles[4] come together in such a way as to effect an animal of such a kind that would hear with its nostrils, smell with its eyes, and see with its ears? If those 'first bodies' leave no kind of position untried, monsters ought to have been produced daily of a sort in which a preposterous arrangement of members and widely different uses would prevail. But since all the kinds and all the parts in each observe their own laws and arrangement and guard the uses attributed to them, it is evident that nothing was made by chance, since the perpetual disposition of the divine plan is preserved. Epicurus, however, we will refute in other circumstances: now let us discuss Providence as we have begun to.

Chapter 7

God, therefore, fastened and bound together the solid parts of the body, which are called bones, knotted and joined one with another by sinews, which the mind might use as checks when it wished to go ahead or stay back.[1] Indeed, without any labor or effort, but with only the least

---

[4] The word is *principia* used in the Lucretian sense of beginnings: 'origins,' 'elements,' 'first particles,' 'atoms.'

[1] Cf. Isidore, *Origines* 11.1.86.

movement, it might moderate and direct the bulk of the whole body. He covered these with the inward organs, those fitting to each part, so that the solid parts might be enclosed and covered. He also mixed with these inward parts veins, streams, as it were, divided through the whole body, so that by coursing through these water and blood might bring moisture to all the members of the body in vital juices.[2] The inward organs, formed in the manner suited to each kind and fitted to its position, He covered by a skin layer. This skin he either adorned with beauty alone, or covered with bristles, or protected with scales, or decorated with distinctive plumage, as the case might be. That was, indeed, a marvelous plan of God's whereby one disposition and one fashioning exhibits innumerable varieties of representations.

For in nearly all things that breathe there is the same grouping and arrangement of members. First, there is the head, and joined to this is the neck; the breast is, likewise, joined to the neck and the shoulders extend from it; adhering to the breast is the belly and subjoined to this cavity are the genital organs; then, lastly, there are the thighs and feet. And not only the members keep their own course of behavior and position in all animals, but even the parts of the members do. In one single head, the ears have a fixed place, the eyes, and the nose as well; then there is the mouth, too, and within it the teeth and tongue. And even though all these things are the same in all animals, yet there is an infinitely manifold diversity of formations, because these parts I have just mentioned are either more drawn out or more contracted and are variously kept together by different lineaments. Why? Is it not something divine that, in such a great number of living creatures, each single animal is most beautiful in the form peculiar to its own kind, so that if anything should be transferred from one to another in turn, of necessity, the result would be such that there could be nothing more confused as to utility,

---

[2] *Ibid.* 11.1.121.

nothing more deformed in appearance? For instance, suppose that you should give a prolonged neck to an elephant or a short one to a camel. Or suppose that you should add feet or hairs to serpents, the stretched out length of body in these requiring nothing else except that marked with spots on their backs and supported by smooth scales, they glide into slippery tracts by winding and turning.[3]

In quadrupeds, however, the same Divine Workman prolonged the construction of the spine, drawn all the way from the top of the head, extended along the outside part of the body, and pointed into a tail. The purpose of this prolonging was so that either the offensive parts of the body might be covered because of their unsightliness or protected because of their tenderness, or so that certain tiny, harmful animals might be warded off from the body by its movement. If this member should be removed, there would be a weak and imperfect animal. But where there is reason and a hand, this tail is not necessary, nor is a covering of hair. Each creature is most apt and fitting in its own kind, so much so that nothing more disgraceful could be imagined than a naked quadruped or a covered man.

But, although the very nakedness of man contributes marvelously to his beauty, still this does not apply also to the head. So God covered the head with hair, and, because it was to be on the top, He adorned it as the top point of the structure.[4] This ornament was not collected into a circle or made even into the shape of a hat, lest it be unsightly to have some parts bare; but in some parts it was supplied bountifully and in others withheld according to the beauty of each place. The forehead, therefore, is encircled and the hair comes forth from the temples in front of the ears. The top part being surrounded as in a crown, and all the back part of the head being covered, the result is an appearance of great beauty. Then,

---
3 *Ibid.* 12.4.2.
4 This is doubtless a borrowing from Varro. Cf. Augustine, *Principia dialecticae* 6; also Isidore, *Origines* 11.1.28.

too, it is incredible how much the nature of the beard matters in distinguishing the maturity of bodies or the difference of sex or the splendor of manliness and strength,[5] so that it seems that the plan of the whole work would not have endured in any way at all, if the arrangement were in any way different from what it now is.

Chapter 8

Now I will show the construction plan of the whole man and of the individual members which are exposed or hidden in the body, and I will explain their uses and habits. When God decided to make man, alone of all the animals, a creature for heaven—and all the others for earth —He raised him upright to behold the heavens and He made him a biped, very probably so that he might look upon the place of his origin.[1] The others, however, He bent toward the earth, so that, since there is no expectation of immortality for them, with the whole body stretched out close to the ground, they might be subject to their stomachs and to food. And so of man alone the right reason, the upright position, and countenance, in close likeness to that of God the Father, bespeak his origin and his Maker.[2] His mind, nearly divine, since it has been assigned the domination not only of the living creatures of the earth, but also of his own body, placed in the top of his head as though on a lofty summit, gazes out upon all things and beholds them.[3] God did not make this

---
5 Cf. Isidore, *De differentiis rerum* 17.53.

1 Cf. *Inst.* 2.1.14-19 (vol. 49, this series); Cicero, *De natura deorum* 2.56.140; Isidore, *De differentiis rerum* 17.47-50.
2 This is a period piece of apologetic writing and serves as an interesting patristic commentary on our traditional Catechism question: Is this likeness (i.e., of man to God) in the body or in the soul? The answer: 'This likeness is chiefly in the soul,' does not, therefore, exclude entirely the notion here stressed by Lactantius. God is spirit, but it is helpful to consider that even our bodies bear some likeness to their Maker.
3 Cf. Cicero, *De natura deorum* 2.56.140; Isidore, *De differentiis rerum* 17.49.

hall or court spread out or prolonged, as in the dumb animals, but like a circle or globe, because the roundness of a circle is of perfect shape and form. The mind, therefore, and that divine fire He covered, as it were, with that vault (of the head).[4] And when He had clothed its top part with a natural garment, He furnished and adorned as well the front part, called the face, with the necessary attendant services of its parts.

First, He enclosed the orbs of the eyes in concave sockets, and Varro thinks that the forehead received its name from the boring of these.[5] God wished them to be neither more nor less than two, because there is no number more perfect, with regard to appearance, than two. So there are two ears also, and it is incredible how much beauty their symmetry brings out, both because each part is adorned similarly, and because voices coming from both sides may be gathered in more easily. Their very shape was fashioned in a wonderful way, because He did not want their openings to be bare and unprotected, which would have been both less beautiful and less useful, since the voice could fly past the narrow passageways of simple caverns if the openings themselves (like those small vessels which are applied to vessels with a narrow opening which are to be filled) did not confine it, after receiving it in hollow windings and keeping it from repercussion.

These ears, then, might get their name *(aures)* from the drinking in *(hauriendis)* of voices,[6] whence from Vergil: 'And with these ears I drank in his voice';[7] or because the Greeks name the voice itself *audēn* from 'hearing' *(auditu)*, and the ears *(aures)*, as though they should have been *audes*, they named by the change of a letter. God, the Maker, did not want to fashion them of soft skins, which by hanging down

---
[4] Cf. Cicero, *De republica* 3.1.1; cf. also Augustine, *Contra Julianum Pelagianum* 4.12.
[5] Cf. Isidore, *Origines* 11.1.35; *De differentiis rerum* 17.53. The Latin for concave sockets is *concavis foraminibus;* therefore, *frons* is made to be related to *foratus.*
[6] *Ibid. Origines* 11.1.46; *De differentiis rerum* 17.55.
[7] Vergil, *Aeneid* 4.359.

and drooping would lessen beauty; nor did He want them to be made of hard and solid bones lest they be useless in their immovableness and rigidity. But He arranged for what would be between these extremes, that a softer cartilage might bind them, and that they might have, at the same time, a befitting and flexible strength. There was constituted in these just the function of hearing as in the eyes that of seeing was placed.

The delicacy of workmanship of the eyes is especially inexplicable and marvelous, because their orbs, which are like gems in that part where they have to see, He covered with transparent membrane, so that the images of objects placed before them, being reflected as in a mirror, might penetrate to interior perception.[8] Through these membranes, therefore, that power of perception called the mind sees through the things which are outside it, lest you might suppose that we see by the incursion of the images, as some of the philosophers prate, because the function of seeing ought to be in that which sees, not in what is seen; or lest you think it happens by the impact of the air upon the pupil, or by the outpouring of the rays, because, if this were so, we would see after we moved our eyes, when the air having contacted the pupil or the rays being poured forth should come to that which would have to be seen. But since we see at the very same moment of time, and since generally, even while we are doing something else, nevertheless, we do behold all things that are placed before us, it is very true and very evident that it is the mind which by means of the eyes sees through to the things placed opposite, as if through windows covered with translucent glass or transparent stone. For this reason, the mind and will are often discerned from the eyes. Now Lucretius, when he was refuting this, made use of an exceedingly inept argument. 'For if the mind,' he says, 'sees through the eyes, it should see better through the sockets of eyes plucked and torn out since more light enters doorways when the doors are pulled back

---

[8] Cf. Isidore, *De differentiis rerum* 17.53.

than when they are obstructed.'⁹ Beyond doubt his eyes, or rather those of Epicurus who was his teacher, had been torn out, so that he did not see that eyeballs plucked out of their sockets, and the fibers or cords of the eyes broken, and blood flowing through veins, and pieces of flesh from the wounds filling up, and scars being spread to the widest extent could admit no light, unless, perhaps, he wished eyes to be produced in the manner of ears so that we would be doing our beholding not so much by the eyes as by openings. And nothing would have been more ugly in appearance and more impractical in function than this.

What a little bit would we be able to see if the mind had to focus its attention from the inmost recesses of the head through the infinitesimal fissures of cavities! So that if one wished to look through a pipe, certainly he would behold no more than the capacity of the pipe would embrace. There was need, therefore, for organs for seeing rather than for accumulations into an eyeball in order that vision might be spread in extent, and that even those things which have a position very near to the face would be able to be beheld freely. Consequently, then, the ineffable power of Divine Providence fashioned two identical eyeballs and controlled them so completely that they could not only be directed and turned entirely, but also be moved and bent partially. The balls themselves He wished to be filled with a clear, liquid substance, and in the middle of these are held enclosed sparks of light which we call pupils. In these delicate apertures is contained the 'special sense' and accoutrements of seeing.¹⁰ Through these eyes, therefore, the mind directs itself to see, and, in a marvelous manner, there is mingled and joined into one the vision or object seen of the two lights.

---

9 Lucretius 3.359ff., 367ff.
10 Cf. Isidore, *De differentiis rerum* 17.54.

Chapter 9

At this point, we may reprehend the vanity of those who, while they wish to show that the senses are false, gather together many things about which the eyes can be mistaken. Among these, they stress even the fact that everything is seen double by those in a rage or intoxicated, as if, indeed, the cause of this error were obscure. Now this happens by reason of the fact that there are two eyes. But listen to how it happens. The power of sight of the eyes rests upon the intention of the mind. And so, since the mind, as was said above, uses the eyes as though they were windows, this happens not only to the insane or intoxicated, but also to the sane and sober. For if you should hold something too close, it will be seen double, because the interval and space whereby the keenness of vision of the two eyes comes together is fixed.

Likewise, if you should call away your mind again, to relax the intention of your mind from thinking, as it were, then the sight of the two eyes is drawn apart and each begins to see separately. If you should strain your mind again and direct your gaze, whatever was being seen double comes together into one (single vision). Why, then, is it strange if the mind, weakened by poison and the power of wine, cannot direct itself for the purpose of seeing, just as the feet weakened from benumbed or stiffened sinews cannot control walking? Or if the force of a madness raging in the brain severs the harmony of functioning of the eyes? And this is, indeed, true, so much so that in no way can it happen to one-eyed men, if they become insane or intoxicated, that they see anything double. Wherefore, if a reason appears why the eyes are deceived, it is manifest that the senses are not false. Either they are not deceived, if they are clear and sound or unmutilated; or if they are deceived, the mind, however, is not deceived which knows their error.

Chapter 10

But let us return to the works of God. In order that the eyes be more protected from injury, He covered them over with coverings of hairs whence Vatro fancied that they were called eyes.[1] The eyelids themselves which are given their name from their movement, that is palpitation,[2] are ramparted by hairs standing in order and furnish an exceedingly fitting enclosure for the eyes. The constant motion of these, taking place with an incomprehensible speed, on the one hand does not impede the course of seeing and on the other restores and renews the gaze. The pupil,[3] that is, a transparent membrane which must not be dried up or parched, wears out unless it shines clear and clean with an ever present humor. Now consider this. Are not the very edges of the eyebrows equipped with short hairs, with ramparts as it were, a protection for the eyes lest anything fall upon them from above, and, at the same time, do they not present a pleasing appearance?[4]

The nose which arises from the ends of the eyes, stretched as though upon an equalizing yoke, at one and the same time both separates and also protects the sight of the two eyes. Below also the not unseemly hill-like swelling of the cheeks gently rising from every part makes the eyes more protected. This was foreseen by the Supreme Artificer, that if any very vehement blow should perhaps befall, it might be repelled by these prominent areas.[5]

The upper part of the nose down to its middle portion is solidly constructed, but the lower part is made pliant by the cartilage inherent to it in order that it might be tractable to

---
1 He uses the verb *occulo* (to cover over) and unites *oculus* (eye) with it.
2 *Palpebrae* (eyelids) and *palpitatio* (their movement).
3 The word is *acies* (keenness of vision) which is often used for the eye itself. Cf. A. Blaise, *op. cit.* 44.
4 Cf. Isidore, *Origines* 11.1.36,39; *De differentiis rerum* 17.54.
5 *Ibid. De differentiis rerum* 17.56.

the hands. In this member, although simple, there are constituted, however, three functions: one, conducting the breath; the second, receiving odors; and the third, the passing through its hollows of the excretions of the head.[6] With how marvelous, with how divine a plan did God arrange these very things so that even the opening of the nose itself would not mar the appearance of the face in any way! And this surely would have been the case if there were to be but one single opening. But just as if by a wall leading through the middle, He fortified and divided it, and He made it quite beautiful by this very division.

We learn from this how much the dual number compacted in one simple structure contributes to the perfection of things. For although the body is one, yet it could not endure entire unless there were parts both left and right. Thus the two feet, and likewise the hands, have power not only for the utility and function of moving and doing, but they also confer a quality of marvelous beauty. So also in the head, which is the summit, as it were, of the whole divine work, by the Supreme Artificer the hearing has been divided between two ears, sight between two eyes, and smell between two nostrils; because the head, in which resides the power of sensing, even though it is one, is separated into two parts by a dividing membrane. The heart, too, which seems to be the residence of wisdom, even though it is one, has two interior folds wherein are contained the fonts of living blood which are divided by a wall between, in order that, just as in the world itself the principal substance of things, either double from single or single from double, controls and contains the whole, so in the body the whole compacted or arranged in twos might present an inseparable unity.

And how useful and how becoming is the fashioning and opening of the mouth (made transversely, as it is) cannot be described. Its usefulness rests in the two functions of taking

---

[6] *Ibid.* 17.57.

food and of speaking.⁷ The tongue is enclosed within it. This determines the voice by its movements in the production of words, and it is the 'interpreter of the mind.'⁸ Yet it cannot alone, and of itself, perform the function of talking, but it must push against its own edge with the palate, or it must be helped by the striking of the teeth and compression of the lips. The teeth, indeed, have a great deal to do with talking, for, on the one hand, infants do not begin to talk before they have teeth, and, on the other hand, old people, when they have lost their teeth, so stammer and babble that they seem to be returning again to infancy. But these matters have to do only with men, or with birds, for in them the tongue, sharpened and vibrating by certain movements, expresses innumerable variations and diverse types of sounds.

The tongue has besides another function. It performs this in all, not in dumb beasts alone; it collects the food broken and chewed by the teeth, gathers it into balls by its own action, and transmits it into the stomach. So Varro thinks that the name of tongue was imposed upon it from the binding of the food.⁹ It also aids the beasts in drinking. For they drink water with it extended and cupped, and the water gathered by the fold of the tongue they flush with quick movement to the palate lest it flow back on account of slowness and delay. Thus this is covered, as it were, by the concave shell of the palate, and God has surrounded it by the enclosure of the teeth as if by a wall.

Our very teeth, lest by being exposed and uncovered they should be rather a horror than a mark of beauty, God embellished with soft gums which are named from the fact that the teeth spring from them,¹⁰ and then with the covering of

---

7 *Ibid.* 17.58; *Origines* 11.1.51.
8 Lucretius 6.1149.
9 Cf. Cicero, *De natura deorum* 2.54.134. The Varronian etymology is again interesting, *lingua* (tongue) related to *ligando* (a binding).
10 Cf. Isidore. *Origines* 11.154; *De differentiis rerum* 17.60. The etymology here accepted is that *gingiva* (gum) is derived from *gigno* (to spring or rise from).

the lips. The hardness of the teeth, just as that of a grinding stone, is greater and rougher than in the other bones in order that they may serve for chewing food and nourishment.

The lips, too, which in the beginning, so to speak, stuck together, how beautifully has the Creator separated them! The upper one under the center of the nostrils, He marked with a certain slight indentation, a kind of valley; the lower, He spread outward smoothly for the sake of appearance. For with regard to what concerns getting a taste, he is mistaken who thinks that this sense resides in the palate. It is the tongue by which tastes are discerned, but yet not entirely: the parts of it which are more delicate on either side draw the taste by the finest of sensory apparatus (taste buds). And although there be no lessening of taste in the actual taking of food or drink, yet, in some inexpressible manner, the taste penetrates to the sense (organ) in the same way as the taking in of an odor causes no loss whatever of the matter of the odor.

How beautiful are the other parts can scarcely be expressed. The chin is drawn down gradually from the cheeks and is finished off below so that a faintly indicated division seems to mark its lowest edge. There is a stiff and also well rounded-off neck,[11] just as though the shoulders were lowered from the head by a pliable yoke. Arms are strong and contracted by sinews for strength, a flourishing physical strength by the brawn of outstanding muscles of the upper arms; the joint of the elbows is both useful and becoming.

What shall I say of the hands, those ministers of reason and wisdom? The Master Artificer fashioned these with a plain and moderately concave surface so that whatever must be grasped can fitly occupy this surface. He terminated them in the fingers in which it is difficult to settle whether appearance or utility is the greater. For their number is perfect and complete; their order and gradation most appropriate; the curvature of matching joints is flexible; the form of the nails, rounded and tightly grasping the ends of the fingers with

---

11 Cf. Isidore, *Origines* 11.1.61.

curved protection lest the softness of the flesh falter in the function of holding, furnishes great ornament. But, on the other hand, there is determination for usefulness in marvelous ways, because of the fact that one, separated from the rest, is produced with the hand itself yet is extended rather early apart from it, and this, as if standing out against the others, proffers itself, and possesses either alone or chiefly the whole faculty of holding and doing, as if it were the rector and moderator of all. From this also it has received its name of thumb because it prevails among the others both in force and power.[12] It has just two outstanding joints (the others have three each), but one is connected with the hand by flesh for reason of beauty. For if the thumb, too, had been separated by three joints, the ugly and unlovely appearance would have taken from the beautiful effect of the hands.

Next, consider the elevated breadth of the chest, and how by being exposed to sight it manifests the wonderful dignity of its condition. And this is because God seems to have formed only man as upright and able to lie with head thrown back—for almost no other animal can lie upon its back—but to have fashioned the beasts as if lying on one side and to have pressed them to the earth. And, therefore, their chests are narrow and removed from sight and cast toward the earth. Man's is broad and erect, because being full of reason bestowed from heaven the breast ought not to be slight or indecent.[13] The nipples also, swelling slightly and circled with darker orbs, add something to appearance. They are given to women for nourishing offspring, but only for ornament to men, lest the breast seem malformed and mutilated, as it were. Next, below is the surface of the stomach; the navel marks the center of this by a not unbecoming indication made for this reason, that the fetus might be nourished thereby while it is in the uterus.[14]

---
12 *Pollex* (thumb) as though from *polleo* (to hold sway over). Cf. Isidore, Origines 11.1.70; *De differentiis rerum* 17.63.
13 *Ibid. Origines* 11.1.92; *De differentiis rerum* 17.64,65.
14 *Ibid. Origines* 11.1.99; *De differentiis rerum* 17.66.

Chapter 11

Of necessity, it follows that I should begin to speak about the inner organs also. Not beauty has been assigned to these parts, since they are concealed, but incredible utility, because there had been need for this earthly body to be nourished by some extraction from food and drink just as the earth itself is by rain and hail. The most Provident Artificer made a receptacle in the center of the body for the foods from which, when they have become digested and liquified, vital juices would be bestowed to all its parts.

But although man consists of body and a life-principle,[1] that receptacle which I mentioned above provides food for the body alone; to the life-principle, however, God has assigned another abode. For He made a certain kind of inner part, soft and of loose texture, which we call the lung. He did not fashion it in the manner of a bag, lest the breath should be exhaled at only one time or breathed in just once. For this reason, then, He made the inner organ full, to be sure, but able to be blown into and capable of holding air,

---
1 This section causes difficulty. It is not quite safe to equate 'life breath' with 'soul' here, although the two meanings are given for the word *anima* which Lactantius uses. In ancient Latin, *anima* meant merely 'the life-principle,' whereas *animus* meant the 'mind' or 'heart' or 'soul' as the seat of intelligence. In later Latin, the distinction ceased to hold, and by Christian times the two words were used for 'the soul.'

We must remember that Lactantius is an early writer and in his day Christian psychological principles had not been expounded with preciseness. In fact, in this particular passage, our author seems to be laboring under confusion. He does not subscribe to Tertullian's doctrine of the corporeality of the soul (*De anima* 5-8), but it is evident here that he does not regard the soul as entirely incorporeal, either. To avoid danger of theological and psychological confusion, therefore, the term *life-principle* is being adopted here as a translation of *anima*, though it would certainly seem more sound to speak of man as composed of body and soul. The discussion, however, is concerned with the physical makeup of man, and, as we continue in the chapter, it is quite clear that Lactantius means the life-principle in relation to the respiratory system. Cf. the article '*Anima*' in the *Thesaurus Linguae Latinae* 2.1.69ff.; also A. Blaise *op. cit.*, 82ff., and J. H. Waszink, *Quinti Septimi Florentis Tertulliani De anima* (Amsterdam, 1947), Introduction pp. 15-18 and pp. 48-49.

so that it might draw in breath gradually, while the vital air is spread throughout that loose texture, and then let the same out again gradually when it relaxes itself. This very alternation of the drawing in and letting out of breath sustains life in the body.

Since, then, there are two principles in man, one of air which nourishes the life-principle, the other of foods which nourish the body, there must be two pipes through the neck, one for food, one for air. One of these leads from the mouth to the stomach, the other from the neck to the lung. The nature and purpose of these two differ.

The one pipe, which is the passage from the mouth, is made soft so that it may always adhere to itself when closed, just as the mouth itself, because drink and food make a passageway for themselves, since they are corporeal, when the throat is moved and opened. The breath, on the other hand, which is incorporeal and slight, because it could not make passage for itself, has received an open way which is called the windpipe.[2] It consists of flexuous and soft bones, as though made of rings compacted and clinging together in the manner of hemlock, and this passageway is always open. For the breath can have no rest from moving; and, since it is always moving, it is restrained, as it were, from a certain rushing out by a portion of a joint let down in an advantageous way from the cerebrum. This is named the uva, and it serves as a check lest the air coming in with suddenness and bearing pestilential contagion might either spoil the tenderness of its domicile, or spread its total power for working harm throughout the interior receptacles. For this reason, also, the nostrils are opened slightly, and for this, too, they are so named, because through them either odor or breath does not cease to flow.[3]

This tube for the breath, however, opens not to the nostrils only, but to the mouth also in the extreme palatal area, where

---

2 Cf. Isidore, *De differentiis rerum* 17.61.
3 *Nares* (nostrils) as though from *no, nare* (to swim or float). Cf. Isidore, *Origines* 11.1.47; *De differentiis rerum* 15.57.

wens of the throat facing toward the uva tend to raise themselves into a tumor.[4] The cause and explanation of this are not obscure. For we would not have the faculty of talking if, just as the passage of the esophagus (throat) is to the mouth only, the windpipe opened into the nostrils only. The 'expert craftsmanship' of God, therefore, opened up a way for the voice from that tube for the breath, so that the tongue might be able to perform its own proper service and to cut by its movements the unhampered course of the voice itself into words. If this flow were blocked off in any way, dumbness would result necessarily. And anyone who thinks that there is another cause why men are dumb is surely in error. For they do not have, as is generally supposed, a tied tongue, but they pour forth that vocal breath through their nostrils, just as though they were lowing or mooing, because either there is no passageway whatsoever for the voice to the mouth, or it is not open in such a way that it can emit a full voice. This is what generally takes place in nature. It also may happen by some accident that this approach, blocked off by some sickness, does not transmit the voice to the tongue and thereby causes dumbness in those who have had the ability to speak.

When this happens, the hearing also is necessarily obstructed, so that, because the apparatus cannot emit the voice, it cannot even admit it. A cause of speaking, therefore, is this opened up passageway. There is proof of that also provided when we use the baths. Since the nostrils cannot bear the heat, the hot air is taken through the mouth; and, likewise, if perchance the phlegm or mucous has closed up the spiraments of the nostrils during colds, we can breathe through the mouth, lest the breath be caught because the means of passage is obstructed.

When foods have been received into the stomach and when they have been mixed with the liquids that have been taken, and when they have been heated by the body heat, their

---

4 The reference here is to the thyroid glands, no doubt, and the swelling associated with goiter.

juices are spread in an indescribable way throughout the parts of the body and inundate and invigorate the entire body. What a marvelous work of God are the intestines also, with their multiple coils and their length with many convolutions yet all connected into one system or chain! When the stomach expels the macerated food from itself, little by little that is pressed out by means of those convolutions of the inner parts, so that whatever juice remains in it, whereby the body is nourished, is divided among all its parts.[5] And yet, so that it may not stick and adhere to any part by chance, which could happen on account of the turnings of those coils often coming back upon themselves, and which would not take place without harm, He has smeared the intestines on the inside with a thicker mucous, so that the purgaments of the stomach may by means of the lubrication make their way more easily to their outlets.

That construction plan, too, is most accurate by which the bladder (which incidentally the birds do not have), since it is separated from the intestines and has no tube whereby it may draw urine from them is filled up, is distended with liquid. It is not difficult to see how this happens. The parts of the intestines which receive the food and drink from the stomach are more open and accessible than the other coils and much more fine. These surround and contain the bladder. When the mixed food and drink come to these parts, a rather solid excrement forms and passes through, but all the liquid seeps through that fineness; and the bladder, whose membrane is equally thin and fine, absorbs and gathers it so that it may emit it where nature has provided the outlet.

Chapter 12

Something must be said also about the uterus and conception, since we are discussing the inner organs. Then

---

5 Cf. Isidore, *De differentiis rerum* 17.68.

we may not seem to have passed over anything. Although these organs lie in concealment, they are not able to keep their reason and purpose concealed. The vessel in males which contains the semen is two-fold, a little interior to the receptacle for waste water. Just as there are two kidneys, there are, likewise, two testes; so there are two seminal vesicles, but cohering in one structure, which can be seen in the bodies of animals when they are cut open. The right one contains the male seed, the left one the female (and in the entire body on the whole the right side is the masculine, the left, feminine). Certain people think that seed comes from the marrow only; some think that it flows from the whole body to the genital tube and congeals there, but how this is done the human mind cannot comprehend.[1]

Likewise in women, the womb is divided into two parts, and these, spread apart and bent back, are folded around like the horns of a ram. The part which twists to the right is the masculine part, that which is on the left, feminine.[2] Varro and Aristotle think that conception takes place thus. They say that the seed is not in males only, but also in the females, and that from this fact those like to the mothers are procreated, but that their blood semen has been purged. Then, if this is rightly mixed with the male's, the two, congealed and coagulated at the same time are formed. First, then, the heart of a man is fashioned, because in it resides life and all wisdom, and then the whole is consummated by the fortieth day.[3] Perhaps these facts have been gathered from abortions. In the fetuses of birds, however, there is no doubt but that the eyes are formed first; this is seen often in eggs. Whence I do not think that the forming takes its start from the head.

They think that the likenesses (to parents) are brought about in the bodies of children in this way. When the seeds

---
[1] Sources of this material are Varro, very probably, and Aristotle, *De generatione animalium* 4.1.
[2] Cf. Isidore, *Origines* 11.1.135.
[3] *Ibid.* 11.1.143; cf. Aristotle, *op. cit.*, 4.3.

which have been mixed among themselves coalesce, if those of the male are in the ascendancy, then the offspring, whether male or female, will be like the father; if the woman's prevail, the offspring of either sex will resemble the mother. Now that of the two parts prevails which is the richer; for in a certain way it embraces and includes the other. Hence, it generally comes about that the features of the one only stand out. If there has been an equal mixing of even semen, the features are also mingled so that the offspring is common, or it seems to resemble neither parent, because it does not have all from the one of the two entirely, since it has borrowed part from each.[4] For we see in the bodies of animals either that the colors of parents are confounded and the third becomes like neither of the parents, or that they are so expressive of both parents that a concordant mixture with different colored parts is effected throughout the whole body.

Different natures also are thought to come about in this way. When it chances that a seed from a male parent falls into the left part of the uterus, the opinion is that a male is begotten, but since it is conceived in the female part, it suffers some female characteristics to hold sway in it more than its masculine splendor: either a beautiful figure, or exceeding whiteness or lightness of the body, or delicate limbs, or short stature, or a soft voice, or a weak mind, or several of these characteristics. Likewise, if seed of a feminine stock flows into the right part, a female is, of course, begotten, but, since it is conceived in the masculine part, then some characteristics of maleness hold sway more than the usual sex classification would permit: either strong limbs, or excessive height, or a ruddy complexion, or a hairy face, or an unlovely countenance, or a heavy voice, or a daring spirit, or several of these. If, however, a masculine seed comes into the right part and a feminine into the left, the two fetuses come forth rightly, so that for the feminine the beauty of its nature holds through-

---

4 Aristotle 4.1; 4.3; cf. Isidore, *Origines* 11.1.145.

out all things, and for the masculine manly strength is preserved both as to the mind and the body.⁵

How marvelous, indeed, is this very institution of God which fashioned the two sexes, male and female, for the preservation of the individual kinds! By the union of the two sexes through the excitement of pleasure, a young child was to be produced, lest the condition of mortality should cause the extinction of the whole race of living beings.⁶ But greater strength was assigned to the males so that women might be more easily forced to suffer the marital yoke. So the male was named man, because strength in him is greater than in woman. Hence, too, courage (or valor) has received its name.⁷ Likewise, woman, as Varro interprets it, is from the word for softness, one letter changed and one taken away, as though (it should have been) *mollier,* rather than *mulier.*⁸ When the fetus is sustained by the woman, and when the time of bringing it forth has begun to draw near, her swelling nipples are distended with sweet juices, and her fecund breast abounds with a font of milk for the nourishment of the child. Nothing else would be fitting than that a wise living creature should draw its nourishment from the breast.⁹ And this was arranged most exceptionally, that the rich white fluid should enrich the tenderness of the new body until it should be equipped with teeth and endowed with strength for taking stronger foods. But let us get back to our subject, so that we may briefly explain the other parts which remain to be treated.

Chapter 13

Now I could explain to you the marvelous workings of the genital parts of the body also if modesty did not hold

---
5 Aristotle, Book 5, *passim.*
6 Cf. Cyprian, *De zelo et livore* 15.
7 The word-play is on *vir* (man) and *virtus* (courage, strength, manliness).
8 Cf. Varro, *De lingua Latina* 5.73; Cicero, *Disputationes Tusculanae* 2.18.44; Isidore, *Origines* 11.2.17,18; *De differentiis rerum* 17.82.
9 Aristotle 4.8; cf. Isidore, *De differentiis rerum* 17.65.

me away from a discussion of this type. And so let those matters which ought to be reverenced be veiled by us by a covering of reticence. With reference to the matter at hand, it is sufficient to complain that impious and profane men commit the greatest crime, who, in themselves, turn this divine and admirable work of God, foreseen and planned by His unfathomable design for the propagation of the race, into either the basest gain or filthy works of obscene lustfulness, so that they no longer seek anything from this most holy institution of sex other than empty and sterile pleasure.

Now what? The remaining parts of the body do not lack plan and beauty, do they? How fitted for the function of sitting is the flesh gathered and rounded into the buttocks! And this is more firm than in other parts, lest it should give way to the bones with the pressure of the weight of the body.[1] Likewise, consider the length of the thighs, drawn out and made strong by wider flesh parts by which is sustained the weight of the body more easily. The knees mark the limit of this length as it is gradually contracted into a narrow portion, and their beautiful joints provide a most suitable bending for the feet for walking and sitting. And the legs are not drawn out in an even shape all the way lest an unbecoming appearance should deform the feet, but they are both strengthened and adorned by well-turned calves which gently swell and gradually lessen.

In the soles of the feet, also, there is the usual construction-plan, yet very different from that in the hands. For since these are the foundation, as it were, of the whole construction, the Wondrous Artificer did not form them with a round shape, lest man be unable to stand on them or need other feet for standing as do the quadrupeds; but He made them longer and more extended in shape, so that they might make the body steady by their flatness, whence their name was given

---

1 Cf. Isidore, *Origines* 11.1.101; *De differentiis rerum* 17.70.

to them.² The toes, the same in number as the fingers, displaying beauty in appearance rather than utility, are, therefore, joined and short and arranged in gradation. The largest of these, since it was not necessary for it to be separated from the others, as is the case in the hand, has been arranged so that it seems to differ from the others only in size and in the slight space between. This beautiful closeness of the toes strengthens the tread of the feet by no slight aid, for we cannot be stirred to running unless, the toes being pressed to the ground and leaning against the soil, we take an impetus and a leap.³

I think that I have given an explanation of all the parts of which the plan can be understood. Now I come to those which are either doubtful or obscure.

Chapter 14

It is granted that there are many things in the body whose force and purpose no one can perceive except the One who made them. Or does someone think that he can explain the advantage, or the effect, of that slight transparent membrane by which the stomach is netted over and covered? What of the twin-like likeness of the kidneys? Varro says that these are so called 'because streams of waste moisture arise from them.'¹ This is far from the case, because lying on either side of the spine, they cohere and are separated from the intestines. What is the function of the spleen? What about the liver? These organs seem to be made up of disordered blood, as it were. What of the very bitter moisture of the gall? What is the reason of the globe of the heart? Unless perhaps we shall think that they ought to be

---

2 Ibid. *Origines* 11.1.113; *De differentiis rerum* 17.71. *Planta* (soles) is related to *planities* (levelness).
3 Ibid. *De differentiis rerum* 17.72.

1 The Varronian etymology is that *rienes* (an old form of *renes*, kidneys) is from *rivi* (streams).

believed who hold that the affection of anger is placed in the gall, that of fear in the heart, and that of joy in the spleen.[2] But they hold that the function of the liver is to digest the food in the stomach by means of its warmth and embracing position. Some think that the desires of sexual relations are placed in the liver.

In the first place, the sharpness of human sense cannot perceive those things because their functions lie concealed, nor, when opened out, do they demonstrate their uses. For if such were the case, perhaps the animals which are more gentle would have either no gall at all or less than the wild beasts; the more timid would have more of heart, the more lustful the more of liver; and the more lascivious would have the more of spleen. As, therefore, we know that we hear with our ears, see with our eyes, and smell with our nostrils, so surely we would know that we are angry with the gall, that we desire with the liver, that we rejoice with the spleen. But since we do not at all perceive from what part those affections come, it is possible that they may come from another source, and that those organs may have an effect other than what we think. On the other hand, we cannot be sure that those who hold these things speak falsely. I think, however, that all things which pertain to the movements of the mind and soul are so obscure and of such a lofty plan that it is beyond man to see through them clearly. Nonetheless, this ought to be certain and undoubted that so many parts and so many kinds of organs have one and the same function, namely, that they contain the life-principle within the body. But what particular function is assigned to each, who can know, except the Artificer to whom alone His own work is known?

Chapter 15

Concerning the voice, now what account can we render? Grammarians, of course, and philosophers define the voice

---

2 Cf. Isidore, *De differentiis rerum* 17.66.

as air struck by breath, whence words get their name.¹ But this is manifestly false. For the voice is not produced outside the mouth, but within it; therefore, that opinion is more likely the true one which holds that the breath which has been compressed, presses out the sound of the voice when it has been dashed against the obstacle of the jaws. This is like what happens when we blow breath into an open pipe placed under our lips. That breath, reverberated by the hollowness of the pipe and rolled back from the bottom, while striving for an outlet, and pierces by its onrush the descending breath, produces sound, and the wind, rebounding of itself, is animated into vocal breath. But, indeed, whether this is true let God, the Artificer, see. For the voice seems to arise, not from the mouth, but from the depths of the breast. And, in fact, even when the mouth is closed, a sort of sound can be given forth from the nostrils. Besides, too, the voice is not effected by the very great breath by which we pant; it is effected as often as we wish by a light and not compressed breath. It has not been understood, therefore, in what manner this takes place or just what it is at all. And do not think that I am now falling into the opinion of the Academy,² because not all things are incomprehensible. It must be admitted that many things are not known which God has wished to be beyond the intelligence of man, so, on the other hand, it must be admitted that there are many things which can be perceived by the senses and grasped by reason. But we shall be making this an entire disputation against the philosophers; therefore, let us complete the matter which is our course at present.

---

1 Cf. Augustine, *Principia dialecticae* 5. The common source is probably again Varro. *Verbum* (word) is related to *verbero* (to beat, blast, or lash).
2 Later followers of Plato had reduced some of his theories on ideas to absurdities of doubt and cynicism.

Chapter 16

Who does not know (except the one who has no mind at all) that the nature of the mind, too, is incomprehensible? Since it is not known in what place the mind itself is, or what sort it is, various opinions, therefore, have been discussed by the philosophers concerning its nature and location.[1] But I will not dissimulate what I myself think, not that I affirm that this is so, because to act thus in a doubtful matter is the part of a fool. But I am speaking so that, when the difficulty of the thing has been set forth, you may have a notion of how tremendous is the grandeur of the divine works.

Certain ones have claimed that the seat of the mind is in the breast. But if this is so, how great a marvel is it that a thing situated in an obscure and dark habitation is engaged in such great light of reason and intelligence! Then, consider the fact that to it the senses from every part of the body come together, so that it seems to be present in any region of the members of the body!

Others have said that the seat of the mind is in the brain. And these have used probable arguments, to be sure. They held that it was reasonable, certainly, for that which had the government of the entire body to reside rather in its highest part, as though in a citadel; and that nothing should have a higher position than that which moderates the whole by reason, just as the Lord and Ruler of the world Himself is in the highest place. Then (they have added) that the ministering organs of each sense, that is, of hearing and seeing and smelling, have been situated in the head, and the passages of all these are to the brain, not to the breast. Otherwise, it would be necessary for us to be slower in exercising our senses, (having to wait) until the faculty of sensing should

---

[1] Cf. Cicero, *De natura deorum* 2.59.147. Cf. also the *Disputationes Tusculanae* 1.9.19-20 for some of these various treatments of the philosophers.

descend by a long route through the neck to the breast. These, in truth, do not err much, or, perhaps, not at all.

For the mind, which holds dominance over the body, seems established in the top of the head, just as God in heaven; but when it is engaged in thought, it seems to pass to the breast and to withdraw to some secret recess, as it were, to elicit and draw forth counsel as though from a hidden treasury. And so it is when we are intent upon reflection, and when the mind, occupied, has hidden itself deep within, we are accustomed neither to hear the sounds about us nor to see what is before us.[2] But whether this is so, it is certainly wonderful how it is done, since there is no passage from the brain to the breast. And even if it is not so, still it is no less to be wondered at that, by some divine plan, it happens that it seems to be so. Or can anyone fail to marvel that that living and heavenly sense power which is called mind or soul[3] is of such mobility that it does not even rest when it is asleep; and is of such celerity that, in a single instant of time, if it wishes, it surveys the whole heaven, flies over seas, traverses lands and cities, and, in short, places before its own gaze all things which it pleases, no matter how far and wide they may be removed?

And does one wonder if the divine mind of God, intent upon all the parts of the world, discourses over and rules all things, governs all things, is everywhere present and everywhere diffused, when the force and power of the human mind enclosed within a mortal body is so great that not even by the barriers of this heavy and sluggish body with which it is encumbered can it be in any way restrained from granting to itself impatient of rest the free power of wandering? Whether, therefore, the mind dwells in the head or in the breast, is anyone able to fathom what power of reason brings it about that that incomprehensible sense power either inheres in the inmost part of the brain or in that two-directioned

---

[2] Cf. Theophrastus, *De sensibus* 42.
[3] The words used are *sensus, mens,* and *animus.*

blood which is enclosed in the heart, and not from this very thing conclude how great is the power of God? For the soul does not see itself, or what sort it is, or where it is, and, if it did see, yet it would not be able to see in what way an incorporeal thing is joined to a corporeal one.[4] Or even if the mind has no fixed location but runs about scattered throughout the whole body—which is possible and was held by Xenocrates, a disciple of Plato, inasmuch as the sense power is present in every part of the body—it cannot be understood what the mind itself is, nor of what sort, since its nature is so delicately subtle, that, though infused into solid organs by a living and, as it were, ardent sense power, it is mingled with all the members.

Beware, however, that you never think probable what Aristoxenus taught,[5] namely, that there is no mind at all, but that the power of thinking arises from the construction of the body and the union of the organs, as in the case of the harmony of string instruments. For musicians call harmony the stretching and sounding of the strings into complete measures, without any dissonance. They want it, therefore, that the soul is in man in a manner similar to that whereby agreeable modulation exists in string instruments, namely, that the firm uniting of the separate parts of the body and the vigor of all the members agreeing as one effect that sensible motion and temper or adjust the mind just as well-stretched strings produce the harmonious sound. And as in the case of the strings, when anything has been interrupted or relaxed, the whole system of the music is disturbed and broken, so in the body, when some part of the members has received harm, the whole body is weakened. And, when all parts are corrupted and disturbed, the sense power is destroyed and this is called death.

---

4 Here again Lactantius faces difficulty because the terminology has not yet been precisely fixed for Christian concepts of a philosophical nature. We sense his struggle to treat of the soul as incorporeal when the notion is so necessarily vague in his own mind.
5 Cf. Cicero, *Disputationes Tusculanae* 1.22.51.

But, actually, if that one had had any mind, he would never have transferred the harmony of strings to man. For the strings cannot play of their own accord, so how can there be in them any comparison and similarity with a living person? But the soul thinks and is moved of its own accord. If there were in us anything like harmony, it would be moved by an external striking as the strings by the hands; it would be mute and inactive without the touch of the player and the striking of his fingers. Surely, that one ought to have been struck by the hand, so that he might have had the opportunity to do some experiencing of sensation, for his mind set away from his members was badly benumbed.

Chapter 17

A discussion of the life-principle[1] remains for us, although the system and nature of it cannot be perceived. But for this, we do not think that the life-principle is not im-

---

1 Here again it seems certain that Lactantius means no more than the 'life-principle' which he mentioned in ch. 11 (cf. n. 1). The same word *anima* is used. In the following chapter, he uses both *anima* and *animus* and contrasts the two, so we may not accuse him of word selection that has not been reasoned out.

It is difficult to choose accurate English equivalents for the words which Lactantius uses in a technical sense. If, on the matter of the 'soul' and related terms, St. Augustine's terminology was 'quite floating,' as Etienne Gilson states in his *Introduction a l'étude de Saint Augustin*, Paris 1943 (p. 57, n. 1), still more so must have been that of Lactantius.

Strictly speaking, the *anima* is the animating principle of the body considered with respect to the vital principle which it exercises. *Animus* (a term which comes from Varro; cf. St. Augustine, *De civitate Dei* 7.23.1) is the term used to designate the vital principle which is, at the same time, a rational substance, i.e., man's soul. Therefore, as St. Augustine says, 'the *animus* is the highest grade of *anima*' *(loc. cit.)*. At times, the word *mens* is used interchangeably with *animus*. This is the superior part of the rational substance, the *animus*, and in ch. 18, it is used as a synonym for it. Another term that must be defined is *sensus*, for which we are adopting the English, sense-perception. St. Augustine explains this as 'the passion or feeling occurring when the soul is not in ignorance of what is happening in the body' *(De quantitate animae* 23.41). Cf. Gilson, *op. cit.*, pp. 56-87.

mortal, since whatever thrives and always moves by itself, and cannot be seen or touched must be eternal.[2] As to what this life-principle is, however, there is not yet agreement among philosophers, and perhaps there never will be.[3] Some said it was blood; some fire; some wind, whence the soul *(anima)* or mind *(animus)* got its name, because in Greek *wind* is *ánemos*. Yet none of those seems to have said anything. For the system of the life-principle must not be immediately posited in the material of the blood since the life-principle seems to be extinguished either when the blood is poured out from a wound or is consumed by the heat of fevers. It is just as if the light which we use should come into question as to its nature, and the answer should be given that it is oil, since the light is extinguished when that is consumed, because these things are quite different, for the one is the food of the other. The life-principle, therefore, seems to be like a light, since it is itself not blood but is nourished by the moisture of the blood as the light is by oil.

Those who thought it was fire used this argument, that the body is warm when the life-principle is present and cold when it departs. But fire lacks perception, and it is seen, and it burns when touched, whereas the life-principle is endowed with sense-perception, cannot be seen, and does not burn. Whence it is clear that the life-principle is in some way like to God.

But those who think that it is wind are deceived in this, the fact that we seem to live by drawing breath from the air. Varro thus defines it: 'The soul is air conceived in the mouth, warmed in the lungs, heated in the heart, diffused into the body.'[4] These notions are most plainly false. For I declare that the reason of things of this kind is not so obscure to us that we do not even understand this, what cannot be true. If anyone should say to me that the heaven is of brass, or

---

2 Cf. Cicero, *De republica* 6.25.27.
3 *Ibid. Disputationes Tusculanae* 1.9.20; cf. Isidore, *Origines* 11.1.7f.; *De differentiis rerum* 30.100f.
4 Cf. Varro in Probus on Vergil's *Eclogues* 6.31.

glass, or, as Empedocles says, that it is 'frozen air,' should I agree immediately because I do not know of what material the heaven is?[5] For as I do not know the one thing, so I do not know the other. The life-principle, therefore, is not air conceived in the mouth, because the life-principle is produced much before air can be conceived in the mouth. It is not, indeed, introduced into the body after birth, as it seems to certain philosophers, but right away after conception when the divine necessity has formed the fetus in the womb, and because it so lives within the body of the mother that it is increased by growth and it delights to beat with frequent pulsations. In short, there must be an abortion for the young, living being within to die. The other attempts at definition look to this fact, that during the nine months during which we were in the womb, we seemed to be dead. But none of these three opinions is true. And yet those who believe these things must not be said to be false to such an extent that they said nothing at all, for we do live at once by blood and heat and breath. But since the life-principle exists in the body by the union of all these, they did not express suitably what it was, since it cannot be expressed any more than it can be seen.

Chapter 18

There follows another and in itself an inextricable question: whether the life-principle and the soul are the same, or whether one is that by which we live and the other that by which we perceive and judge.[1] Arguments are not lacking to support each view. Those who say that they are one follow this theory, that we cannot live without perception nor perceive without life, and, therefore, that which cannot be separated cannot be distinct; but whatever it

---
5 Cf. Arnobius 3.17.

1 Cf. especially ch. 17, n. 1. Cf. Isidore, *Origines* 11.1.11; *De differentiis rerum* 29.94f.

is, it has the function of living and the purpose of perceiving.[2] So two Epicurean poets speak without distinction of the soul and the life-principle.[3]

Those who hold that they are different argue somewhat as follows. That the mind is one thing and the life-principle another may be understood from this, that the mind may be extinguished with the life-principle still unimpaired, as is accustomed to happen to the insane. They speak also from the fact that the life-principle is put to rest by death and the mind[4] by sleep. Indeed, so much is the mind put to rest by sleep that not only is it unaware of what it is doing or where it is, but it is also deceived by the contemplation of false objects. How this very thing takes place cannot be perceived; why it takes place can be. For we are able to rest in no way unless the mind[5] is held occupied by representations of visions. But the mind, oppressed with sleep, lies hidden as though fire buried with ashes drawn over it, which, if you move a little, blazes forth again and wakens, as it were. So the mind is called away by images until the members, refreshed with sleep, are invigorated. For the body, although, as long as the sense-perception is awake, it may lie immobile, yet is not at rest, because the sense-perception burns in it and vibrates as a flame and keeps all the members bound to itself.

But after the mind has been withdrawn from attention to beholding images, then, at last, the whole body is dissolved by rest. The mind is also withdrawn from deep thought when, under the force of darkness, it begins to be alone with itself. While it is intent upon those things which it considers, suddenly sleep creeps upon it and cogitation itself turns little by little to the nearest forms or 'apparitions'; thus it begins to

---

2 This is a distinction effected by careful use of words. Again, we have a special connotation for *ratio*.
3 One is Lucretius (cf. 3.421ff.); perhaps the other is Horace (cf. *Epist.* 1.4.16). Lactantius was aware of the fact that these words were not clearly distinguished by writers in general.
4 Again, the word is *animus*. In the sentence immediately preceding, the word for mind is *mens*.
5 *Mens.*

see also those things which it had placed before its eyes for itself. Then, it proceeds further and finds diversions for itself that it may not interrupt a very healthful slumber of the body. For just as the mind during the day is diverted by real sights so that it will not sleep, so during the night it is diverted by false ones so that it will not be awakened. If it perceives no images, then it is necessarily either awake or asleep in perpetual death. For the sake of sleeping, then, has the system of dreaming been bestowed by God and, indeed, to all living creatures in common. But it has been bestowed upon man especially, because when God gave this arrangement for the sake of rest, He left to Himself the power of teaching man future events by dreams. Even historical accounts testify that there have been dreams whose outcome has been immediate and remarkable, and the responses of our seers have consisted in dreams partly. Wherefore they are not always true nor always false, as Vergil testifies, who 'would have there be two gates of dreams';[6] because those which are false are seen to be for the reason of sleeping; those which are true are sent by God that we might learn by this revelation of an imminent good or evil.

Chapter 19

We may come to question also the production of the life-principle, whether it is from the father, or rather from the mother, or both.[1] This question is, in my opinion, still an uncertain one. There is nothing true in the three views; neither from both nor from one or the other are

---

6 Vergil, *Aeneid* 6.893.

1 Jerome makes an interesting comment on this point and mentions the views of Lactantius in *Contra Rufinum* 2.8. Rufinus claims, says Jerome, that Lactantius, along with Tertullian and others, felt that the souls or life-principles are given to men at the time of the transmission of the human semen. Jerome would have more explicit reference concerning the other writers, but he is certain of Lactantius and accuses Rufinus of lying in assigning such a theory to that writer.

souls produced. A body, of course, can be born of the bodies since something is conferred by both; of life-principles, no life-principle can be produced because nothing can leave a tenuous and incomprehensible thing. So the manner of producing life-principles lies with God Himself, and Himself alone.

'In fine, we are all sprung from a heavenly seed;
All, all have that same Father,'[2]
as Lucretius says. For from mortals there cannot be generated anything but what is mortal. Neither he who feels that he has in no way transmitted himself or produced life from his own life ought to be regarded as a father, nor should one who, if he does feel that he has, claim that he has comprehended when or how this was done. From this it is evident that life-principles are not given by parents, but by one and the same God, the Father of all, who alone holds the law and principle of being born, since He alone effected them. For the part of the earthly parent is nothing other than, with a sense of pleasure, to emit or receive the moisture of the body which is the matter of being born. Beyond this work man stops and has no further power. Therefore, men wish for children to be born, because they themselves do not cause it. All the rest is God's work, namely, the conception itself, and the forming of the body, and the breathing in of the life-principle, and the safe bringing forth, and whatever follows for preserving the human life. It is His gift that we breathe, that we live, that we grow. Besides that, through His kindness we are unharmed in body; He provides nourishment from various sources; He endows man with wisdom also, which an earthly father can in no way bestow. And so it happens often that feeble-minded children are born of intelligent parents and intelligent children of feeble-minded parents—which some people assign to fate and the stars. But this is not the place to discuss fate. It is enough to say this: even if the stars do contain the outcome of things, nonetheless, all things are done by God who both

---

2 Lucretius 2.991-992.

made and ordered the very stars.[3] They are fools, therefore, who detract this power from God and assign it to His works.

He wished it to be in our power whether we use this celestial and beautiful gift of God. He bound man himself to the symbol or mystery of strength which He granted whereby he might acquire life. Great, indeed, is the power of man, great his reason, great the mystery.[4] If a man does not fail from this or betray his faith and devotion, he is blessed; he, in short, that I may end quickly, must become like to God. He errs, whoever measures man by flesh, for this mere body, which we have put on, is but the receptacle of man. The *man himself* can neither be touched nor beheld nor grasped, because it lies hidden within that which is seen. And if anyone is delicate and soft in this life, which the manner of it demands, if he devotes himself to fleshly desires in contempt of virtue, he will fall and be pressed to the earth; but if, on the contrary, he eagerly and constantly defends, as he should, his status, the right one which he has attained, if he does not serve the world which he ought to trample upon and overcome, he will merit eternal life.

Chapter 20

I have addressed these things to you, Demetrianus, for the time being only briefly, and more obscurely, perhaps, than was fitting due to the necessity of circumstances and of time. But please be content with these, since you will have more and better things to read if heavenly indulgence comes to my aid. Then, I shall urge you more clearly and more certainly to the learning of philosophy. For I have determined to write as many things as I can which have to do with the state of the blessed life, and, to be sure,

---

[3] Cf. St. Thomas' discussion of fate in the *Summa theologica* 1.116.
[4] The word is *sacramentum* which had not yet received its theological connotation.

in opposition to the 'philosophers' since they are seriously harmful in distorting the truth. Incredible is the might of their eloquence, and the subtleness of their argumentation and discourse deceives easily. These philosophers we will vanquish partly by our own arms and partly, indeed, by those taken from their own bickering among themselves so that it may appear that they have rather drawn error in upon themselves than removed it.

Perhaps you wonder that I dare such a great task. But shall we suffer the truth to be extinguished or oppressed? Indeed, I shall fail the more gladly even under this burden. If Marcus Tullius, the unsurpassed paragon of this type of eloquence, was often overcome by those unlearned and unskilled in eloquence, simply because they were striving for the truth, why should we despair that Truth itself will avail by its own proper force and brilliance against fallacious and captious oratory? They, indeed, are accustomed to profess that they are patrons of truth; but, who can either defend a thing which he has not learned, or make clear to others what he does not himself know? I seem to promise a great thing, but there is need of the help of heaven that opportunity and time be granted me for achieving this aim. And if life ought to be desired by a wise man, then, I would wish to live for no other reason than to accomplish something that is worthy of life and that may be of use to readers (although not for eloquence, because the stream of eloquence in me is slight); something, at any rate, that may assist for living, and that is especially necessary. When this is accomplished, I shall think that I have lived enough and that I have fulfilled a human duty, if my labor has directed toward the path of heaven some men whom it has freed from their errors.

THE WRATH OF GOD

(DE IRA DEI)

INTRODUCTION

THE DE IRA DEI *(The Wrath of God)* is a special work on an important theme. The treatise, promised by Lactantius in his major work, *Institutiones divinae* 2.17 (vol. 49, p. 160), was written in the year 313-314 as a refutation of false notions held about anger in God, chiefly those which were being popularized by the Epicureans.

The Epicureans imagined God as utterly inert, completely aloof from this world, devoid of the passions of anger or kindness as inconsistent with His nature. The Stoics believed that God could be kind but not angry. A conception of some Hebrews, on the other hand, was that God was severe, and sometimes even cruel. A major difficulty, therefore, was faced by those minds which had been trained in the principles of the Greek schools of thought and whose new faith forbade the rejection of any part of the Old Testament.

Many attempted a reconciliation. Arnobius, for instance, the teacher of Lactantius, warmly subscribed to the notion of the impassibility or *apatheia* of God held by the Epicureans.

Lactantius insists that such a theory is destructive of a belief in Divine Providence and even in the existence of God. If God exists, He cannot be inoperative, because to live is to operate. He must engage in action, and this action is the administration of the world (17.4).

With reference to the Stoic doctrine, the refutation of Lactantius shows that the loving of the good comes from the hatred of the evil, and the hatred of evil from the love of good. The two cannot be separated (5.9).

If we remove anger from God, we dissolve religion (22.2). Thus, man's greatest dignity, his real purpose in life, is destroyed. The God who holds power must also possess wrath on which power rests (23.4). The interpretation of Lactantius is quite sound theologically; indeed, it is not dissimilar to that of Augustine: the anger of God is not a disturbance of His mind, but a judgment, whereby punishment is meted out to sin *(De civitate Dei* 15.25).

The problem, on the whole, is given good treatment by Lactantius. The author antedates the great Christian expounders of doctrine by at least a century. As in his *Institutes,* therefore, he relies heavily on the Sibylline oracles and the pagan philosophers rather than upon Christian sources. For comment on his doctrine and its interpretation, the following studies are of value:

Micka, E. F. *The Problem of Divine Anger in Arnobius and Lactantius,* in *Catholic University of America Studies in Christian Antiquity* 4, Washington, 1943.

Rapisardi, E. 'La polemicadi Lattanzio contro l'epicureismo,' *Miscellanea di Studi di Letteratura Christiana Antica* 1 (1947), 5-20.

THE WRATH OF GOD

Chapter 1

 HAVE OFTEN NOTICED, Donatus,[1] that many people believe that which even some philosophers have held, namely, that God does not get angry. This is so either because the divine nature is only beneficent and it is not fitting to its most eminent and excellent power to harm anything, or because it has care for nothing at all, so that neither from its kindness should any good happen to us nor from its wickedness any evil. We must refute their error, because it is a very great one, and because it tends to overthrow the foundation of human life, and so that you yourself may not be deceived, drawn on by the influence of men who think that they are wise. Nor, however, are we so arrogant as to glory in the comprehension of the truth by our own ability, but we follow the doctrine of God who alone can know and reveal His secrets. The philosophers, having no part of this doctrine, have believed that the nature of things can be grasped by conjecture. Which is not at all possible, because the mind of man, walled in by the darksome dwelling-place of his body, is removed far from an accurate view of truth. And in this respect, divine nature is different from human, namely, that ignorance belongs to the human, knowledge to the divine nature.

On this account, we have need of some light for dispelling the darkness by which man's intellect is obscured, since, while

---

[1] This work is addressed to a certain Donatus. We have no way of knowing whether he is the Donatus to whom the *De mortibus persecutorum* was addressed. Cf. the *Paradoxica* of Cicero for a similar beginning sentence: 'I have noticed often, Brutus, that Cato . . . .'

ours is the condition of mortal flesh, we are not able to divine by our senses. But the light of the human mind is God, and he who knows Him, and has received Him within himself, will acknowledge the mystery of truth with an enlightened heart. With God and heavenly instruction removed, however, everything is full of error, and rightly did Socrates, though he was the most learned of all the philosophers, claim that he knew nothing but one thing, that he knew nothing,[2] and this for the purpose of convincing of their lack of knowledge the others who thought they knew something. For he understood that learning had in itself nothing certain, nothing true, nor did he himself, as some believed, pretend to be learned to confute the others, but in some measure he saw the truth; and even at his trial he testified, as is given by Plato, that 'there was no human wisdom.'[3] And he so much despised, derided, spurned the learning in which philosophers then boasted that he professed as the greatest learning the fact that he had learned that he knew nothing.[4]

If, therefore, there is no human wisdom, as Socrates taught, as Plato handed down, it is apparent that the knowledge of truth is divine and is in the power of no one but God. God, then, must be known in whom alone is truth. He is the Father of the world and the Establisher of things, He who is not seen by the eyes and scarcely perceived by the mind. And His religion is accustomed to be impugned in many ways by those who have been able neither to attain true wisdom nor to grasp the reason of the great and heavenly secret.

Chapter 2

Although there are many steps by which an ascent is made to the dwelling of truth, it is not easy for anyone at all to be

---
2 Cf. Cicero, *Prior Academics* 2.23.74; *Posterior Academics* 4.16.
3 Plato, *Apology* 23A.
4 *Ibid.* 21D.

conducted to the summit. For when the eyes are blinded by the brilliance of the truth, those who cannot keep a firm hold are rolled back upon the level ground. The first step is to understand the false religions and to cast aside impious cults of things made by human hands. The next step, then, is to perceive with the mind that there is one supreme God whose power and providence brought about the world from the beginning and watches it in its continuance. The third step is to know His Minister and the Messenger whom He sent or delegated upon the earth, by whose teaching, being liberated from the error in which we are held and involved, and instructed in the worship of the true God, we might learn justice.[1] From all of these steps, as I have said, there is a rapid and easy fall to ruin, unless the feet are fastened with unshakable stability.

From the first step we see shaken off those who, although they understand the false things, yet do not find the true; and although they have despised the frail, earthly images, still they do not bring themselves to the worship of God, whom they know not, but marveling at the elements of the universe they venerate the sky, the land, the sea, the sun, and the other stars. But I have already demonstrated the stupidity of these in the second book of the *Divine Institutes*.[2]

We say that those fall from the second step who, though they feel that there is one supreme God, yet at the same time are ensnared by the philosophers and, captivated by their false arguments, think about that only Majesty in a way other than that of strict truth. For they either say that God has no form, or they think that He is not moved by any affection because every affection is a mark of weakness, of which in God there is none at all.

---

[1] These three steps provide an outline of Lactantius' major work, *Institutiones divinae*. They are also a clear statement of the method of Christian apologetics, most certainly of its functioning in the case of winning over those imbued with the teachings of the schools during the first centuries of the Christian era.
[2] Cf. chs. 5, 6 (vol. 49, this series, pp. 111-120).

But those fall headlong from the third step who, although they know the Ambassador of God, the very same Establisher of the divine and immortal temple, however, either do not receive Him or receive Him otherwise than faith demands. These I have partly refuted in the fourth book of the above-mentioned work.³ Later, I will refute them more carefully when I undertake to reply to all the sects which, while they have been dissipating the truth, have lost it.

Now, however, our discussion is against those who, having fallen from the second step, have wrong notions about the supreme God. For certain ones say that He neither is pleased nor angered with anything, but that, free from care and in repose, He enjoys the good of His own immortality.⁴ But others take away anger from God and leave kindness to Him, holding that a nature endowed with highest virtue, as it ought not to be hurtful, so ought to be kindly.⁵ Thus, all the philosophers agree in the matter of God's anger, but they differ about His kindness. But, in order that the discussion may proceed in order to the matter proposed, we must make an arrangement of this kind and follow it. Since anger and kindness are different and incompatible, either anger must be attributed to God and kindness withdrawn, or both must be equally withdrawn, or anger must be taken away and kindness attributed to Him, or both must be attributed to Him. The nature of the matter can accept nothing further beyond these theories; it is necessary for the truth which is sought to be found in some one of them. Let us consider them separately so that both reason and method may bring us to the shelters of truth.

---

3 Cf. *Inst.* 4.10ff. (vol. 49, this series, pp. 263ff.).
4 These are the Epicureans whose philosophical system, composed of three parts (*Ethica, Physica,* and *Canonice* [axioms]) was intended to free humanity from the old fears and traditions. They were pure materialists and upheld the teachings of Democritus and the old Atomism.
5 These are the Stoics, a sect founded by Zeno of Citium in about 300 B.C. The system was basically ethical; knowledge was the basis of virtue; a devotion to duty was fostered; and brotherhood of man was the ideal.

Chapter 3

First of all, no one has ever said of God that He is angered only, and not moved by kindness; for it is not consistent with a notion of God that He be equipped with power to harm and hinder, but not be able to be of help and to do good. What means, therefore, what hope of salvation has been proposed for men if God is the author of evils only? If this should be so, that venerable majesty would be considered as belonging not to the power of a judge, who may save and set free, but to the office of a torturer and executioner. Since, however, we see that there are not only evils in human affairs, but also goods; certainly, if God is the author of evils, there must, of necessity, be another who works in opposition to God and gives us the goods. If so, by what name must he be called? Or why is he who does evil better known to us than he who does good? But if there can be nothing besides God, it is absurd and foolish to think that the divine power, than which nothing is greater, nothing better, could harm, and could not benefit; and so there is no one who would dare to say this, because it has no sense and it could not be believed in any way. And since this is the general opinion, let us pass on and seek the truth elsewhere.

Chapter 4

What follows is of the school of Epicurus. He teaches that just as there is no anger in God, so there is not even kindness. For since Epicurus thought that to do evil or do harm was foreign to God (an action which is generally sprung from the emotion of anger), he also took from Him beneficence because he saw it to be a consequence that, if God possessed anger, He would have kindness also. And so, lest he concede a vice to Him, he made Him deprived of a virtue also. 'From this,' he says, 'He is blessed and incorrupt, because He cares for nothing, and He neither has any concern Himself, nor does He show it for another.'[1] Accordingly, he is not God if he is not moved (which is proper to a living being), and if he does not do anything that is impossible to man (which is proper to God), if he has no will whatsoever, no action, in short, no administration which is worthy of a god. What greater, what more worthy administration can be assigned to God than the governance of the world, than the care of living things, and especially of the human race to which all earthly things are subject? What beatitude, then, can there be in God if quiet and immobile He is ever inactive; if He is deaf to those who pray, if blind to those who worship Him? What is so worthy, so befitting to God as providence? But if he cares for nothing, provides for nothing, He has lost all divinity.

He who takes away all force, therefore, all substance from God, what else does he say except that there is no God at all? Marcus Tullius, in fact, relates that it was said by Posidonius that Epicurus believed this, that there were no gods, but that the things which he spoke about the gods he had said for the sake of driving away ill will, and so in his words he left the gods, but in very fact he removed them to whom he assigned no motion, no function.[2] And if this is so, what is more deceitful than that, which ought to be foreign to a wise and serious man? Indeed, if this man believed one thing and said another, what else ought he be called but a wicked, double-tongued deceiver, and, on that account, a fool? But Epicurus was not so crafty as to speak such things with the intention of deceiving, since he consigned these beliefs even to writings for perpetual remembrance; but he erred by his ignorance of the truth.

Being influenced from the beginning by the likeliness of the truth of a single opinion, he necessarily ran into those which followed. For his first opinion was that it is not fitting

---

[1] Epicurus, frg. 243 (Usener, p. 243.33); cf. Cicero, *De natura deorum* 1.17.45.
[2] Cicero, *ibid.* 1.44.123; cf. 1.30.85.

for wrath to be in God. And when this seemed to him true and unassailable, he could not check the consequences, because with one affection cut away, necessity itself forced him to take away from God the other affection also. So, he who is not angered, surely is not moved by kindness either, which is contrary to anger. Accordingly then, if there is neither anger nor kindness in him, surely there is neither fear nor joy nor grief nor compassion. For there is one plan for all the affections, one connected movement, which cannot be in God.[3] But if there is no affection in God, because whatever is affected is a weakness, therefore, neither is there any care of anything nor any providence in Him.

The disputation of the wise man extends to just this point. He was silent about the other things which follow, namely, that there is no care in Him nor providence, and, therefore, that there is not any reflection nor any sense in Him, by which it comes about that He does not exist at all. So when he had descended step by step, he stopped on the last step because he then saw the precipice. But what advantage is it to have kept silent and to have concealed the danger? Necessity forced him to fall even against his will. He said what he did not mean because he so ordered his argument that he necessarily came down to that point which he was avoiding. You see, therefore, where one arrives when anger is withdrawn and taken away from God. Finally, either no one believes that, or only a few, and they even wicked and evil, who hope for impunity for their sins. But if this, too, is found to be false, namely, that there is neither anger nor kindness in God, let us come to that which was put in as a third theory.

Chapter 5

The Stoics and some others are thought to have had a somewhat better notion about divinity, in holding that kind-

---
[3] Cf. Epicurus, frg. 366 (Usener, p. 244.7).

ness resides in God but not anger. It is a very favorable and popular cant that this weakness of mind does not belong to God, that He who cannot be injured should believe that He has been injured by anyone; or that that serene and holy majesty should be aroused, disturbed, enraged, which is a mark of earthly frailty. For this opinion regards anger as an upsetting and disturbance of the mind, which is foreign to God. Because if anger is not becoming to a man even, provided he is wise and respectable—since, if ever it invades the mind of anyone, just as a raging tempest it excites such great waves that it changes the condition of the mind, the eyes take fire, the mouth quivers, the tongue stammers, the teeth chatter, and now a red flush suffuses and marks the countenance and now a white pallor[1]—how much more is such unseemly mutation unbecoming to God? And if a man who has authority and power should spread harm widely by his wrath, shed blood, overturn cities, destroy peoples, and reduce provinces to desolation,[2] how much more should it be credible that God, who has power over the whole human race and the very universe, would destroy all things, if He were angered?

They hold that so great, so pernicious an evil, however, ought to be absent from God. And if wrath and disturbance are absent from God because ugly and injurious, and if He does not do evil to anyone, there remains no other conclusion but that He is a gentle, tranquil, propitious, and kindly preserver. Thus, at length, He may be called both the common Father of all, and the best and greatest, which the divine and heavenly nature demands. For if among men it seems praiseworthy to help rather than to harm, to let live rather than to kill, to save rather than to destroy, and if not undeservedly innocence[3] is counted among the virtues, and if he who does these things is loved, esteemed, adorned with all benedictions

---

[1] Cf. Seneca, *De ira* 1.1.4.
[2] *Ibid.* 1.2.1.
[3] The root meaning of the word is not preserved in English. *Nocere* means *to harm*, and *innocens* is *one not causing harm*.

and honored with promises, and, in short, is judged because of his merits and benefits to be most like to God, how much more is it proper that God Himself, excelling in divinely perfect virtues and removed from every human failing, should act toward the whole race of men with heavenly kindness!

Things like that are said speciously and popularly, and they entice many to credence. Those who think these things approach, indeed, quite near to the truth, but they, in part, fall by considering the nature of the case only a little. For if God is not angry with the impious and the unjust, then, to be sure, neither does He love the pious and the just. So the error of those who take away both anger and kindness together is a more consistent one. For, in opposite things, it is necessary either to be moved toward each side or toward neither. Thus, he who loves the good also hates the evil, and he who does not hate the evil does not love the good, because, on one hand, to love the good comes from hatred of evil, and to hate the evil rises from love of the good. There is no one who loves life without a hatred of death, and no one seeks light but he who flees darkness; for those things are so connected by nature that one cannot exist without the other.

If a master has in his household servants, a good one and a bad one, certainly he does not hate them both, nor does he bestow benefits and honor upon both—and if he does, he is both unfair and foolish. But the good one he addresses kindly, and praises him, and puts him in charge of his house and family and all his goods; the bad one, however, he punishes with reproaches, beatings, nakedness, hunger, thirst, and shackles, so that this one may be an example to the others not to do wrong, and the former an example for serving well. Thus, fear may check some and honor encourage others.[4] The one who loves, therefore, also hates, and he who hates also loves; for there are those who ought to be loved and those who should be hated. And just as he who loves confers good things upon those whom he loves, so he who hates calls evils down

---
4 Cf. Cyprian, *Ad Demetrianum* 8.

upon those whom he hates; and this argument, because it is true, can in no way be destroyed. Vain, therefore, and false is the opinion of those who, when they grant one thing to God, withdraw another from Him, an error no slighter than the error of those who withdraw both. The former, as we have pointed out, in part do not err but retain that which is the better partial theory,[5] whereas the latter, whom reason and the truth of this argument convict of error, having taken a completely false opinion, fall into the greatest error. For they ought not to have reasoned thus: God is not subject to anger; therefore, He is not moved by kindness either. But they ought to have reasoned this way: God is moved by kindness; therefore, He is also moved to anger. If it had been certain and undoubted that God is not subject to anger, then, it would have been necessary to come to that other conclusion. But, since the question of anger is more ambiguous, while that of kindness is plainly evident, it is absurd to want to overturn what is certain by what is uncertain, because it is easier to establish uncertain things from what are certain.

Chapter 6

These are the opinions of the philosophers about God; no one of them has ever said anything else besides these things about God's anger. But if we have grasped that these things which were said are false, one last resort remains in which alone the truth can be found which has never been taken up nor at any time defended by the philosophers, namely, that God's anger is a consequence of His kindness. We must look to this opinion and spread it abroad for upon it rests the sum total, and it is the hinge of piety and religion. And neither can any honor be owed to God if He grants nothing to one worshiping Him, nor any fear if He does not become angry with one who does not worship Him.

---

5 i.e., the Stoics who attribute kindness to God.

Chapter 7

Although the philosophers have often, through ignorance of the truth, wavered from reason and fallen into inextricable errors (for usually there happens to them what happens to a traveler not knowing his way and not admitting that he does not know it; he wanders about while he is ashamed to seek direction from those whom he meets), still no philosopher has ever propagated the theory that there is no difference between man and the beasts. Nor has anyone at all, one who wished to seem even but slightly wise, ever equated the rational animal with the mute and irrational ones. This, certain ignoramuses do, themselves like the very beasts, who, since they wish to devote themselves to their appetites and to voluptuousness, hold that they have been born according to the same principle as all things which breathe, a wicked thing to be said by man. For who is so unlearned not to know, who so unwise not to realize that there is in man something divine? I do not come yet to the powers of the soul, and intellect, by which there is a manifest kinship with God for man; but, does not the position of the body itself and the shape of the face declare that we are not equals of the dumb beasts? Their nature is prostrate to the ground and to their pasture, and it has nothing common with heaven which it does not behold. Man, however, in an upright position and with his face held aloft to behold the world, compares his countenance with God and reason recognizes Reason.[1]

And on this account, 'there is no animal,' as Cicero says, 'except man which has any knowledge of God.'[2] For he alone is endowed with wisdom, so that he alone understands religion, and this is the chief or the only difference between man and the dumb animals. As to the other things which seem to be proper to man, although such things are not in the beasts,

---
[1] This is the theme of the *De opificio Dei;* cf. especially ch. 8, p. 25.
[2] Cicero, *De legibus* 1.8.24; cf. Seneca, *De ira* 1.3.6-8.

similarities can be seen. Speech is peculiar to man; yet, even in the beasts there is a certain resemblance to speech. They distinguish one another by their voices; and when they are angry, they give forth a sound like to quarreling; and when they see each other after a long lapse of time, they give indication of pleasure by their voice. To us, of course, their voices seem unlovely, as ours do perhaps to them, but to themselves, because they understand themselves, they are words. Finally, in every affection they give forth certain sounds by which indications they express the feeling. Laughter also is peculiar to man, and yet we see certain signs of gladness in other animals, when they leap and frolic for sport, turn down their ears, contract their mouths, smooth their foreheads, and relax their eyes in sportiveness. What is so proper to man as plan and providence for the future? Yet there are some animals which contrive several openings from their lairs in different directions, so that if any danger befalls, there may be a way of escape for those shut in. They would not do this unless they had knowledge and cogitation.[3] Others provide for the future, as 'Ants when they plunder a great heap of corn, mindful of the winter, and lay it up in their dwelling';[4] or as bees 'which alone know a country and fixed abodes; and mindful of the winter which is to come, they practice labor in the summer, and lay up their gains as a common stock.'[5]

It would take long if I should try to trace out the things very much like human policy which are accustomed to be done by the different classes of animals. But if of all these things which are usually ascribed to man there is found a likeness in the beasts also, it is clear that religion is the only thing of which neither any vestige nor any suspicion can be found in the beasts. Justice is a property of religion which comes in contact with no other animal. Man alone has it; the other animals are arranged and provided for man. The worship of

---

[3] Here instinct, of course, is meant, a 'sense-intelligence.'
[4] Vergil, *Aeneid* 4.402-403.
[5] *Ibid. Georgics* 4.155-157.

God, however, is ascribed to justice, and he who does not take this upon himself will live the life of the beasts, removed from the nature of man, even though he remain of a human appearance. Since, then, we differ from the rest of the animals in this one respect almost, that we alone of all perceive the divine might and power while there is no understanding of God in them, surely, it cannot be that in this respect either the dumb animals would be more wise or human nature not wise, because it is on account of man's wisdom that all things which live and the whole nature of things are subject to man. Wherefore, if reason, if the power of man excels in this and surpasses other things having life, because alone he grasps knowledge of God, then it is evident that religion can in no way be dissolved.

Chapter 8

But religion is dissolved if we believe Epicurus when he says such things as this: 'For the nature of gods must ever in itself of necessity enjoy immortality together with supreme repose, far removed and withdrawn from our concerns; since, exempt from every pain, exempt from all dangers, strong in its own resources, not wanting aught of us, it is neither gained by favors nor moved by anger.'[1] When he says these things, does he think that any worship ought to be rendered to God, or does he overturn all religion? For if God does anything good to anyone, if He returns no thanks for the devotion of a worshiper, what is so empty, so foolish, as to build temples, make sacrifices, bestow gifts, deplete one's private fortune for no gain?[2] But it is fitting that an excellent nature be honored, the argument runs. What sort of honor can be due to one having care for nothing, one who is an ingrate? Or can we be bound in any way to him who has nothing in common with

---

1 Lucretius, *De rerum natura* 2.646-651.
2 Cf. Cicero, *De natura deorum* 1.41.115.

us?[3] 'Farewell to god,' says Cicero, 'if he is such that he is held by no favor, no love of men. For why should I say, "May it be well for him," for it can be well for no one?'[4] What could be more contemptuously spoken against God? 'Farewell,' he said, that is, 'Away with him, let him be gone, inasmuch as he can be of help to no one.' But if God neither has nor displays any concern, why should we not do wrong, as long as we may escape the knowledge of men and get around the public laws?[5] Whenever an opportunity of hiding favors us, let us consider the matter; let us take away what belongs to others, either without bloodshed, or even with it, if there is nothing more besides the laws which ought to be feared.

While Epicurus thinks these things, he destroys religion at its foundations;[6] and, when this is removed, confusion and disturbance of life will ensue. But if religion is not able to be taken up so that we may keep our hold both on wisdom, whereby we differ from the beasts, and on justice, whereby the common life is more safe, how can religion itself be kept or protected without fear? For what is not feared is contemned; what is contemned is surely not cherished. Thus it comes about that religion and majesty and honor rest upon fear, but there is no fear when no one is moved to anger. Therefore, whether you draw kindness away from God, or wrath, or both, of necessity religion is taken away without which the life of man is filled with foolishness, crime, and enormity. For conscience greatly checks men, if we believe that we are living in the sight of God; if we realize that not only what we do is seen from above, but also that what we think or say is heard by God. And it is of value to believe this, as some think, not for the sake of truth but of utility, since laws cannot punish the conscience, unless some terror impends from above to restrain sins. Then, all religion is false and divinity does not exist at all, but all things have been confected by wise men in order

---

3 *Ibid.* 1.41.115-116.
4 *Ibid.* 1.44.124.
5 *Ibid.* 1.30.85.
6 *Ibid.* 1.2.3.

that life may be more upright and innocent.⁷ This is a big question and one foreign to the material which we have proposed, but because it necessarily comes up, it has to be touched upon although briefly.

Chapter 9

When the opinions of philosophers of former times were in agreement about Providence, and when there was no doubt but that the world had been formed by God and by reason and that it was ruled by a plan, first of all, there arose, in the time of Socrates, Protagoras who said that it was not clear to him whether there was any divinity or not. And this discussion of his was judged so impious and against truth and religion to such an extent that the Athenians both banished the man himself from their territory and burned the books [in which his doctrines were contained] in a public assembly.¹ It is not necessary to discuss his opinion because he expressed nothing certain. After this one came Socrates himself and his pupil, Plato, and those who branched from the school of Plato, as though streams into different directions, the Stoics and Peripatetics. These were of the same opinion as the earlier ones. Later, however, Epicurus said that there was a god, indeed, because it was necessary that there be in the world something outstanding, and distinguished, and blessed, but still he held that there was no providence; and, as a result of this, the world itself he regarded as fashioned neither by any plan nor by design nor by art, but that the nature of things had conglobated by certain minute and inseparable seeds.² And I do not see what notion more repugnant than this can be spoken. For if there is a God, surely He is provident as God, and it cannot be otherwise than that divinity be assigned to

---

7 *Ibid.* 1.42.118.

1 Cf. Minucius Felix 8.3.
2 Cf. Epicurus, frg. 368 (Usener, p. 247.35); Cicero, *Disputationes Tusculanae* 1.27.66.

Him, except that He retain past things, know present things, and foresee future things. So, when that one removed providence, he also denied that there was a god. But when, on the other hand, he professed that there was a god, at the same time he also conceded that there was a providence, for one without the other cannot be at all, nor can it be understood.

However, in those times after philosophy had already ceased flourishing, there arose a certain man of Melos, Diagoras, who said that there was no god whatsoever, and for this opinion he was named an atheist, and likewise the Cyrenean, Theodorus; the two of them, because they had been able to find nothing new—everything having been said and discovered already!—preferred to make denials contrary to truth on anything which all prior to them had agreed without ambiguity.[3] These are the ones who have calumniated the doctrine of providence, adhered to and defended for so many ages, by so many geniuses with really philosophical minds. What is our question then? Shall we refute those small and weak philosophers by reason, or by the authority of eminent men, or rather by both? But we have to hurry lest our discussion wander farther from the subject matter.

Chapter 10

Those who do not wish to hold that the world was made by divine providence say that it was either massed together by prime bodies joined together among themselves at random, or that it suddenly sprang into existence by nature. That nature, however, as Strato says,[1] has within itself the power of producing and reducing, but it has no sensible aspect or figure, so that we may understand that all things were generated of their own accord, as it were, with no artificer or author. Each

---

3 Cf. Cicero, *De natura deorum* 1.12.23, 63; Minucius Felix 8.3.

1 Cf. Cicero, *De natura deorum* 1.13.35.

of these is a wild and impossible hypothesis. But this happens to those who are ignorant of truth. They think up anything at all rather than believe that which reason demands. In the first place, those minute seeds, by whose chance coming together they say that the world has cohered, where or whence are they, I ask? Who has ever seen them? Who has felt them? Who heard them? Or did Leucippus alone have eyes?[2] Did only he have a mind? He, surely, alone of all men was blind and without heart to say things that not even a sick person could babble in delirium nor one sleeping could dream.

The old philosophers argued that all things were made up of four elements.[3] He would not accept that, lest he seem to follow the footsteps of others, but he wished there to be of these very elements other beginnings[4] which could be neither seen, nor touched, nor perceived by any part of the body. 'They are so minute,' he says, 'that there is no blade of iron so fine by which they can be cut and divided.' Whence he put on them the name of 'atoms.'[5] But it occurred to him that, if there were one and the same nature for all, they could not effect the diverse things with such great variety as we see exists in the world. So he said that some were smooth, and some rough, and some round, and some angular, and some hooked.[6] How much better had he kept silent than to have put his tongue to uses so miserable, so inane! Indeed, I am afraid that he who thinks that these things ought to be refuted is no less in a delirium. Nevertheless, let us answer as though we were replying to someone saying something.

If they are smooth and round, certainly they are not able to attach themselves one to another so as to form a body, so

---

2 Leucippus, fl. 440 B.C., a Greek philosopher, disciple of Zeno the Eleatic, was the originator of this atomic theory. Cf. F. Coppleston, *A History of Philosophy*, Vol. 1, for a general introduction to the ancient philosophers and to the systems referred to by Lactantius in this treatise.
3 Cf. Lucretius 1.763ff.
4 The word is Lucretius' *primordia;* cf. 1.265ff.; 2.730ff.; 842ff.
5 *Ibid.* 1.528ff. The Greek word means 'that which cannot be cut.'
6 Cf. Cicero, *De natura deorum* 1.24.66; Lucretius 2.333ff.; 381ff.

that if any of thousands should wish to draw together into one coagmentation, the very softness of the particles would not allow their coming together into a mass.⁷ But if they are sharp and cornered and hooked so that they can cohere, they are, therefore, divisible and separable; of necessity the hooks and corners project so they can be cut off. Thus, what can be lopped off and parted will be able to be seen and held.

'These,' he says, 'fly about through the void in ceaseless motion and are borne hither and thither, just as we see the specks of dust in the sun when it sends its rays and light through a window.⁸ From these, trees and herbs and all fruits arise; from them, animals and water and fire and all things are produced; and are again resolved into the same.'⁹ This can be endured as long as it is a question of small things. But then he went on. 'From these even the world has been put together.' He fulfilled the requirement of perfect insanity! It would seem that nothing further could be added, but he found something which he might add. 'Since everything,' he said, 'is infinite and there cannot be anything empty, it is necessary, therefore, that there be innumerable worlds.'¹⁰ How great had been the power of atoms that such inestimable masses were conglobated from such tiny bodies?

First of all, I would inquire what is the plan or origin of those seeds of his. If all things are from them, whence shall we say, therefore, that they themselves come? What nature has provided such a great supply for bringing about even innumerable worlds? But let us concede that he raved with impunity about worlds; let us speak of this one in which we are and which we see.

He says that all things are made from separate little bodies.¹¹ If this were so, nothing would ever need seed of its own kind: birds would be born without eggs, or eggs would come with-

---
7 Lucretius 2.453-455.
8 *Ibid.* 2.114ff.; cf. Isidore, *Origines* 13.2.1.
9 Cf. Lucretius 1.744ff.; 820ff.
10 Cf. *ibid.* 2.1048ff.
11 Cf. *ibid.* 1.160-162.

out birth; and, likewise, other living things without coition; trees and things which are produced from the land would not have their own seeds which we handle and sow daily. Why does a cornfield spring from corn, and, again, corn from a cornfield? In short, if the coition and conglobation of atoms brought about all things, everything would grow together in the air, inasmuch as atoms fly about in empty space. Why without earth, without roots, without moisture, without seed can no herb, no tree, no fruits spring up and grow? From this is clear that nothing is produced from the atoms since every single thing has its own peculiar and fixed nature, its own seed, its own law given from the beginning. Finally, Lucretius, as though forgetting the atoms which he was propounding, by which he was confuting those who say that all things are made from nothing, made use of these very arguments which were powerful against himself. For he said: 'If things come from nothing, any kind might be born of anything; nothing would require seed.'[12] And then later: 'It must be considered, therefore, that nothing can come from nothing since things have need of seed so that each may be fashioned and led out into the gentle realms of air.'[13]

Who would think that he possessed a brain when he said such things as these and did not see that they were contradictory? That nothing is made from atoms is clear from this, that the seed of each thing is fixed, unless we will believe by chance that the nature of fire and of water is from atoms. What about the fact that fire is struck out if materials of the strongest hardness are rubbed together with a very vehement blow? Are the atoms hidden in the iron or in the flint? Who shut them in? Or why do they not spurt forth of their own accord? Or how could the seeds of fire remain in exceedingly cold matter?

I dismiss flint and iron. If you hold in the sun a glass ball full of water, from the light which is refracted from the water

---
12 *Ibid.* 1.159-161.
13 *Ibid.* 1.205-207.

fire is enkindled, even in the most severe cold. It should not be believed, should it, that the fire is also in the water? But still fire cannot be kindled from the sun, not even in summer. If you breathe upon wax, or if some light vapor touches anything, say the surface of marble or a plate, gradually in the tiniest drops water condenses. Likewise, from the exhalation of the land or sea a vapor is formed, and this mist either disperses and moistens whatever it touches, or collected on high mountains and snatched aloft by the wind it is compressed into a cloud and sends down the greatest showers.[14] Yet, where do we say that the fluid atoms are? In the vapor? In the exhalation? In the wind? But nothing can have position in that which is neither touched nor seen.

What shall I say, therefore, of the animals in whose bodies we see that nothing has been formed without plan, without order, without utility, without beauty to such a degree that the most skilled and careful arrangement of all the parts defies accident and chance? But let us imagine that the limbs and bones and sinews and blood were able to come together from atoms. What of the senses, thought, mind, memory, and ability? From what seeds can they be put together? 'From the minutest,' he says. There are, then, other larger ones. In what way are they not able to be cut?

To go on, if things which are not seen are from invisible seeds, it follows that those which are seen are from visible seeds. Why, then, does no one see them? But whether you consider the invisible things which are in man or the tangible things which come under one's notice, who does not see that both are based on a plan? How, then, can things coming together without plan effect anything reasonable? For we see that there is nothing in all the world which does not have in itself a very great and marvelous construction-plan. Inasmuch as this is above the understanding and capacity of man, to what more rightly than to divine providence ought it be assigned?

---

14 Cf. *ibid.* 1.305ff.; 6.470ff.; 6.451ff.

If reason and artistic skill fashion an image of man and a statue, shall we suppose that man himself is made from pieces rushing together at random? And what likeness of truth is there in the thing fashioned, when very great and exceptional workmanship can imitate nothing else except the shadow and extreme lineaments of the body? Can human skill give to its work either movement or any feeling? I omit the function of seeing, hearing, smelling, and the marvelous uses of the other members, either apparent or concealed. What artificer could fashion the heart of man, or his voice, or his wisdom itself? Does any sane person think, therefore, that what man cannot make with reason and plan could be accomplished by the indiscriminate coming together of cohering atoms? You see into what ravings they have fallen while they are unwilling to grant to God the accomplishment and care of things.

Let us concede to them, however, that the things which are earthly are made from atoms. Are the things which are heavenly also? They say that the gods are incorrupt, eternal, happy, and to them alone they give immunity, so that they may not be seen to be formed by the concourse of atoms. For if the gods also had come from these, that would be able to be dissipated, the seeds resolving at times and recurring to their own nature. Therefore, if there is something which atoms have not brought about, why do we not understand that this is the case with other things, too? My question is, before those beginning-bodies had generated the world, why did not the gods build a dwelling for themselves? Surely, unless the atoms had come together and made heaven, the gods would still be hanging in the empty middle.[15] By what plan, therefore, by what arrangement of the confused heap did the atoms collect themselves, that from some of them, in space below, the earth should be conglobated, and that in space above, the sky should be spread, marked with such a great variety of stars that nothing more beautiful could ever be imagined? Can he who sees things so great and of such a kind believe that they were

---
15 Cf. Epicurus, frg. 354 (Usener, p. 238.21).

brought about by no plan, by no providence, by no divine reason, but that such great marvels have been compacted from fine and minute particles? Is it not like a prodigy either that there was born a man to say these things or that there existed those who believed them, such as Democritus who was the pupil, or Epicurus whose entire folly flowed forth from the font of Leucippus?[16]

But to hold the notion that the world was made by nature, which is without perception and form, as others say[17]—this is truly much more absurd. If nature made the world, it must have made it by plan and reason: for only that makes something which possesses either the will or the knowledge of making. If it lacks perception and form, how can there be made from it that which has both perception and form? Unless, perhaps, someone thinks that the fabric of living things, so delicate and so wondrous as it is, could have been fashioned and quickened by a non-perceiving agent, or that the very sight of heaven so providently tempered for the enjoyment of living creatures suddenly came to be in some way, without an establisher, without an artificer? 'If there is anything,' says Chrysippus, 'which brings about those things which man, endowed as he is with reason, cannot do, that surely is greater and stronger and wiser than man. Now man cannot make celestial bodies; therefore, that which brings about or has brought about these surpasses man in art, in purpose, in prudence, in power. Who, then, can it be except God?'[18]

But if nature, which they consider to be, as it were, the mother of things, has no mind, it will never bring about anything nor fashion anything. For where there is not thought,

---

16 Democritus lived from c. 460 to c. 370 B.C., a wealthy citizen of Abdera in Thrace. He adopted the atomic theory of his master Leucippus (cf. n. 2).
    Epicurus, c. 342 to c. 271 B.C., was an Athenian. He founded a philosophic community. He is the great master and hero of Lucretius' poem, *De rerum natura*.
17 Cf. Cicero, *De natura deorum* 1.20.53.
18 Cf. *ibid*. 2.6.16; 3.7.17; 3.10.25. Chrysippus who was in charge of the Stoic school from 232-207 B.C. elaborated and corrected the earlier Stoic system of Zeno.

neither is there any motion or efficacy. But if it uses plan for undertaking anything, reason for disposing it, art for effecting it, energy for consummating it, power for ruling and controlling it, why should it be called nature rather than God?

Or if a concourse of atoms, or a nature, bereft of mind, has brought about those things which we see, I ask why it could make the sky and not a city or a house; why it made mountains of marble, but did not make columns and statues.[19] But should not the atoms also have come together for effecting these things, inasmuch as they leave no position which they do not try? With regard to nature which has not a mind, it ought not to be wondered that she forgot to make these things.

What, therefore, is the conclusion? Surely, God Himself, when He began this work of the world, than which nothing can be more disposed as to order, nor more fit as to utility, nor more adorned as to beauty, nor greater as to size, made the things which could not be made by man; and, among these, He made man himself, too. He gave to him a share of His own wisdom and equipped him with reason, as much as his earthly frailness could take, that he might make for himself what would be necessities for his use.

If, however, in the commonwealth, so to speak, of this world, there is no providence which rules, no God who administers; if no perception at all holds sway in this nature of things, whence, then, shall the human mind be believed to have sprung, which is so skillful, so intelligent? For if the body of man was made from dust, whence man took his name,[20] then the soul, which has wisdom, which is the ruler of the body, to which its members yield as to a king and commander, which can neither be seen nor comprehended, could not come into a man unless from a wise nature. And as the mind and soul govern the whole body, so does God govern the world. Nor is it likely, indeed, that lesser and lowly things have

---
19 *Ibid.* 3.37.94.
20 Cf. Isidore, *Origines* 11.1.4; *De differentiis rerum* 17.47. Cf. also *Inst.* 2.10 (vol. 49, this series, pp. 140-141). The etymology accepted is that *homo* (man) is from *humus* (earth).

power of control and that greater and supreme things do not. In short, Marcus Cicero in his *Tusculans* and *Consolation* says that 'no origin of souls on earth can be found. For there is in souls nothing mixed or compacted or which may be produced or fashioned of earth, nothing—not even anything moist, or airy, or fiery. In these natures, there is nothing which may have the power of memory, of mind, of thought, which may hold past things, foresee the future, and be able to embrace the present; these are attributes solely divine, and there will never be found a means by which they can come to man except from God.'[21] Except for two or three vain calumniators, then, it is accepted that the world is ruled by Divine Providence, just as it was also thus made. And since there is not anyone who dares to prefer the opinion of Diagoras and Theodorus[22] or the inane invention of Leucippus or the fickleness of Democritus and Epicurus to the authority either of those seven early ones who were called 'Wise'[23] or of Pythagoras or Socrates or Plato or of the other very fine philosophers who have judged that there is a providence, that opinion whereby they think that religion was instituted by wise men because of terror and fear, in order that uncultivated men might refrain from sins, is also false.

But if this should be true, then we have been fooled by the sages of old. And if, for the sake of deceiving us and, therefore, the entire human race, they invented religion, then they were not wise, because lying does not fall within the character of a wise man. But they may have been wise. Then what great delight of lying was it that they deceived not only the unlearned, but Plato also and Socrates, and that they so

---
21 Cf. Cicero, *Disputationes Tusculanae* 1.27.66; *Consolatio*, frg. 13.
22 Diagoras, a lyric poet of Melos, seems to have been active in the last quarter of the 5th century B.C. According to Cicero (*De nat. deor.* I.2.63), he was renowned for his atheism.
  Theodorus of Cyrene was his contemporary. He was a mathematician, a teacher of Plato and Theaetetus (cf. Plato, *Theaetetus* 147D-148B). He was taught by Protagoras, the Sophist, who held that man is the measure of all things.
23 The Seven Sages, the traditional list of the seven wise men among the early Greeks; cf. Coppleston, *op. cit.*

easily deluded Pythagoras, Zeno, Aristotle, leading men of the greatest sects? There is, however, a Divine Providence, as all these whom I have mentioned believed, by whose force and power all things which we see were made and are ruled. Such a great magnitude of things, such a disposition, such a constancy in preserving orders and times could neither come about in time without a provident artificer, nor remain for so many ages without an indwelling power, nor be governed in perpetuity without a knowing and perceiving ruler. Reason itself declares this. Whatever is, therefore, which has reason must have arisen from reason. Reason is characteristic of a sentient and wise nature. That wise and sentient nature can be nothing other than God. So the world, since it has reason whereby it is ruled and kept in existence, was, therefore, made by God. And if the establisher and ruler of the world is God, then rightly and truly has religion been founded; for to the Author and Common Parent of things honor and veneration are due.

Chapter 11

Since we have treated the matter of providence, it follows that we should show whether it is to be believed as the quality of many gods, or rather of only one. We have demonstrated sufficiently, I think, in our *Institutes*[1] that there cannot be many gods, because if the divine might and power were distributed among more than one, it would have to be lessened. What is lessened is certainly mortal. But if it is not mortal, it can neither be lessened nor divided. Now God is one, in whom force and consummate power can be neither diminished nor increased. If, however, there should be many gods, while they have individually some power and will, the sum itself decreases, nor will they be able to have individually the whole which is held in common with the many; for to each one so

---

[1] *Inst.* 1.3ff. (vol. 49, this series, pp. 22-93).

much will be lacking as the others will possess. There cannot be, therefore, in this world many rulers, nor in one house many masters, nor on one ship many pilots, nor in one herd many leaders, nor in one hive many queens.² Not even in the sky can there be many suns, just as there are not several souls in one body.³ Thus does all nature harmonize into unity. But if the world 'A spirit within nourishes, and the mind diffused throughout the limbs stirs the whole mass and mingles itself with the great body,'⁴ it is apparent from the poet's testimony that the god-inhabitant of the world is one, since the whole body cannot be inhabited and ruled except by one mind. So it is necessary, then, that the whole divine power be in one, by whose nod and command all things are ruled. He is so great that He cannot be described in words nor grasped by the senses of man.⁵

Whence, then, did there come about the persuasive idea of many gods? Actually, all those who are cultivated as gods were men, and the same were the earliest and greatest kings. These, having attained immortal memory, were treated after death with divine honors either on account of the courage with which they had excelled the race of men, or on account of the benefits and inventions with which they had adorned human life. Not only men were honored, but also women. And both the oldest Greek writers, whom they call Theologoi, and also the Romans, following and imitating the Greeks, teach this; and chief among them, Euhemerus and our own Ennius who point out the births, marriages, progenies, commands, deeds, passings, tombs of all of them.⁶ Following their lead, Tullius, in his third book *On the Nature of the Gods,* dissolved the public religions; but the true one, however, which he did not know, neither he himself nor anyone else

---

2 This may be a Vergilian echo because the text uses the word *kings* with *swarm*.
3 Cf. Minucius Felix 18.7.
4 Vergil, *Aeneid* 6.726-727.
5 Cf. Minucius Felix 18.8.
6 Cf. Cicero, *De natura deorum* 3.21.53; 1.42.119.

could introduce. To this extent even he testified that the false was indeed manifest, but that the truth was hidden. 'Would that I were able,' he said, 'to come upon true things as easily as to overcome those that are false.'[7] This, indeed, he proclaimed, not dissimulatingly as an Academician, but truly and according to his judgment, because the truth can never be withdrawn from human senses. That which human foresight could attain to, it has attained to, in order to uncover false things. And whatever is feigned and fabricated, because it is supported by no reason, is easily dissolved.

There is, therefore, one principle and origin of things, God, as Plato in the *Timaeus* both understood and taught. And His majesty, he declares, is so great that it can be neither grasped by the mind nor expressed by the tongue.[8] Hermes admits the same, who Cicero says is considered in the number of the gods among the Egyptians.[9] He means that Hermes, in fact, who, because of his strength and understanding of many skills, was called *Termaximus;*[10] and he was more ancient by far than not just Plato, but even Pythagoras and those Seven Sages. According to Xenophon, Socrates states in a discussion that the 'form of God ought not to be investigated,'[11] and Plato in the *Laws* that 'what God is precisely ought not to be inquired since this can neither be discovered nor expounded.'[12] Pythagoras also acknowledges that there is but one God. He said that Mind, which is diffused and extended through all the natures of things and which gives vital sensitivity to all living beings, is incorporeal.[13] Antisthenes in the *Physics* said

---

7 Cf. *ibid.* 1.32.91.
8 Cf. Plato, *Timaeus* 28C; Cicero, *De natura deorum* 1.12.30; Minucius Felix 19.14.
9 Cicero, *ibid.* 3.22.56.
10 Hermes Termaximus or Trismegistus (i.e., 'Thrice greatest'). He was an Egyptian philosopher of great antiquity. 'Thoth, the Very Great,' the reputed author of the philosophico-religious treatises known as *Hermetica;* cf. Isidore, *Origines* 8.11.49.
11 Cf. Xenophon, *Memorabilia* 4.3.13; Cicero, *De natura deorum* 1.12.31; Minucius Felix 19.13.
12 Cf. Plato, *Laws* 7.821A; Cicero, *De natura deorum* 1.12.30.
13 Cf. Cicero, *ibid.* 1.11.27; Minucius Felix 19.6.

that there is one natural god, although tribes and cities have their own native gods.[14] Aristotle, along with his followers, the Peripatetics, and Zeno with his, the Stoics, have held about the same belief.

It would be a lengthy task to track down the opinions of the individual thinkers, who, although they have made use of diverse names, yet have concurred in admitting that there is one power which rules the world. But although philosophers and poets and those, in short, who reverence the gods often acknowledge the one supreme God; still, however, no one has ever inquired into the matters of His worship and honors; no one has ever treated them, under an impression, no doubt, whereby they believe that God is ever beneficent and incorrupt, and they think that He would neither feel angry toward anyone nor be in need of any worship. So religion cannot exist where there is no fear.

Chapter 12

Now, since we have responded to the impious and detestable wisdom, rather senselessness, of certain writers and teachers, let us return to the problem. We said that, if religion is removed, neither wisdom nor justice can be held on to; wisdom, because the understanding of divinity, in which we differ from the beasts, is found in man alone, and justice, because, unless God who cannot be deceived restrains our passions, we will live wickedly and impiously. Therefore, that our actions are watched by God has connection, not only with the usefulness of common life, but also with the truth; for, if religion and justice are withdrawn, we are reduced in our loss of reason either to the stupidity of cattle or to the wildness of beasts. It is even more of a degradation because the beasts spare the animals of their own kind. What would be more

---

14 Cf. Cicero, *ibid.* 1.13.32.

fierce than man, what more unmerciful, if, the fear of a higher being taken away, he should be able to either escape the force of laws or despise it? It is the fear of God alone, therefore, which guards the society of men among themselves; through it life itself is sustained, fortified, governed. But that fear is taken away if man should be convinced that God is without anger. God is moved and indignant when injustices are done. Not only ordinary usefulness, but also reason itself and truth convince us of this. Again, we have to go back to the points made above, so that, since we showed that the world was made by God, we may now show why it was made.

Chapter 13

If one considers the entire administration of the world, he will certainly understand how true is the opinion of the Stoics who say that the world was arranged for our benefit.[1] For all the things of which the world consists and which it generates from itself have been ordained to the usefulness of man. Man uses fire for the purpose of heat and light and of softening foods and the working of iron. He uses the springs for drinking and for bathing; the rivers for irrigating fields and marking land boundaries. He uses the earth for reaping a variety of fruits, the level ground for grains, the hilly parts for planting vineyards, the mountains for the cultivation of forests and lumber. He uses the sea, not only for commerce and the bearing of supplies from far-off regions, but also for its yield of all kinds of fish.[2]

If he makes use of these elements to which he is so near, there is not a doubt that he uses also the sky, since the functions of celestial bodies have been tempered to the fertility of the earth from which we live. The sun with ceaseless coursings

---

[1] Cf. Cicero, *De natura deorum* 2.61.154.
[2] Cf. *ibid.* 2.60.151f; 1.39.98ff.

and unequal intervals completes yearly cycles, and either in its rising leads forth the day for labor or at its setting brings on the night for rest, and, then, by its recess farther south and, again, by its approach closer to the north, it makes the changes of winter and summer. As a result, through the winter moistures and frosts, the earth increases in strength and richness, on the one hand; and, on the other hand, by means of the summer heat either the grassy growths are hardened in maturity or those which are in moist places ripen with in-warming and heating. The moon also, governess of the night time, regulates her monthly courses, by turns of light alternately lost and regained, and she lights up the nights, dark with gloomy shadows, with the brightness of her shining so that summer journeys, and expeditions, and works may be accomplished without trouble and inconvenience, inasmuch as

> By night the light stubble, by night
> The dry meadows are better mown.[3]

The other stars also, by their risings or settings in fixed positions, serve for the advantages of the seasons. And they provide direction to ships so that they will not wander into the immense deep by a devious course, since the pilot who observes them rightly comes through to the shore port of his destination. Clouds are drawn and formed by the blowing of the winds, that the sowed crops may be watered with rains, that the vines may be rich in grapes and the trees in fruits. And these things are displayed in succession or by turns throughout the year so that there might not be lacking, at any time, that by which the life of man is sustained.

But (it may be said) the same earth nourishes other living things, and by the produce of the same earth even the dumb beasts are fed. God has not labored also for the sake of the beasts, has He? Not at all, because they are without reason. We understand, moreover, that these very beasts were made by God in the same way for man's use, some for food, some for clothing, some for help in his work, so it is clear that

---

[3] Vergil, *Georgics* 1.289-290.

the Divine Providence wished to equip and adorn the life of men with an abundance of materials and supplies, and, for this reason, He filled the sky with birds and the sea with fishes and the earth with quadrupeds.[4] The Academics, in arguing against the Stoics, usually ask why, if God made all things for the sake of men, many things contrary and harmful and injurious to us are also found both in the sea and on land.[5] The Stoics refuted this, most foolishly not considering the truth. For they say that there are many things in the productions and numbers of animals, the utility of which still lies hidden, that will be discovered in the process of time, just as necessity and use have now discovered many things unknown to former ages. What utility, then, can be found in mice, in beetles, in serpents which are burdensome and harmful to man? Or does some healing lie hidden in them? If there is, it may be found at some time, surely to serve against evils, although they complain now that these are entirely evil! They say that the viper, when burned and reduced to ashes, cures the bite of the same beast. How much better it would have been for that not to exist at all than for it to be sought as a remedy for itself from itself![6]

They could have answered, however, rather briefly and very truly in this manner. When God made man as His image, the creation which was the summation of the divine workmanship, He breathed wisdom into him alone, so that he might subjugate all things to his power and sway and make use of all the advantages of the world. He put before him, however, both good things and evil, because He gave him wisdom, the whole reason of which rests in discerning good and evil. For no one can choose the better and know what is good unless he knows, at the same time, how to reject and avoid what things are evil. Both are mutually connected with each other, so that if one is removed, the other has to be taken away. Since good

---
4 Cf. Cicero, *De natura deorum* 2.63.158f.
5 Cf. Cicero, *Prior Academics* 2.38.120.
6 Cf. Plutarch, *De Stoicorum repugnantiis* 21.4.

and evil things, therefore, have been set down, wisdom, at last, performs its work and, indeed, seeks the good for utility and rejects the evil for safety.[7]

Therefore, as innumerable goods have been given which it might be able to enjoy, so also evils have been placed for it to avoid. For if there were no evil, no danger, nothing, in short, which could harm man, the whole matter of wisdom would be removed, nor would it even be necessary for man. If only goods are set before his sight, what is the need of thought, understanding, knowledge, and reason, since wherever he extends his hand, there is that which is suited and arranged to nature? As an example, if anyone should wish to place a completely arranged full-course dinner before infants who as yet have no taste, surely they will each reach for that to which either impulse or hunger or even chance has attracted each one, and whatever they take will be for them life-sustaining and healthful. What harm will it do them to remain as they are and always to be infants and ignorant of affairs? But if you mingle bitter things, or useless things, or even poisonous things, they will certainly be deceived due to their ignorance of good and evil, unless there comes to them the wisdom through which they may possess the rejecting of evils and the choosing of goods.

You see, then, that we need wisdom much more on account of evils. Unless these had been set before us, we would not be rational animals. And if this reasoning is true, which the Stoics could see in no way, that argument of Epicurus is dissolved also where he says: 'God either wishes to take away

---

[7] On this matter of evil as being known only by contrast with the good, cf. the doctrine in St. Thomas, *Summa theologica* I.48. In Article 1, he states: 'One opposite is known through the other as darkness is known through light. Hence also what evil is must be known from the nature of good.' And in Article 3: 'Evil exists in good as in its subject.'

On the will and its movement by and choice of the good, cf. St. Thomas, *S.T.* I, 11, qq. 1-10.

Here in Lactantius the word *sapientia* (wisdom) can be equated with the 'intellect-directed willing' or 'choice' of later writers. It is 'moral wisdom.' Cf. A Blaise, *Dictionnaire latin-français des auteurs chrétiens*, p. 738.

evils and he cannot, or he can and does not wish to, or he neither wishes to nor is able, or he both wishes to and is able. If he wishes to and is not able, he is feeble, which does not fall in with the notion of god. If he is able to and does not wish to, he is envious, which is equally foreign to god. If he neither wishes to nor is able, he is both envious and feeble and therefore not god. If he both wishes to and is able, which alone is fitting to god, whence, therefore, are there evils, and why does he not remove them?"[8] I know that quite a number of philosophers who defend the notion of providence are accustomed to be disturbed by this argument and, unwilling, they are almost forced to confess that God cares for nothing, which Epicurus is especially aiming at. But when the reasoning has been examined, we easily bring this formidable argument to dissolution.

For God is able to do whatever He wishes, and there is no feebleness or envy in Him. He can, therefore, remove evils. But He may not wish to; nor is He, on that account, however, envious. This is the reason that He does not take them away, since He granted wisdom at the same time, as I have explained, and there is more good and pleasure in wisdom than there is annoyance in evils. For wisdom brings it about that we know even God and, through that knowledge, we seek immortality, which is the highest good. And so, unless we first recognize the evil, we shall not be able to recognize the good. But Epicurus did not see this, nor anyone else, that if evils are taken away, wisdom is equally removed; nor do any vestiges of virtue remain in man, the nature of which consists in sustaining and overcoming the bitterness of evils. So for the sake of the slight gain of having evils removed, we should be deprived of a very great good, a real good, and one proper to us. It stands, therefore, that all things are proposed for man, evils and goods as well.

---

8 Cf. Epicurus, frg. 374 (Usener, p. 252.30). It has been suggested by Schwenk (cf. note in Brandt's text, p. 103) that this section should be used for the lost or mutilated part of Cicero's *De natura deorum*, book 3. Cf. Minucius Felix 12.2; Cicero, *op. cit.* 1.2.3.

Chapter 14

It follows that I should discuss why God made man himself. As He fashioned the world for the sake of man, so man himself He formed for Himself, to be, as it were, an overseer of the divine temple, a spectator of His works and of heavenly things. For it is he alone who, possessing senses and capable of reason, is able to 'understand' God,[1] who can admire His works, perceive His strength and power. Wherefore he has been endowed with judgment, intelligence, prudence. And so, too, he alone beyond other living creatures has been formed of upright body and stature so that he seems to have been 'called' or raised to the contemplation of his Parent. For this reason, he alone has received speech and language as interpreter of thought so that he might be able to declare the majesty of his Master.[2] Finally, on this account, all things have been subject to him so that he himself might be subject to God, his Maker and Artificer. If, then, God wished man to be His worshiper and for this reason granted him so much honor that he might hold dominion over all things, surely, it is most just to love both the God who has bestowed such great gifts and man who has been joined to us by a fellowship of divine sanction. It is not right for a worshiper of God to be violated by a worshiper of God. Whence we understand that man was fashioned because of religion and justice. Marcus Tullius is a witness of this in his work on *Laws* where he speaks thus: 'But of all the things which are treated in the discussion of learned men, certainly nothing is more outstanding than that we are plainly understood to have been born for justice.'[3] Now since this is quite true, God, therefore, wishes all men to be just, that is, to hold God and man dear, to

---
1 The word is *intellegere*, 'to get to know,' to know God through the intellective faculty, though not to fully grasp or comprehend Him.
2 Here, again, is one of Lactantius' favorite themes. Cf. *Inst.* 2.1 and 8 *passim* (vol. 49, this series); cf. also Cicero, *De natura deorum* 2.56.140; Lucretius 6.1149.
3 Cicero, *De legibus* 1.10.28.

honor God, actually, as a Father and to love man as a brother.[4] Upon these two, all justice rests. But he who does not acknowledge God, or harms man, lives unjustly and against his nature and, in this way, he breaks the divine institution and law.

Chapter 15

Here, perhaps, someone may ask how it is that sins have come to man or what depravity has twisted the rule of divine institution to worse things so that, although he is born to justice, man performs unjust works. I have already explained above[1] that God has set forth simultaneously good and evil, and that He, indeed, loves the good but hates the evil which is repugnant to the good. Nevertheless, He has permitted the evil for this reason, that good may come from it, because, as I have often taught, we understand that the one cannot exist without the other. And, finally, the world itself has been put together from two elements, opposed and yet joined to one another, fire and moisture. And light could not have been made unless there had been darkness, because there cannot be a higher without a lower, nor a rising without a falling, nor heat without cold, nor soft without hard. Thus we, too, have been made up of two equally opposing parts, soul and body, one of which is assigned to heaven because it is light and intractable, the other to earth because it is within grasp; the one is substantial and eternal, the other is frail and mortal. Therefore, good adheres to the one, evil to the other. To the one is associated light, life, justice; to the other darkness, death, injustice. Hence, there arose in man the depravity of his nature so that it was necessary for law to be established whereby the vices could be prohibited and the duties of virtue enjoined.

---
4 Cf. Matt. 22.40.
1 In ch. 13, p. 91.

Since, therefore, there are good and evil things in human affairs, the scheme of which I have set forth, it is of necessity that God is moved with reference to each. He is moved to kindness when He sees just things done, and to wrath when He beholds the unjust. But Epicurus is in opposition to us and he says: 'If there is in God a movement of joy unto kindness and of hatred unto wrath, then He must have both fear, and inclination, and desire, and the other affections which belong to human feebleness.'[2] It is not of necessity that he who is angry should fear, or that he who rejoices should grieve. In fact, those who are prone to anger are less timid, and those who are joyous by nature grieve less. What need is there to speak of the human affections to which our frailty yields? Let us consider the divine necessity—I do not like to say *nature* because God is believed to have never been born.[3] The affection of fear has matter in man; in God it has not. Man, since he is subject to many chances and dangers, fears that some greater force exists which may strike, despoil, lacerate, afflict, and destroy him; God, however, on whom there falls neither need, nor injury, nor pain, nor death, can fear in no way because there is nothing that can bear force against Him.

Likewise, the reason and cause of desire in man is manifest. For, because he was made fragile and mortal, it was necessary that another and different sex should be constituted, by union with which offspring could be brought forth to further the continuance of the race.[4] But this desire has no place in God because frailty and death are foreign to Him; nor is there any woman in whose union with Him He could rejoice; nor does He need succession who is always going to be. The same things can be said about envy and passion which are found in man for certain evident reasons, but in God in no way at all. But, truly, kindness and wrath and pity have matter in

---
[2] Cf. Epicurus, frg. 366 (Usener, p. 244.19).
[3] The word-play is not retained in English: *natura* (nature) and *natus* (having been born).
[4] Cf. *De opificio Dei* ch. 12, n. 4, p. 40.

God, and rightly does that supreme and singular Power use them for the preservation of things.

Chapter 16

Somebody may ask what that matter is. First, men, when they are afflicted with besetting evils, generally flee to God, placate Him, beseech Him, believing that He can drive evils from them. Therefore, God has a reason for feeling pity, and He is not so harsh and contemptuous of men that He refuses aid to those in trouble. Then, too, there are very many who are convinced that justice is pleasing to God; and these venerate Him because He is the Lord and Parent of all, and they offer Him gifts and sacrifices with persevering prayer and frequent promises. They attend His name with praises; they take pains to oblige Him with good and holy works. It is, therefore, on this account that God is both able to be and ought to be gratified. And if there is nothing so suited to God as beneficence, and also nothing so foreign than that He be ungrateful, it is necessary that He offer something to those who are very good and living holy lives, and that He make return to them that He may not suffer the blame of ingratitude, which is reproachful even in man.

On the contrary, however, there are others, vicious and nefarious men, who pollute all things with lusts, plague others with killings, defraud them, steal and perjure; they spare neither their relatives nor their parents, and they ignore laws and even God Himself. Therefore, wrath in God has matter. For it is not right for Him, when He sees such things being done, not to be moved and to rise up in vengeance against the criminals and to destroy those baneful and harmful ones, in order to have regard for all the good. On this score, in the very wrath there is gratification. So the arguments are found to be empty, either of those who, when they object to God's being angry, mean that He is pleased, since not even this can be done without anger, or of those who think that there is no movement of the mind in God. Because there are some affections which do not happen to be found in God, like desire, fear, avarice, grief, envy, they have said that He is utterly free from all affection. He is free of these because they are affections of vices; but, those which are of virtue, that is, anger toward the evil, love toward the good, compassion for the afflicted, since they are becoming to His divine power, these God experiences as His own, and they are just and true. And, certainly, unless He has these, human life will be disturbed and the state of affairs will come to such great confusion that, with the contempt and surpassing of laws, only boldness will reign. Finally, it will come about that no one may be safe unless he excels in strength; thus through highway robbery, as it were, on a general scale the whole earth will be destroyed.

Now, however, since the evil expect punishment and the good kindness and the afflicted help, there exists place-rank for virtues and crimes are more rarely committed. But, generally, it seems that the wicked are the more fortunate, and the good the more wretched, and the just are harassed by the unjust with impunity. We will consider later why things like that happen. Meanwhile, let us unravel the question of anger, whether there is any in God, or whether He cares for nothing at all and is not moved at those things which are done sinfully.

Chapter 17

'God,' says Epicurus, 'cares for nothing.'[1] Therefore, He has no power—for it is necessary that he who has power exercise care—or if He has power and does not use it, what is the reason of negligence so great that, I will not say our race, but

---

1 Cf. Epicurus, frg. 360.

even the world itself, is vile and worthless to Him? 'On this account,' he says, 'He is incorrupt and blessed, because He is always quiet.'[2] To whom, then, has the administration of such great affairs yielded, if these things which we see controlled by the highest plan are neglected by God? Or how is he who lives and feels able in any way to be quiet? For quiet is a quality of either sleep or death. But not even does sleep have quiet. For when we are asleep, the body, indeed, is resting, but the mind, not at rest, is in motion. It forms for itself the images which it may perceive so that it exercises its natural motion by a variety of visions, and it calls itself away from the false until the members are satiated and strengthened from rest.[3] Everlasting rest, therefore, belongs to death alone. But if death does not touch God, then God is never at rest. And what can the activity of God be, therefore, except the administration of the world?

Now if God exercises care for the world, then God cares for the life of men, and He takes note of the acts of individuals, and He wants them to be wise and good. This is the will of God; this is the divine law. He who follows it, he who observes it is dear to God. It is of necessity, therefore, that God be moved to anger against one who has violated or spurned this eternal and divine law. 'If God does harm to anyone, then,' he says, 'He is not good.' By no slight error are they deceived who defame censure, both human and divine, with the name of bitterness and malice, thinking that one who inflicts punishment on the harmful ought to be called harmful. If this is so, then we have harmful laws which have sanctioned punishments for those breaking them, harmful judges who inflict capital punishment on those convicted of crime. But if both the law is just which pays back to a harmful man what he deserves, and if a judge is called sound and good when he punishes evil deeds—for he who punishes the evil guards the safety of the

---
2 *Ibid.;* cf. Cicero, *De legibus* 1.7.21; *De divinatione* 2.50.104; *De natura deorum* 1.20.52.
3 Cf. *De opificio Dei* ch. 18, p. 53.

good—so God, too, when He opposes the evil, is not harmful. That one is harmful, however, who either harms an innocent man or spares a harmful one that he may do more harm.

We might ask those who imagine God immobile this question. If someone should have property, a home, an establishment, and if his slaves, despising the patience of the master, should invade everything, should themselves enjoy his goods, and if his household should honor them, and, on the other hand, should despise their master and ridicule and abandon him, could he be wise who would not avenge the insults, but would allow those over whom he has power to enjoy his possessions? What patience so great could be found in anyone, if it ought to be called patience and not a certain insensible stupor? But it is easy to bear contempt. What if those things which are spoken of by Cicero should take place? 'For I ask, if any head of a family, when his children had been put to death by a slave, his wife slain, his home burned, should not exact from that slave the severest possible punishment, whether he should seem to be kind and merciful or inhuman and most cruel.'[4] But if to pardon crimes of that sort is the mark of cruelty rather than of dutifulness, it is not, therefore, a mark of virtue in God not to be moved at those things which are done unjustly, because the world is as though the house of God and men are His slaves, as it were.[5] And if His name is a mockery to them, what sort of patience, or how great is it, to yield His own honors, and to see base and unjust deeds done and not be indignant, which is fitting and natural to Him to whom sins are displeasing? To be angry, therefore, is the part of reason; for faults are removed and license is restrained, and this certainly is acting justly and wisely.

But the Stoics did not see that there is a difference between right and wrong, that wrath is just and also unjust, and because they did not find a cure of the thing, they wished to do away with it altogether. The Peripatetics, however, held that

---
4 Cicero, *In Catilinam* 4.6.12.
5 Cf. Cicero, *De natura deorum* 2.62.154.

it should not be done away with but moderated; we have replied to them sufficiently in the sixth book of the *Institutes*.[6] That the philosophers did not know what was the nature of anger is clear from their definitions which Seneca has enumerated in the books which he wrote *On Anger*. 'Anger is,' he says, 'the desire of avenging an injury; or, as Posidonius says, the desire of punishing him by whom you think you have been hurt unfairly. Some define it thus: anger is the incitement of the mind to injure him who has either done an injury or wished to injure. Aristotle's definition is not much different from our own, for he says that anger is the desire of paying back pain.'[7] This is the unjust anger of which we spoke above, which resides even in the dumb beasts, and truly this should be restrained in man, lest through rage he should rush forth to exceedingly great evil. This cannot exist in God because He cannot be harmed, but it is found in man because he is frail. For injury inflames pain and pain causes a desire for revenge.

Where, then, is that just anger which causes reaction against offenders? This is surely not the desire for revenge since injury does not precede it. I do not speak of those who sin against the laws; for, although a judge can be angry with them without blame, still let us pretend that he ought to be of a calm mind when he inflicts punishment on the guilty, since he is a minister of the laws, not of his own mind or power, but thus they claim who try to root out anger. But I speak most of all about those who are within our power, for example, our slaves, children, wives, pupils. When we see these offend, we are aroused to reprove them. For it is necessary that things which are bad should displease one who is good and just, and he to whom evil is displeasing is moved when he sees it done. Therefore, we rise to punishment, not because we have been injured, but in order that discipline be preserved, morals corrected, and license suppressed. This is just anger.

---

[6] Cf. especially ch. 15 (vol. 49, this series, pp. 434-435).
[7] Seneca, *De ira* 1.2; 3.2; cf. Cicero, *Tusc.* 4.9.21.

And just as it is necessary in man for the correction of evil, so certainly is it in God from whom example comes to man. As we ought to restrain those who are subject to our power, so also ought God to restrain the sins of all. And in order that He do this, He has to get angry, since it is natural for a good person to be moved and aroused at the sin of another. Therefore, they ought to make a definition thus: Anger is a movement of a mind arising to the restraint of offenses. For the definition of Cicero, 'Anger is the desire of revenge,'[8] is not very different from the ones given above. So, then, the anger which we are able to call either fury or rage ought not even exist in man because it is completely vicious; but, that anger, on the other hand, which has to do with the correction of vices ought not to be taken from man, nor can it be taken from God, because it is both useful and necessary for human affairs.

Chapter 18

'What need is there,' they say, 'of anger, since offenses can be corrected without this affection?' But there is no one who is able to watch calmly a person guilty of committing an offense. Perhaps he who presides over the laws can, since the crime is not performed under his eyes, but it is brought to him as a matter of doubt from elsewhere. Nor can an evil deed ever be so manifest that there is no place for defense; and, therefore, a judge cannot be moved against him who may be found innocent; and, even after the detected crime shall come into the light, he uses no longer his own, but the opinion of the laws. But it may be granted that he does what he does without anger, for he has precedent which he may follow. We, of course, when an offense is committed at home by those of our own, whether we see it or perceive it, have to be indignant, for the very sight of sin is unworthy. He who is not

---

8 Cicero, *Tusc.* 4.19.44.

moved at all, either approves of the faults, which is more shameful and unjust, or he avoids the bother of correcting them, bother which a calm spirit and quiet mind shuns and rejects unless anger has goaded and aroused it. When he, however, who is moved, still with extreme leniency either forgives more often than necessary, or even always, that one is plainly destroying the life of those whose daring for greater crimes he fosters, and he is providing himself with perpetual matter for annoyance. Therefore, the restraint of anger in the case of sins is harmful.

Archytas, the Tarentine, is praised who, when he had discovered that everything in his field was ruined through the fault of his overseer, said, 'You wretch! I would have killed you with beatings if I had not been angry.'[1] Men think that this is an unique example of temperance, but, because they are influenced by authority, they do not see how foolishly he spoke and acted. For if, as Plato says, no prudent man punishes because there has been an offense, but lest there be offense, it is apparent what a bad example that wise man displayed.[2] If slaves feel that their master goes into a rage when he is not angry and is restrained when he is angry, they will certainly not commit light offenses, lest they be beaten; but, they will transgress as seriously as they can, so that they may arouse the ire of the perverse man and escape unpunished. I would praise him if, when he had been angry, he had merely given space or bent to his wrath so that, when the excitement of his mind settled in the course of time, his chastisement would be within measure. Punishment, therefore, on account of the greatness of his anger ought not to have been given, but it ought to have been deferred, lest it should either inflict a more than just penalty on the offender or provoke the rage of the punisher. Now, indeed, what fairness is there, finally, or what wisdom when one is punished for a slight fault and not pun-

---
[1] Archytas of Tarentum lived in the first half of the 4th century B.C. He was visited by Plato and had a great reputation in antiquity. Cf. Valerias Maximus 4.1. Ext. 1; Cicero, *Tusc.* 4.36.78.
[2] Cf. Plato, *Laws* XI.934A; Seneca, *De ira* 19.

ished for a very great one? If that man had learned the nature of things and their causes, he never would have admitted so unseemly a restraint, so that a worthless slave should rejoice that his master was angry with him. For just as God has equipped the human body with many different senses necessary for the use of life, so, too, He has assigned to the mind various affections on which the plan of life rests; and just as He gave sexual desire for the sake of propagating children, so He gave anger for the sake of correcting faults.

But those who do not know the ends of good and evil things, just as they use sexual desire for corruption and base pleasure, so they use the affection of anger for harm when they are angry with those whom they hate. At times, they are angry also with those who do not offend, even with their equals, even with their superiors. From here, it is a matter of leaping daily to inhuman crimes; hence, tragedies often arise. Archytas, then, would have been deserving of praise, if, when he had been angry at some citizen or equal who had injured him, he had restrained himself, however, and had mitigated the impulse of his fury with patience. This control of self is glorious when, by it, some great impending evil is restrained, but it is wrong not to punish the offenses of slaves and children, for they go on to greater evil through impunity. In this case, anger should not be restrained, and it should even, if it lies still, be stirred up.

What we say about man on this score, we also say about God who made man like to Himself. I do not mention the figure of God, since the Stoics say that God has not any form, and another mass of material should spring up if I wished to refute them. I speak only of the spirit. If it belongs to God to think, to be wise, to understand, to foresee, to excel, and since of all the animals man alone has these abilities, then, he has been made to the image of God. But it is on this account, too, that he proceeds to vice; because, mixed with earthly frailty, he cannot preserve incorrupt and pure that which he received from God, unless by the same God he be imbued with precepts of justice.

Chapter 19

But since man is made up, as we have said,[1] of two parts, soul and body, virtues are contained in one part and vices in the other, and these struggle against each other. For the goods of the soul, which consist in restraining lusts, are opposed to those of the body; and the goods of the body, which consist of every kind of pleasure, are inimical to the soul. But if strength of soul resists the desires and checks them, then, indeed, will man be like to God. Whence it is clear that the life-principle of man, which grasps divine strength, is not mortal. But there is that distinction, namely, that, since virtue has bitterness and the enticement of pleasure is sweet, many are overcome and are drawn to the sweetness. And since these have pledged themselves to the body and to earthly things, they are pressed to the earth, nor are they able to attain to the favor of the divine bounty since they have stained themselves with the defilements of vice. But they who, following God and obeying Him, despise the desires of the body, and, preferring virtue to delights, preserve innocence and justice, these God recognizes as like to Himself.

Since He has laid down that most holy law, then, and wishes all men to be innocent and good, is it possible for Him not to be angry when He sees His law despised, virtue discarded, pleasure pursued? But if He is the administrator of the world, as He ought to be, surely He does not despise that which in all the world is the very greatest thing. If He is foreseeing, as befits God, surely He looks out for the interest of human kind, He provides that human life may be fuller and better and safer. If He is the Father and Lord of all, certainly He is pleased with the virtues of men and aroused by their vices. Therefore, He both loves the just and hates the wicked.

'There is no need,' that one says, 'for hatred, for He has determined, once and for all, a reward for the good and

---
[1] Cf. ch. 15, p. 95.

punishment for the evil.' But if someone lives justly and innocently and, at the same time, neither worships God nor cares for Him at all, as Aristides[2] and Cimon[3] and several of the philosophers did, shall he enjoy impunity from the fact that, although he obeyed the law of God, he spurned God Himself? This is something on account of which God can be angry with one rebelling against Him; it is as though it were in full accord with His integrity. If He can be angry with this one on account of pride, why not more so with the sinner who has contemned the law together with the Law-giver? A judge is not able to give pardon because he serves the will of another; but God can because He is Himself the Determiner of His law and its Judge; and when He laid it down, certainly He did not take away from Himself all power, but He holds the right of pardoning.

Chapter 20

If He can pardon, then He can be angry too. 'Why, then,' someone will say, 'are those who sin often happy and those who live devoutly often wretched?' Because both the fugitives and the disinherited live freely, and those who are under the discipline of a Father or a Master live more strictly and frugally.[1] For virtue is proved by evils and gets established; vices by pleasure. But neither should that one, however, who sins, hope for perpetual impunity, for there is no lasting happiness. 'But the last day indeed must a man always wait for,

---

[2] Aristides, an Athenian statesman and soldier, born about 520 B.C. His reputation for honesty became proverbial. He died a poor man, c. 468 B.C.

[3] Cimon (c. 512-449 B.C.), also an Athenian statesman and soldier, the son of Miltiades. He helped Aristides to form the Delian League. Tradition regards the two as magnanimous characters.

---

[1] This is a rather direct, practical, prosaic, and almost familiar manner of dismissing an age-old problem. It is warm and home-like in its unquestioning acceptance of fatherly discipline, and it is certainly sound advice.

and no one ought to be called happy before his departure
and the last of his funeral rites,'² as the poet says rather
pleasantly. It is the end which proves the felicity, and no one,
living or dead, can escape the judgment of God. He has power
both to cast down the living from on high and to inflict
eternal tortures upon the dead. 'No,' our objector says, 'if God
is angry, immediately He ought to work vengeance and punish
each one in accord with his merits.' But if He did this, no one
would be left. For there is no one who does nothing wrong,
and there are many things which incite to sin—age, drunkenness, need, opportunity, reward.³ The frailty of the flesh with
which we are clothed is prone to sin to such an extent that,
unless God gave indulgence to this compulsion, perhaps too
few would be living. For this reason, He is most patient and
He restrains His wrath. Because virtue in Him is perfect, it
is necessary that His patience also be perfect, since it is itself
a virtue, too. How many from being sinners later became
just, from being bad became good, from excessive, temperate!
How many who were base in early life and condemned by
common judgment afterwards, however, turned out to be
laudable! This certainly would not be the case if punishment
followed upon every offense.

Public laws condemn those who are manifestly guilty, but
there are very many whose sins are concealed; very many who
silence the accuser either by entreaty or bribe; very many who
elude trials by favor or influence. And if divine censure should
condemn all those who escape human punishment, there
would be but a few odd men, or even none at all on the earth.

Even that one cause of destroying the human race could
have been just, namely, that men, despising the living God,
give divine honor to frail earthly figments or images as though
to heavenly beings, adoring works made by human hands.
And although God their Maker raised them up to the contemplation and knowledge of God, fashioning them with raised

---

2 Ovid, *Metamorphoses* 3.135-137.
3 Cf. Terence, *Andria* 603.

countenance and upright posture, they have preferred to bend themselves to the earth and cattle-like to crawl upon the ground. For he is low, and curved, and bent forward who turns from the sight of heaven and God, his Father, and honors the earth, that is, things made and fashioned of earth which he should have trampled upon. In such great impiety, therefore, and in such great sins, the patience of God brings it about that men, condemning the errors of their previous lives, correct themselves. I must bring this point to a close. There are many good and just people, and they, in rejection of earthly cults, acknowledge the majesty of the One God. And, although the patience of God is very great and most fitting, nevertheless, even though late, He punishes the guilty and He does not allow them to proceed further when He has seen them to be incorrigible.

Chapter 21

There remains one last question. Perhaps someone has said that so true is it that God does not get angry that even in His precepts He forbids man to get angry. I could say that anger in man ought to be curbed, because often he is unjustly angry, and has the temporary disturbance of anger, since he is temporal. And so, lest those things be done which the lowly and men of mediocre station and even great kings do through anger, his temper ought to be moderated and suppressed, because of the danger that being without control of his mind he might commit some unpardonable crime. God, however, is angry, and not for the present moment, since He is eternal and has perfect virtue and is never angry unless rightly. But, however, the matter is not considered settled just in this way. For if God forbade anger entirely, He would have been a reprehender of His own workmanship in a way, since in the beginning He had given anger (its seat, the liver) to man, inasmuch as the cause of this reaction is believed to be contained in the moisture of the bile. Therefore, not entirely does He forbid anger since that emotion has been given as a necessary part of the creation, but He forbids the continuation of anger. For the wrath of mortals ought to be mortal, and if it should last, enmities are strengthened unto everlasting ruin. Then, again, since He has commanded man to be angry, indeed, and yet not to sin, certainly He did not tear out anger by its roots, but He tempered it, so that in all chastisement we might hold to measure and justice.[1] He who orders us to be angry, therefore, Himself surely gets angry; He who charges us to become appeased rather quickly, certainly He is Himself placable. He commands what is just and applicable to common circumstances. But, because I have said that wrath in God was not temporal as it is in man,[2] who becomes heated to a rage with a passing disturbance and is not able to govern himself easily because of his feebleness, we ought to understand, since God is eternal, that His anger also lasts forever. On the other hand, since God is possessed of the highest virtue, we ought to understand that He has His wrath in His power and is not ruled by it, but that He Himself governs the wrath as He wishes, which is not at all repugnant to a higher being. For if His anger were absolutely immortal, there would be no place for satisfaction or grace after a wrong-doing, although He Himself orders men to make peace before the sun sets,[3] but the divine wrath endures forever against those who continue in their sin. So God is appeased, not by incense, not by sacrifice, not by precious gifts, all of which are corruptible, but He is appeased by an improvement of one's way of life, and he who puts a stop to his sinfulness makes God's anger mortal.[4] And for this reason, He does not punish each offender at the time

---

[1] Cf. Ps. 4.5; Eph. 4.26.
[2] Ch. 12, p. 89.
[3] Cf. Eph. 4.26.
[4] This seems quite daring use of words, but it is indicative of the power of repentance and of prayer. Cf. Ps. 50.18: 'A contrite and humble heart, O God, Thou wilt not despise.'

of the offense so that man may have the opportunity of recovering and correcting himself.

Chapter 22

I wanted to mention these points about the anger of God, my very dear Donatus, so that you might know how to refute those who imagine God to be immobile. There remains for us to use this epilogue in the Ciceronian manner of peroration. Just as he did in the *Tusculans* when he was treating of death,[1] so we in this work ought to apply the divine testimonies to which credence can be given in order to subdue the erroneous persuasion of those who, in believing that God is without anger, destroy all religion. Without religion, as I have shown,[2] we are leveled to either the inhumanness of beasts or the stupidity of cattle; for in religion alone, that is, in the acknowledging of the Supreme God, is wisdom. All the prophets, filled with the Divine Spirit, speak of nothing else than the favor of God toward the just and His anger against the wicked. Their testimonies, indeed, are enough for us, but since those who toss 'wisdom' about in their beards and cloaks[3] do not believe them, I had to refute them also with reason and arguments. Thus they consider, so preposterously, that human affairs give weight to divine, when divine things should rather give weight to human. Let us leave these things now lest we, too, do nothing about them and simply get involved and prolonged *ad infinitum*. Let us seek, therefore, those testimonies which they can either believe or, at least, not contradict.

Numerous authors, and those very great ones, have handed

---

1 Cicero, *Tusc.* 1.47.112f.
2 Ch. 12, p. 88.
3 The sarcasm is directed against those who think that they are wise, the clever rhetoricians who flaunt their sophistries, but who possess little other than the most superficial 'wisdom.' The philosophers wore long hair and cloaks. Cf. *Inst.* 3.25 (vol. 49, this series, p. 231).

down many of the Sibylline utterances.[4] For example, of the Greeks, there were Aristonicus[5] and Apollodorus,[6] the Erythraean, and of our own writers, Varro[7] and Fenestella.[8] All these relate that the Erythraean Sibyl was exceptional and noble beyond the rest. Apollodorus, to be sure, glories in her as his own compatriot and fellow-citizen. Fenestella, however, also relates that an embassy was sent to Erythraea by the Senate to convey the oracles of this Sibyl to Rome, and that the consuls, Curio and Octavius, should see to it that these be placed in the Capitol, which had then been restored under the supervision of Quintus Catulus. Among the pronouncements of this Sibyl, verses like this about the Supreme God and Maker of things are found: 'The incorruptible and eternal Fashioner who dwells in the sky holdeth forth good to the good, a much greater prize, but for the wicked and unjust He worketh anger and wrath.'[9] Again, in another place, when she was enumerating the deeds by which God is most especially aroused, she brought in these details: 'Flee unlawful worships; serve the living one. Abstain from adultery and impure relations. Rear a family of children of your own. Do not kill. For the immortal one will be angry with whoever commits sin.'[10] God is angry, therefore, with sinners.

---

4 As a single prophetess, the Sibyl was variously localized (cf. the account in the *Inst.* 1.6; 8-12, vol. 49, this series) and legends are numerous. In his *Res divinae*, Varro listed ten Sibyls. The content of their prophecies was put into the form of Greek hexameters. Collections of the verses were made for later use. Jewish and Christian interpolations helped to give to the Sibyls a position in Christian literature and art somewhat akin to that accorded to the Old Testament prophets.
5 Aristonicus, an Alexandrian grammarian of the Augustan Age. He wrote commentaries and did text studies on Homer, Hesiod, and Pindar.
6 Apollodorus, an Athenian of the 2nd century B.C. A pupil of Aristarchus, he wrote a rationalistic account of Greek religion that was much used by later writers.
7 Marcus Terentius Varro (116-28 B.C.), a voluminous writer. Most of his works, encyclopedic in nature, are lost. The ancients perhaps used him most for his *Antiquitates rerum humanarum et divinarum*.
8 Fenestella (c. 50 B.C.-A.D. 20), an antiquarian-annalist who wrote a Roman history from its origins to his own day.
9 *Sibylline Fragments* III.17-19 (Rzach edition) p. 236.
10 *Ibid.* III.763-766.

Chapter 23

But since there are reported by most learned writers to have been very many Sibylline oracles, as I have said,[1] the testimony of one may not be enough for the confirmation of the truth, which is my purpose. Indeed, the scrolls of the Cumaean Sibyl, in which the fates of Romans have been inscribed, are kept in hiding, but the books of nearly all the rest are not forbidden to the perusal of all. Of these, one Sibyl, announcing to all the nations the anger of God because of the wickedness of men, began in this way: 'Since great danger is coming upon a world not obedient, I reveal the commands of God unto the last age making prophecies to all men city by city.'[2] Another also said that the flood of a previous age had been caused by the anger of God against the unjust, so that the malice of the human race might be extinguished: 'From the time when the God of heaven was angry with the very cities and with all men, the sea covered the earth, a deluge having burst forth.'[3] In a similar vein, she prophesied a conflagration that would afterwards take place, whereby the impiety of men would again be destroyed: 'And then, God, no longer being gentle but bristling with anger, will destroy the race of men and wipe out all of it by a great burning.'[4] From this comes the note in Ovid about Jupiter that

> He remembers that it is also in the fates
> that there will be a time in which the sea,
> in which the earth, and the vault of heaven
> will be snatched and burned by fire, and
> the well-wrought mass of the world will labor.[5]

And this must happen at the time when the honor and worship of the Supreme God has perished among men. That same

---
1 Ch. 22, p. 111; *Inst.* 1.6; 1.8-12 *passim* (vol. 49, this series).
2 *Sibylline Fragments* VIII.1-3.
3 *Ibid.* IV.51-53.
4 *Ibid.* IV.159-161.
5 Ovid, *Metamorphoses* 1.256-258.

THE WRATH OF GOD   113

Sibyl, however, attesting that He was appeased by the repentance of evil deeds and reformation of conduct, added this: 'Pitiable mortals, change now, and do not provoke the great God to all sorts of anger.'[6] Likewise, a little later: 'He will not destroy; He will stop His anger again if all will render worthy reverence in their minds.'[7] And another Sibyl declares that the Father of things heavenly and earthly ought to be loved so that His indignation should not rise against men for their destruction: 'Lest perchance the immortal God should ever be angry and destroy the entire living race of men and their shameless progeny, it is necessary to love God the Father, wise and ever-living.'[8]

From this much it is clear that the thinking of philosophers who think that God is without anger is foundationless,[9] and among His other praises, they insert that which is most useless. They draw away from Him what is especially salutary for human affairs, that on which the very notion of majesty rests. This kingdom and earthly empire, unless fear protects it, is dissolved. Take away anger from a king and the result will be, not only that no one will obey him, but even that he will be hurled headlong from his eminence. Why, actually, snatch away this emotion from any obscure man, and who will not despoil him? Who will not deride him? Who will not heap injuries upon him? And thus he will be able to have neither clothes, nor a place, nor food, with others making off with whatever he might have. Much less, then, may we think that the majesty of a heavenly empire can stand without anger and fear. Apollo at Miletus,[10] when consulted about the religion of the Jews, put this description into his answer: 'The God, the King and Father of all, before whom tremble the

---
6 *Sibylline Fragments* IV.162-163.
7 *Ibid.* IV.169f.
8 *Ibid.* V.358-360.
9 Lactantius uses the Greek word in his text, *a-orgēton*.
10 Apollo of Miletus, or the Milesian Apollo, is a reference, no doubt, to the god's temple at Miletus and to a prophetess or Sibyl who functioned there. The selection given here can be found among the fragments of Porphyry, edited by G. Wolff in 1856, p. 142.

earth, and heaven, and the sea, whom the murky regions of Tartarus and the devils dread.'

If God is so mild as those philosophers will have Him, how is it that, at His nod, not only the demons and ministers of such great power, but even the heavens and earth and the whole system of nature tremble? If no one serves another except through force, then all authority rests upon fear, but fear rests upon anger. For if one is not aroused against somebody who is unwilling to obey, that one will not be able to be forced to submission. Let each one consult his own feelings. He will understand immediately that no one can be subjected to authority without anger and chastisement. Where there is not anger, there will not be authority either. But God has authority; therefore, it is necessary for Him to have wrath also, on which authority rests.

Chapter 24

Wherefore, let no one under the influence of the empty talk of philosophers 'refine' himself to a contempt of God, which is the greatest impiety. We all ought to love Him because He is our Father, and reverence Him because He is the Lord, do Him honor because He is kind, and fear Him because He is severe. Each aspect of God is venerable. Who would not, in keeping with piety, love the parent of his life? Or who with impunity would despise Him who, as ruler of all things, exercises true and everlasting power over all? If you consider Him as a Father, He provides us with our entrance to the light that we enjoy; through Him we live; through Him we have entered into the lodging of this world. If you think of Him as the Lord, He nourishes us with innumerable provisions; he sustains us; we dwell in His house; we are His family. And if we are less obedient than we should be, and less dutiful than the immortal worth of our God and Father demands, it is, however, of utmost profit to us for gaining pardon if we retain our knowledge and worship of Him, if we cast aside goods that are low and earthly and meditate upon those of heaven that are divine and everlasting. To be able to do this, we have to follow God, we have to adore Him and love Him, since in Him is the substance of things, the principle of the virtues, and the source of all good.

For what is greater in power than God, or more perfect in reason, or more gleaming in brightness? And since He has begotten us to wisdom and created us to justice, it is not right for man, abandoning God, the Giver of sense and life, to wait in service upon the frailties of earth, or, cleaving to a search for temporal goods, to sever himself from innocence and piety. Vicious and death-bringing pleasures do not make a person happy; nor does opulence, the enkindler of lusts; nor does inane ambition; nor the halting honors by which a human soul, ensnared and shackled to the body, is doomed to eternal death. Only innocence, only justice brings happiness, whose legitimate and worthy reward is immortality. From the beginning, God determined this for holy and incorrupt minds which preserve themselves from vices and keep themselves intact and inviolate from every earthly stain.

They cannot be sharers of this heavenly and everlasting reward who have stained their consciences with frauds, rapes, deceits, and who have branded indelible stains upon themselves by abominable injuries and crimes committed. So it is necessary for all the wise, those who wish to be called 'men'[1] deservedly, to condemn frail things, to trample upon things of earth, to despise mean things, that they may be joined with God in a most blessed bond of union.

May impiety be done away with, and let turbulent and baneful dissensions, by which the divine union of human society and public compact is broken into, cut apart, and scattered, be put to rest. As much as we can, let us strive to be

---

1 *Viri* (men) is related to *virtus* (manliness) for Lactantius. Cf. *De opificio Dei* 12, n. 7, p. 41.

good and kind. If we have wealth, if we have resources at hand, let them be used, not for the pleasure of one, but for the welfare of many. For pleasure is as mortal as the body to which it gives service. On the other hand, justice and beneficence are as immortal as the mind and soul which by good works attain a likeness to God. Let God be hallowed by us, not in temples, but in our hearts, for all things are destructible which are made by hand. Let us clean this temple which is defiled, not by smoke, not by dust, but by evil thoughts, this temple which is lighted, not by burning wax, but by the brightness of God and the light of wisdom. And if we believe that God is always present in it, God to whose divinity the secrets of the mind lie open, we shall so live that we may always find Him being merciful to us and never dread him in His being angry with us.

ON THE DEATHS OF THE PERSECUTORS

(DE MORTIBUS PERSECUTORUM)

INTRODUCTION

a. Nature of the Work

THE DE MORTIBUS PERSECUTORUM of Lactantius is pamphlet literature. It is a treatise which could well be listed as outstanding in the field of popular apologetics of the period. The other works of Lactantius, those which he intended as doctrinal and which he wrote for a numerous enlightened public, are Ciceronian in their conception, tone, and language. Here, we do not find evidence of the author's customary attitudes; nor is there indication of the quieting effect of study and the retirement effected by persecution. Rather, in its burning accents, we find a passionate outcry, the chant of Christian victory, the bursting of flood gates, as it were, previously held in restraint through long years of oppression.

The *De mortibus* was occasioned by the surcease under Constantine of persecution and was addressed to the Christians or their sympathizers. A wave of general exaltation followed the triumph of Constantine and the subsequent peace that came to the Church. It was this, no doubt, which impelled our author to give vent to his feelings and add a literary tribute to the flood of material that was being poured forth in ovation to the Emperor and in congratulations to the religious group which had gained the latter's open support.

The theme of the present work is that tremendous idea of the Divine Vengeance exercising itself when the hour, reckoned according to God's time, came upon those who had risked it. It is not a new theme with Lactantius;[1] he had even written

---
1 Cf. *Institutes* 4.27.5; 5.22, 23 (vol. 49, this series).

a complete treatise on God's anger.[2] This work does provide him, however, with the opportunity of crowning the entire structure of his writings with a piece that can summarize his apologetical work and can well serve as a victory paean for the cause to which his pen was dedicated. For this reason, he is hyper-zealous, and at times indiscreet, in attempting to unravel God's designs with the fearless certitude which he applies to the numerous details at his command. The *De mortibus* can be considered, therefore, as the proclamation for the *Institutes* of the 'Fall of Assyria' in the song of triumph of the nations in connection with the ninth and following chapters of Isaia:

> The people that walked in darkness, have seen a great light. To them that dwelt in the region of the shadow of death, light is risen.
> Thou hast multiplied the nation, and hast not increased the joy. They shall rejoice before thee, as they that rejoice in the harvest, as conquerors rejoice after taking a prey, when they divide the spoils.
> For the yoke of their burden, and the rod of their shoulder, and the scepter of their oppressor thou hast overcome, as in the day of Madian.
> For every violent taking of spoils with tumult, and garment mingled with blood, shall be burnt, and be fuel for the fire. . . .
> Woe to them that make wicked laws, and when they write, write injustice to oppress the poor in judgment and do violence to the cause of the humble of my people: that widows might be their prey, and that they might rob the fatherless. What will you do in the day of visitation, and of the calamity which cometh from afar? To whom will ye flee for help? And where will ye leave your glory? And it shall come to pass, that when the Lord shall have performed all his works in Mount Sion, and in Jerusalem, I will visit the fruit of the proud heart of the king of Assyria, and the glory of the haughtiness of his eyes. . . .
> Therefore the sovereign Lord, the Lord of hosts, shall send leanness among his fat ones; and under his glory

---

2 *De ira,* pp. 61-116.

shall be kindled a burning, as it were the burning of a fire.
And the light of Israel shall be as a fire, and the holy one thereof as a flame: and his thorns and his briars shall be set on fire, and shall be devoured in one day.
And the glory of his forest, and of his beautiful hill, shall be consumed from the soul even to the flesh, and he shall run away through fear. . . .
Therefore, thus saith the Lord, the God of hosts: O my people that dwellest in Sion, be not afraid of the Assyrian: he shall strike thee with his rod, and he shall lift up his staff over thee in the way of Egypt.
For yet a little and a very little while, and my indignation shall cease, and my wrath shall be upon their wickedness. . . .
Behold the sovereign Lord of hosts shall break the earthen vessel with terror, and the tall of stature shall be cut down, and the lofty shall be humbled.[3]

Lactantius had lived through the days when the enemy of the Church was in power and furiously exerted its diabolical control. So, he could not be impartial when writing of the abatement of this fury. The hatred of Lactantius for Diocletian and his associates, as well as his deliberate choice of Galerius for blaming as the evil power *par excellence*, seems to impair the soundness of our writer's judgment, and he would appear to be more anxious to prove a thesis than to write an historical account. A vindication of the historicity of his account will follow, however, and in this work the rhetorical gifts of Lactantius are wonderfully intensified by his personal feelings. Hence, such vivid writing reminds one rather of Tacitus than of Cicero, upon whom Lactantius usually modeled his rhetoric. Like Tacitus, he presents a strongly one-sided picture of imperial policies; like him also, he had suffered too much at first hand to be able to conceal his grievances; and like the work of the Silver Age historian, the *De mortibus* of Lactantius almost fanatically moralizes. The pamphlet, put out after the Peace of Milan, breathes a powerful spirit of satisfied justice;

---

[3] Cf. Isa. 9.1-4; 10.1-3, 12, 16-18, 24, 25, 33.

it shows the effects, the practical, terrifyingly practical, consequences of the anger of God.

Lactantius presents in this work an account of the persecutions of the Christians by the Roman state. For the earlier periods, beginning with that of Nero, he is not so profuse with details.[4] For the period of the most intense persecution, however, that of Diocletian and his associates, especially Galerius, he is vivid, dramatic, bitter, and impassioned in style; and, although the story as told by Lactantius has often been questioned, there is no reason whatever to doubt its substantial truth.

b. Authenticity and Date of Work

Although the *De mortibus* is so markedly unlike all of the other works of Lactantius, there is no longer any question about its authenticity, in spite of the fact that it comes down to us in a single manuscript, the *Colbertinus*, preserved in the Bibliotheque Nationale of Paris, number 2627. This manuscript was edited in 1629 by Baluzius who had recently discovered it in a convent library in Moissac. He declared his discovery to be the *De persecutione* of Lactantius which had been mentioned by Jerome. This opinion was not upheld, however, and, after two centuries, Brandt[5] had almost convinced the literary world of the spuriousness of the work when he himself was compelled to retract his thesis because of the convincing arguments of Pichon[6] in favor of Lactantian authorship.[7]

Some points that have raised question are purely extrinsic:

---

4 Chs. 1-6. The remaining forty-six chapters treat of the Diocletian-Constantinian period.
5 S. Brandt, *Ueber den Verfasser des Büches de Mortibus Persecutorum, Neue Jahrbücher für Philol. und Padag.*, CXLVII, 1893, pp. 121-138, 202-223.
6 R. Pichon, *Lactance* (Paris 1901) 337-360.
7 The whole question of the authenticity of the work is handled in Moreau's Introduction, pp. 22ff.

the discrepancy between the title affixed to the work and that given by Jerome, and the name of the author given as *Lucius Cecilius*, whereas Lactantius is ordinarily called *Firmianus Lactantius* or *Coelius Firmianus Lactantius* in the manuscripts. Besides, arguments have been raised about the identity of the addressee. If he is the same Donatus to whom the *De ira Dei* was dedicated, the same author could scarcely have written both works, for the Donatus of the *De ira Dei* is a neophyte who needs much instruction, and the Donatus of the *De mortibus* is a veteran Christian, one who endured the trials of persecution.

It is much more to the purpose to consider intrinsic points in a discussion of the authenticity of a work like the *De mortibus persecutorum*. The matter of vocabulary and style is an important one. Even a translation can show that the short, sometimes abrupt sentences and the overall conciseness of expression in the *De mortibus* are diametrically opposed to the sweeping, majestic periods of the *Institutes* and the customary prolixity of all of the other works of Lactantius. This opposition, however, is more apparent than real. In the *De mortibus*, there are numerous oratorical features of the *Institutes*. Of course, these are not to be found in the highly narrative sections, but the philosophical or pathetic or triumphant sections, and the invectives and apostrophes show close resemblance to the finely wrought works of his days of study.[8] Conversely, the short style so characteristic of the *De mortibus* appears time and again throughout the *Institutes*, for instance, when his philosophical discussions give place to recitations or enumerations.[9] Besides, this rapid and concise style is that imposed upon the author in his *Epitome*[10] by the nature of that type of writing. So, it was not a strange style to Lactantius. Since the genre of a work does determine, to a large extent, the character of its style, hardly any other style

---

8 Cf., for example, 1.2f.; 16.5ff.; 31.5-6; 52.2ff.
9 Cf. *Inst.* 2.7; 7.16, etc. (vol. 49, this series).
10 Cf. General Introduction (vol. 49, this series, pp. xvii-xviii).

could be adequate for the theme of the *De mortibus*. The dogmatic works, destined as they were for a large, enlightened public, are Ciceronian in conception, tone, and language; they are polished masterpieces. The *De mortibus*, on the other hand, was for the author's fellow Christians: explanations, extreme politeness, caution, and condescension are superfluous. The believing Christian is superimposed on the rhetor here; the author addresses the jubilant confessors of the faith in a manner familiar to them. The style is a masterpiece of directness.

Still, it is possible to note details of language and style that are incontestably Lactantian.[11] And in the more general qualities of style, the *De mortibus* is very similar to the other works. There is the same classical quality of vocabulary and syntax, the rarity and banality of metaphors so characteristic of Lactantius, a frequency of etymological figures and repetitions, and a scholarly regard for regular composition. In the matter of citations, too, the work is Lactantian. There is not such a great use of citations as in the other works, but the choice is similar. There are many Vergilian reminiscences and an almost complete absence of biblical quotations. All of these characteristics were united in the fourth century, it has been noted,[12] in only two works, that known to us as the *Institutes* and that known as the *De mortibus*. Moreover, there exists a very strong argument in favor of identifying the two, namely, the presence in the two works of the same clausulae which follow an order of identical frequency. This argument should satisfy those who demand statistical methods.

The most compelling argument for the authenticity of the work, however, is that it is in the spirit of Lactantius. From the *Institutes* to the *De mortibus*, there is a change of tone, but not of sentiment. There are the same dogmatic preoccupations in the one as in the other. The *De mortibus* declares that the

---

11 On this point, the commentary (vol. 2) of Moreau's edition is exceptionally valuable. His notes contain ample citations of parallel passages.
12 *Ibid*. Introduction, p. xviii.

deaths of the persecutors present a terrible lesson to us on the unity of God and the vengeance of His justice. It serves as a practical example or fulfillment of the teaching and prophecy of the *Institutes* (the first two books of which develop the idea of the unity of God; book five, His justice; and parts of books six and seven, warnings of His vengeance) and the *De ira Dei,* a complete treatise on the philosophical notion of anger in God. In the *De mortibus,* also, there is the characteristic Lactantian treatment of demons with the addition of precise details, for he gives vivid descriptions of Galerius and Maxentius and Maximin as devils incarnate. Fundamental to all his works is a spirit of zeal, the almost rash zeal of many converts, in apostolicity, in devotion to the Church's doctrine, in rigid adherence to its policies, even though they be temporal and political. In his partiality, he censures measures that are not indefensible, but this can be understood when we consider the times and circumstances of his writing.

This work of Lactantius—and it unquestionably bears the stamp of his authorship—seems to have been written by one who very recently witnessed the events described therein. A date for the writing of the work cannot be given with certitude. But, since in the treatise Licinius is depicted, along with Constantine, as a protector of the faith of the Christians, the writing must have taken place before the beginning of his break with Constantine and his subsequent attack upon the Church, that is, before A.D. 321. A *terminus post quem* can be given as well. The deaths of Maximin Daia and of Diocletian are recorded, events which occurred in 313 in the case of Maximin Daia and about 316 in the case of Diocletian.

There had been a prevalent belief, however, that Lactantius left Nicomedia around 306 or 407. Since the *De mortibus* describes events which took place in the East subsequent to 306-307, and since these events could have been written only by an eye-witness, it is possible to conjecture that another writer, perhaps a disciple of Lactantius, remained in Bithynia until about 314. Thus did Brandt and his followers reckon.

The hypothesis is not verifiable, because all the dating has rested on the probable period of Lactantius' tutorship of Crispus during 307-308. It is more likely, however, that Lactantius performed this work around 317,[13] and there is no indication that he lived in Gaul before this date. Even if he did leave Nicomedia to avoid the rigorous rule of Galerius, there would be no reason to suppose that he did not return in 311 after the Edict of Toleration. Perhaps, like many others during persecution, Lactantius had been able to keep in hiding near Nicomedia and to keep in touch with the affairs of the Church and the imperial household there. Thus he could have had the first-hand information on the early years of the fourth century.

For more precise dating of our treatise, we must examine notices made on certain events. Because there was friction and open warfare between Licinius and Constantine in 314, the *De mortibus* must have been written after the agreement to forget this incident, because a 'serene peace' exists between the two. The action of Licinius in having Valeria and Prisca, daughter and wife of Diocletian, put to death, however, is not at all glossed over by Lactantius in his treatment of the matter in chapter 51. Since these murders, likewise, occurred in the year 314, it is strange that the writer's attitude toward Licinius seems suddenly almost hostile. The plausible explanation is that the work underwent a redaction at the hands of its author (the major portions of it very probably had been circulated earlier among his co-religionists). We are quite certain that this was the case with the *Institutes* and their panegyrical sections.[14] It is to the point to recall that the defeat of Licinius by Constantine occurred in 324. It was evident before this time that Lactantius, who lived at the court of Constantine, kept his writing in line with the wishes of his protector,

---

13 O. Seeck in *Geschicte des Untergangs der antiken Welt* (Berlin 1920) Vol. 1.4, pp. 476ff., fixes the birth date of Crispus at 307. Therefore, Lactantius could not have instructed him in Latin literature before 316-317.

14 Cf. the Introduction to the *Institutes* (vol. 49, this series, pp. 8-11).

benevolent toward Licinius after the reconciliation of 314 and malevolent toward the end of 318 and 319. This would point toward a later date than the *terminus post quem* of A.D. 313, that suggested by Alföldi,[15] and suggest instead a date closer to the *terminus ante quem*, 321.

This hypothesis seems the more likely in view of an interesting bit of Lactantian attention to detail. In his conclusion, he makes mockery of the great surnames adopted by Diocletian and Maximian, *Jovius* and *Herculius*. But in 315, Constantine was still utilizing in the official imperial decorations of his arch these traditional Roman theological symbols, and again in 324, out of consideration for his pagan subjects, he had coins struck honoring his father-in-law, Maximian Herculius. The conclusion, therefore, is that the mockery of these names must have been made between the years 315 and 324, so we are again compelled to accept the years 318-321 as the most likely for the writing by Lactantius of his pamphlet *On the Deaths of the Persecutors*.

c. *The Historical Significance*

Research in the last three hundred years has, in spite of all its contradictions and controversies, accomplished tremendous progress. This is particularly true of the scholarship that has been devoted to the period of transition between antiquity and the Middle Ages, so-called. The third century, notwithstanding all its chaos and confusion, and the fourth, with its new experiment in Christian domination, are now considered of utmost importance in the history of the Empire and of the Western World. This is the period of the culmination of the fusion, and of its first flowering as well, of the basic elements of our civilization: Graeco-Roman culture and Christianity. Hardly,

---

15 A. Alföldi, *The Conversion of Constantine and Pagan Rome* (Oxford 1948) 45.

then, can any period of history be said to be more important than the epoch of Constantine the Great. The old familiar sources have been subjected to rigorous examination and reinterpretation in the light of the progress of scientific methods in scholarship. Many causes have been responsible for unsound attitudes toward this great period of European history which has only of late years come into its own.[16] It is the period which saw the final breakdown of old Rome and the rise of the new one with its capital on the Bosphorus. It is the period of barbarian invasions and of their infiltration into the culture of Europe and the world. Of utmost importance is the religious aspect of the period. It is the age of the beginning of the Christian Empire.

For this period, we have Lactantius and Eusebius as our chief contemporary Christian authorities. Eusebius,[17] Bishop of Caesarea, was the personal friend of Constantine. He sat at the Emperor's right at the Council of Nicaea. His *Historia ecclesiastica* is the outstanding historical work of this period from the Christian side. Another work of his, called in Latin *Vita Constantini,* is a vast source of material. The critics of this panegyric fail to take account of its purpose; it does not profess to give a complete biographical record, but deals only with the Emperor's actions that were for the advancement of the Christian religion.[18]

Written by an eye-witness of many of the events which are related in it, the *De mortibus persecutorum* of Lactantius constitutes, for the epoch of the tetrarchy and the beginning of Constantine's sole rule, a source of the first rank. Like the writings of the contemporary Eusebius, the work is the product

---

16 Cf. especially the closing section, 'Epilogue' in the *Cambridge Ancient History,* Vol. XII, pp. 700-109; E. K. Rand, *The Building of Eternal Rome,* pp. 145-285; and A. Alföldi, *The Conversion of Constantine and Pagan Rome,* Introduction, pp. 1-5.
17 Cf. Eusebius Pamphili, *Ecclesiastical History,* trans. by Roy J. Deferrari in *Fathers of the Church,* Vols. 19, 29 (New York 1953, 1955). The Introduction, pp. 3-32 of the first volume, furnishes ample biographical material on Eusebius.
18 Cf. *Vita* 1.11.

of an author with personal admiration and friendship for
Constantine, and it displays an unreflective interpretation of
history in the light of modern standards of scientific criticism.
The account that he gives us of the inception and course of
'the Great Persecution' is vividly dramatic, and, although
his story has often been questioned, there is no longer any
reason to doubt his truth. In his views on Galerius, he is supported by Eusebius, and it is not easy to reject the major agreements of these two contemporary writers,[19] in spite of the fact
that they are prejudiced, especially when we consider the
'non-prejudiced' source material on the epoch in question.

The chief pagan historian of the period, Ammianus Marcellinus (born c. A.D. 330), who wrote a continuation of the
history of Tacitus, would have been a most valuable source
for this period, but the first thirteen books of his work, containing events to 353, have been lost. A fourth-century work
that has survived under the name of the Anonymous of Valois[20]
does provide a biography of Constantine, however, and, although it is brief, it is apparently deserving of a high degree
of acceptance.

Eutropius (4th c. fl.), a secretary of Constantine and later
an intimate friend of the Emperor Julian, wrote a *Breviarium
ab urbe condita* which is of real value, written with evident
candor and the aim of providing an unbiased account of his
own times.

The pagan tradition violently opposed to Constantine and
maliciously pejorative of his character can be considered of
no real value for estimating the character of Constantine and
the true nature of events during his lifetime. This tradition
took its rise in the hostile mockery of the writings of his
nephew, Julian the Apostate (332-363). Julian's satire, *The*

---

19 Cf. N. H. Baynes, 'The Great Persecution,' *Cambridge Ancient History*, Vol. 12, p. 665.
20 The writer, probably a pagan, seems to have been a contemporary of Constantine. The fragment, therefore, is valuable for his reign. It is a piece of historical writing which covers the years 293-337. It was first published by H. Valois, and, for this reason, its author is generally called *Anonymus Valesii*.

Caesars, influenced the writing of Sextus Aurelius Victor, *Historia abbreviata,* and apparently also the work of Zosimus, *Historia nova.* This last author, though clear and interesting in his style, was pronounced undependable even by Gibbon.

The other pagan writers are the Panegyrists. Between the years 289 and 321, we have no fewer than fifty-three panegyrics of Roman rhetors in Gaul alone. Those which deal with the Constantinian epoch are the following:

1. A paneygric of unknown origin, delivered to Maximian and Constantine on the occasion of the latter's marriage to Fausta in 307.

2. A panegyric ascribed to Eumenius, delivered at Treves after the execution of Maximian in 310-311.

3. Another, possibly by Eumenius also, giving the official thanks of the citizens of Autun for favors bestowed by Constantine.

4. The eulogy of Constantine delivered at Treves in 313, ascribed to Nazarius.

5. The panegyric, also ascribed to Nazarius, delivered at Rome in 321.

6. The poetic panegyric and letter by the poet Optatian in exile in honor of Constantine's Twentieth Anniversary Celebration. This secured Optatian's pardon.

In the light of this summary of our sources for this period, it is quite evident that we must rely chiefly upon Eusebius and Lactantius as literary sources. To their works in recent years, however, has come confirmation from the field of numismatics.[21] Ancient coins were very often of medallic character, that is, they referred directly to historical events. And far more than our modern coins, they were religious and symbolical expressions of state policy. The Roman imperial coinage is, therefore, a series of medals relating the history and politics of the successive reigns. Coins are of prime significance

---

[21] Cf. H. Mattingly's discussion on coins in the 'Appendix on Sources,' *Cambridge Ancient History,* Vol. 12, pp. 713-720. The great source work on the coins of the period is that of J. Maurice, *Numismatique Constantienne,* 3 vols. (Paris 1908-12).

in telling the economic history of their period, but they perform as well the service of suggesting the unspoken beliefs that governed the minds of men. It is here that the science of numismatics offers its corroboration to the literary accounts of Eusebius and Lactantius. The auxiliary science lends great support in the case of the *De mortibus*. The coins available for the period and studied by Maurice have provided the necessary control and verification of the text. As a result, historians have come to realize that the remarks and descriptions of Lactantius have great historical value. His personal wrath and bias, therefore, need not disqualify this treatise as a source for the very important period in question.

Even if this work were only the reflection of the opinion of one Christian of Constantine's court during the period between the two wars of that emperor against Licinius, it would still be of primary source value. But our pamphlet is something more than the echo of Christian political thought of that time. It is also a book of history which has preserved details of great importance. It is a partisan history, of course, but history just the same. No historian can be impartial if he writes of his own times. Lactantius admits his bias and his purpose.[22] He aims to prevent the falsifications of accounts of his times which are bound to follow. His own bitter and impassioned account serves but to emphasize the horrors which even the unprejudiced could not conceal or deny. Even in this work, so violent and so personal, he can still be likened to his rhetorical model, and, like Cicero, he provides us with real history in what we may call his 'Philippics.'

The pamphlet was written by Lactantius to prove a thesis, a persistent theme of his writings, namely, Providence and the Divine Governance of the world. Because of his subject matter, the deaths of the persecutors, especially those under whom he himself had lived, the work may be called an apocalypse rather than a philosophy of history. It is the climax-like proof of all

---

22 *De mortibus* 52.1.

that he had written, particularly the *Institutes* and *De ira Dei,* the manifestation of God's avenging justice.

The first six chapters give an account of the persecutions from the days of Nero to Aurelian. Though brief, the account merits acceptance. It is to his credit as an historian that he refrained from giving commentary and details for periods on which he was not himself an authority. There are omissions, however. It is hard to explain these. Marcus Aurelius is not mentioned as a persecutor, perhaps because of the generally very high reputation of that emperor. He should not be placed among the monsters whom Lactantius depicts. No such suggested reason can be given, however, for the exclusion from the list of tyrants the name of Maximin the Thracian. The most likely explanation for the sketchiness and omissions of these first chapters is that given by Moreau in his Introduction, that Lactantius added the introductory chapters as a hasty afterthought to his masterpiece of vehement and vindictive triumph, and that, in his eagerness to publish the work, he neglected to be complete in its introduction.[23]

The remaining forty-six chapters of the pamphlet are of eminent value for the period of the tetrarchy and for the first years of Constantine and Licinius. It can be followed in complete confidence for events from 300 to 316. In the recounting of facts, their chronology and their interconnections, Lactantius takes no liberties with the truth. There is no contradiction with what we learn from the other sources—whether it be the burning of the palace of Nicomedia, the abdication of Diocletian, the elevation of Maxentius, the character portrayal of Galerius, or the arguments between Constantine and Licinius that he is recounting. His work is great also because of the fact that it reflects the sentiments of a Constantinian party during the years 313 to 320, immediately after the Edict of Milan. It is also a precious witness to this crucial period in Constantine's own career, a contemporary and first-hand source for the study

---

[23] Cf. Moreau, *op. cit.,* p. 48.

of the political and religious evolution of the great re-founder of the Empire.

The stages and changes in political control recounted in the *De mortibus* may be seen best in a brief chronological listing. It will be remembered that during the third century more than one emperor shared his duties and powers with a colleague. Therefore, shortly after Diocletian assumed full control, his choice of an associate was not truly an innovation. His devising of the tetrarchy, however, was. He and his colleague were to rule as the Augusti in East and West; subordinate to them were to be the two Caesars with right of succession that did not work out according to Diocletian's plan. Lactantius indicates the individualism and desire for power that caused its dissolution. The chart shows the shifting scene.

From Diocletian to Constantine[24]

Year	Eastern Part of Empire	Western Part of Empire
284	Diocles succeeds Numerian	Carinus, son of Carus, still rules in the West
285	Victory of Diocles over Carinus. He rules as sole emperor, is called Diocletian. In June he appoints Maximian as his Caesar.	
286	Diocletian (Jovius)	Maximian (Herculius)
293	Diocletian is Augustus, and Galerius is appointed his Caesar	Maximian is Augustus, and Constantius is appointed his Caesar
305	Diocletian abdicated. Galerius, Augustus; Maximin Daia appointed Caesar	Maximian abdicated. Constantius, Augustus; Severus appointed Caesar
306	Galerius, Augustus; Maximin Daia, Caesar	Constantius died; Severus, Augustus; Constantine proclaimed Emperor by soldiers; Maxentius, usurper at Rome

---

[24] This chart is an arrangement based on the chronological tables given in *Cambridge Ancient History*, Vol. 12, and a chart appearing in L. B. Holsapple's *Constantine the Great* (New York: Sheed and Ward, 1942) p. 2.

307	Galerius, Augustus; Maximin Daia, Caesar	Severus died; Constantine ⎤ all claimed Maximian ⎬ title of Maxentius ⎦ Augustus
308-310	Galerius, Augustus; Maximin Daia, Caesar	Licinius, Augustus; Constantine, Augustus; Maxentius, usurper; Maximian removed
311	Galerius died; Maximin Daia in control	"
312	Maximin Daia in control	Licinius; Constantine; Maxentius defeated at Milvian Bridge; Maxentius killed
313	Maximin defeated by Licinius; Maximin died.	Licinius; Constantine
314-324	Licinius	Constantine
324		War between Constantine and Licinius decided by the victory of Constantine
324-337		Constantine, sole Emperor

In the midst of this political upheaval rises the issue of the great persecution which did not occur at the opening of Diocletian's reign, but only during the winter of 302-303. Diocletian and Galerius, his Caesar, were together at Nicomedia, and the Caesar pressed upon the Augustus the policy of rigorous persecution. Diocletian yielded and a fatal edict inaugurated the period of the most unspeakable destruction and torture known to men until our own day. It is unnecessary here to discuss at length the various views held on this question. For some,[25] persecution of the Christians seems the necessary and logical completion of Diocletian's program of reorganization and reform. As the 'last of the Romans,' this Illyrian emperor was to be the instigator of the most formidable assault upon the Christian faith which men feared would annihilate the Empire. In the light of recent and contemporary evidence, however, it seems that Lactantius' story that Galerius forced

---

25 K. Stade in *Der Politiker Diokletian und die letzte Grosse Christenverfolgung* (Wiesbaden 1926) gives strong arguments for this case.

the issue is the more likely. For the details of the persecution as it concerned the various courts of the time the text is better by far than any commentary.

And although no complete history of the persecution can be written,[26] there is no doubt that for those who lived through it, as for all thinking men today, the victory was that 'which overcomes the world, our faith.'[27] Against that faith emperors and demons were powerless. Such is the theme of the *De mortibus persecutorum*. Its bias cannot destroy its fundamental historical value. Its author is not only a Christian; he is also a Roman who cannot fail to see that the Empire must pass away as did Babylon and Assyria. His natural feeling of patriotism and distress at this is an undertone and must be subjected to the principle of his interpretation of history. Here, the vindication of divine justice is accomplished. God's anger and the deaths of the persecutors are a part of His providence.

---

26 Cf. N. H. Baynes, *op. cit.*, *Cambridge Ancient History*, Vol. 12, pp. 670-674.
27 Cf. 1 John 5.4.

The Book of Lucius Caecilius to
Donatus, the Confessor

ON THE DEATHS OF THE PERSECUTORS

Chapter 1

MY VERY DEAR DONATUS,[1] the Lord has heard the prayers which you made daily, each hour of the day, to Him. He has heard, too, those of the rest of our brethren who by a glorious confession[2] have sought an everlasting crown for themselves as reward of their faith.

Behold, all our adversaries are crushed;[3] tranquility is restored throughout the world; the Church, but recently buffeted by persecution, now rises again; and the temple of God, which had been overturned by the impious, is rebuilt in greater splendor by the mercy of the Lord. God has raised up princes[4] who have done away with the wicked and bloody commands of tyrants, and who have looked out for the human race so that now,[5] the cloud of that most bitter period having been dissolved, so to speak, a joyous and serene peace rejoices

---

1 This Donatus suffered torture nine times under Diocletian. Imprisoned for six years, he was released upon the publication of the Edict of Sardica. Cf. chs. 16, 35, 52. His name is always accompanied by the epithet, *carissimus* (dearest).
2 The word has the technical significance of 'public witness' here.
3 The word *adtritis* is a correction of J. Moreau whose text is mainly followed for this translation. Cf. Introduction.
4 Constantine and Licinius, the rulers of East and West from 313-324.
5 This is a section rich in forceful and abundant contrasts. Cf. Moreau, p. 190. Here, too, there is a very natural connection with the two Constantinian dedications of the *Institutes* 1.1.13-16; 7.27.11-17 (vol. 49, this series). Cf. the discussion in the Introduction, p. 126.

the hearts of all men. Now, after the violent whirlwinds of a dark storm, a clear sky with longed-for light has shown forth. Now, appeased by the prayers of His servants, God has raised up the fallen and afflicted with His heavenly assistance. Now, because the plots of the wicked are done away with, He has dried the tears of those who mourned. Those who had insulted God lie prone upon the earth; those who had overthrown the sacred temple have themselves fallen in a greater ruin; those who had hacked the just to pieces have poured forth their lives that wrought harm, punished by blows sent from heaven and well-deserved tortures.

This punishment came late, indeed, but heavily and deservedly. God had put off their punishment in order to use them as great and remarkable examples from which posterity might learn that there is but one God,[6] and that the same One as Judge exacts in vindication[7] meet punishments from the impious and the persecutors.[8] It has been my purpose to testify about their end in writing so that all might know of it, both those who have been far removed from the events, and those who are going to come after us. I intend them to learn to what extent the Most High God has shown forth His power and majesty in destroying and wiping out the enemies of His name. However, it is not out of place, if, going back to the beginning, from the time that the Church was established, I set forth who her persecutors were and what punishments the severity of the heavenly Judge inflicted upon them.

Chapter 2

In the last days of the reign of Tiberius Caesar, as we read, our Lord Jesus Christ was crucified by the Jews on the ninth day before the Kalends of April (March 23) in the consulship

---
6 Cf. *Inst.* 1.17.3; 2.17.6; 4.3.13ff.; etc.
7 The textual emendation of Moreau has again been followed.
8 This theme is treated at length in the *De ira Dei*.

of the two Gemini.[1] When He rose again on the third day, He gathered together His disciples whom the fright of His arrest had put to flight. He stayed with them for forty days, opening their hearts and interpreting the Scriptures for them, which, up to that time, were obscure and involved; and He ordained them and instructed them for the preaching of dogma and His doctrine, setting down the solemn discipline of the New Testament. When this work was completed, a storm cloud enveloped Him and took Him from the sight of men into heaven.[2]

Then, the disciples (who then numbered eleven), after adding Mathias, in place of the traitor Judas, and Paul, dispersed throughout the whole world to teach the Gospel, just as their Master had commanded them.[3] During twenty-five years, that is, to the beginning of Nero's reign, they laid the foundation of the Church throughout all provinces and states.

And when Nero was already reigning, Peter came to Rome. Through his performance of certain miracles which he worked by the power of God that was given to him, he converted many to the way of justice and set up a firm and faithful temple unto God. This fact was made known to Nero. When he noticed that, not only at Rome but everywhere, a great multitude was daily turning aside from the cult of idols and passing over to the new religion in condemnation of the old, because he was an evil tyrant doing harm, he zealously strove to tear down the heavenly temple and destroy justice. And he was the first of all to persecute the servants of God: he crucified Peter and killed Paul.

However, he did not do this without paying the penalty, for God looked upon the distress of His people. So, cast down

---
[1] Cf. *Inst.* 4.10.18 (vol. 49, this series). The tradition which fixes the year as that of the consulship of the two Gemini shows up in Tertullian, *Against the Jews* 8 and also in Sulpicius Severus, *Chronicles* 2.11.18; 27.5. Cf. also St. Augustine, *City of God* 18.54; *Christian Doctrine* 2.28.42. However, this date is not considered in the Greek tradition nor by Saints Cyprian, Hilary, Ambrose, and Jerome.
[2] Cf. Luke 24.51; Mark 16.19; John 6.62.
[3] Cf. Acts 1.9.

from the pinnacle of empire and overthrown from his high position, the impotent tyrant was suddenly nowhere to be found, so that not even a burial place in the earth was apparent for such an evil beast. Whence some people, raving with foolish ideas, believe that he was carried off from the earth and is reserved living someplace, according to the Sibylline verse: 'The matricide is to come, an exile from the ends of the earth.'[4] And thus he who first persecuted the Church will be the same one, they think, who will also persecute it last and precede the coming of Antichrist.[5] It is not right to believe this of him. But certain of our own writers hold that just as two prophets[6] were carried away living to remain until the end of time and return before the holy and everlasting reign of Christ when that begins to come upon the earth, in the same way, too, will Nero come to be the precursor and advance-man of the devil for the devastation of the world and the overthrow of the human race.

Chapter 3

Some years after this one,[1] another, no less a tyrant, arose, Domitian. Although he exercised a hated sway, still he pressed upon the necks of his subjects as long as possible, and he reigned safely until he stretched out impious hands against the Lord. After he had been incited with the inspiration of demons to the persecution of the just people,[2] then, turned

---

4 Cf. *Sibylline Oracles* VIII.70-71.
5 Cf. *Inst.* 7.16; 17.2-10. The Fathers of the Church see in the Antichrist a false Jewish Messias, or a *Nero redivivus* (a returned-to-life Nero, cf. Victorinus Petavius, *In Apol.* 13.16 [PL 5.338]) or a magician. Cf. Moreau, p. 202.
6 Elias and Henoch. Lactantius follows Tertullian in this; cf. his *Anima* 50.

---

1 Nero died in 68. Domitian began to rule in 81.
2 Moreau, pp. 205-208, summarizes the materials on the persecution of Domitian. Cf. especially M. Goguel, *La naissance du Christianisme* (Paris 1946) 575-584.

over to the hands of enemies, he paid the penalty. It was not enough for vengeance that he was killed at home; even the memory of his name was erased.³ For although he had erected many marvelous works, when he built the Capitol and other noble monuments, the Senate so persecuted his name that it left not a trace of his images or inscriptions. Thereby, with its decrees, it most gravely branded a mark on the dead ruler unto everlasting ignominy.

When the acts of this tyrant were rescinded, the Church was not only restored to its former status, but it even shone forth much more clearly and flourishingly. In the times that followed, when many good princes held the keys and controls of the Roman Empire, suffering no assaults from enemies, the Church stretched forth her power and sway into East and West, so that there was no corner of the globe so remote that the religion of God had not penetrated. And, finally, there was no nation in existence of such wild customs that it did not become gentle and practice works of justice upon embracing the worship of God.

But afterwards the long peace was interrupted.

Chapter 4

Then after some years,¹ there appeared a vile beast, Decius, who tormented the Church. Who would persecute justice save an evil man? And as though he had been carried to that elevation of princedom for this very reason, he began right away to rage against God, so that his fall was thereby immediate.

For setting out against the Carpians who then had seized Dacia and Moesia,² he was immediately surrounded by bar-

---

3 Suetonius, *Domitian* 16, 23.

1 The long 'peace,' according to Lactantius, was from 96 to 249.
2 The reference here is to the frontiers along the Danube River. The Carpians united with Goths, Vandals, etc., in resisting the Romans.

barians and destroyed with a large part of his army. He was not able to be honored with burial even, but despoiled and abandoned, as was fitting for an enemy of God, he lay exposed as food for the beasts and birds.

Chapter 5

Not long after this,[1] Valerian also, seized with a madness that was not any different, raised impious hands against God and spilled much just blood in a short time.[2] But God afflicted him with a new and singular kind of punishment, so that he served for posterity as an example that the adversaries of God always receive wages worthy of their crime.

This Valerian was captured by the Persians, and he lost, not only the power which he had used with insolence, but also the liberty which he had wrenched from others. He lived in the most disgraceful servitude. Sapor, the king of the Persians who had captured him, forced him to bend down and offer him the use of his back whenever he felt like mounting his horse or chariot. And, then, when he had placed his foot on the Roman's back, he said to him with a reproachful laugh that that which the Romans depicted on their tablets and walls was not true.[3] Thus that one lived for some time, so most deservedly triumphed-over that, for a long time, the Roman name was a sport and mockery for the barbarians.[4]

Even this was added to him for punishment, the fact that, although he had a son as emperor,[5] still he found no avenger of his captivity and extreme servitude. Nor was his return even sought for at all. However, after he had completed his

---
1 Valerian's reign was from 253 to 260.
2 The actual persecution was in effect in 257 and 258.
3 The Romans depicted themselves as the lords of the earth.
4 On the Roman-Persian conflict in question, cf. M. G. Higgins, *The Persian War of the Emperor Maurice, The Catholic University of American Byzantine Studies* I (1939) 19-20; A. Christensen, *L'Iran sous les Sassanides* (Paris 1936) 215ff.
5 The Emperor Gallienus (260-268).

shameful life in that disgrace, the skin was torn from him and the covering, stained red from blood, was ripped from his members, so that it might be placed in the temple of the barbarian gods for a memory of a most splendid triumph. This way he would always be a spectacle to our legates that Romans should not place too much confidence in their strength, since they would be beholding the spoils of a captive prince before the shrines of the Persian gods.

When God has exacted such punishments, then, for sacrileges, is it not to be wondered at that anyone should dare afterwards, not only to do, but even to contrive or plan to do anything against the majesty of the one God who rules and holds all things in His power?

Chapter 6

Aurelian[1] was of an insane and rash nature. Although he was of an age to remember the captivity of Valerian, he forgot his crime and its punishments, likewise provoking the wrath of God by his cruel deeds. For to him, it was not even permitted to carry out what he had planned, but he was cut off suddenly in the very beginnings of his madness. His bloody edicts had not yet reached the outer provinces when he himself lay in blood upon the soil of Caenofrurium, a village of Thrace, murdered by his friends because of a certain false suspicion.

It was fitting for the later tyrants to be restrained by so many examples such as these. Yet these were not only not terrified, but they acted against God even more boldly and more presumptuously.

---

1 L. Domitius Aurelianus (273-275) had himself acclaimed as 'lord' and 'god,' and furthered the official cult of the Sun, but he is not regarded as especially opposed to Christianity, nor is there any authority for a persecution under his auspices. The assignment of a list of martyrs to his reign is perhaps due to a confusion of names, his and that of Aurelius, one of Diocletian's names. Cf. the bibliography suggested for this question by Moreau, pp. 226-232.

Chapter 7

Diocletian,[1] who was an inventor of crimes and a manufacturer of evils, although he destroyed everything else, could not refrain from laying hands even on God. He subverted the world (i.e., the Empire)[2] at the same time by both avarice and timidity. He made three men sharers in his power, dividing the world into four parts and multiplying armies, for each one of them strove to have a greater number by far than earlier princes had had when they were sole rulers of the state.[3] The number of receivers had begun to be so much greater than that of givers, the strength of the colonists being sapped by the enormity of impost duties, that fields were deserted and cultivated areas were turned into forests. And in order that all things might be filled with terrors, the provinces, too, were cut up into sections. Many officials and many bureaus were set up in the individual regions and they burdened almost each city. Likewise, there were many financial officers and magistrates and vicars of prefects. The civil acts of these were very rare; only condemnations and proscriptions were frequent; their exactions of innumerable taxes were, I will not say frequent, but perpetual; and the injuries in these exactions were such as were beyond endurance.

Matters which were concerned with the employing of soldiers were also not to be tolerated. In his insatiable avarice, he wished the treasury to be never diminished, but he was always laying up extraordinary funds and resources in order

---

[1] C. Aurelius Valerius Diocletianus (284-305).
[2] Lactantius attributes the destruction of the Empire to Diocletian. He is the greatest of the persecutors; therefore, to Lactantius, he is responsible as well for the greatest social and political ruin.
[3] Cf. W. Seston, *Dioclétien et la Tétrarchie* I (Paris 1946); A. E. R. Boak, 'An Egyptian Farmer of the Age of Diocletian,' *Byzantina Metabyzantina* I (1946) 39-53; H. M. D. Parker, 'The Legions of Diocletian and Constantine,' *Journal of Roman Studies* XXIII (1933) 184; A. Alföldi, *The Conversion of Constantine and Pagan Rome* (Oxford 1948) for recent and accurate treatments of these general topics connected with Diocletian's rule.

to keep those funds which he had accumulated preserved intact. When, because of his iniquities, he made things extremely high-priced, he attempted to fix by law the price of saleable goods. Then, on account of scarcity and the low grade of articles, much blood was spilled; and because of fear nothing purchaseable appeared. Therefore, expensiveness raged much worse, until, after the death of many, the law was dissolved by sheer necessity.[4]

To this there was added a certain limitless desire of building, and for supplying all the workers, craftsmen, carts, and whatever was necessary for constructing the works, there was an additional taxing (no less than the others had done) of the provinces. Here, there were basilicas; here, a circus; here, a mint; here, an armory; here, a house for his wife; here, one for his daughter.

All of a sudden, a great part of the city[5] was razed to the ground. All left with their wives and children as though the city were captured by the enemy. And when these works had been completed at the price of the ruin of provinces, he said: 'They were not done properly; let them be done another way.' Again, it was necessary for tearing down and changing and, perhaps, it would fall again. Thus, he kept on going mad, desiring to equal Nicomedia with Rome.[6]

I pass by the fact that many perished for the sake of their having possessions or fortunes. This was usual and generally permitted because of the customariness of evils. That was an outstanding quality in this ruler, because wherever he had seen a more cultivated field or more ornate building, then, a charge of calumny and capital punishment was prepared for the owner, as though he could not plunder and steal without bloodshed.

---

4 The financial reforms of Diocletian were the least successful of his program.
5 Nicomedia.
6 Lactantius counts this preference for a city other than Rome as a capital city a fault in Diocletian, whereas Constantine is claimed as the avenger of Rome (cf. ch. 48, p. 196) when he does likewise.

Chapter 8

What shall we say of his brother Maximian who was called Herculius?[1] He was not unlike him, for they could not have stuck together in such a faithful friendship unless there were one mind in the two, the same thought, a like will, and equal judgment. They differed in this respect alone, that there was greater avarice in one but more timidity, and in the other less avarice but more spirit, not for the doing of good, but of evil. For although he held Italy, the very seat of empire, and had the richest provinces subject to him, Africa and Spain, he was not so careful in guarding the riches, the supply of which lay at hand. And since there was need, very wealthy senators were not lacking who were said to have affected the imperial power by providing witnesses in such a way that the eyes of the senate members were constantly being torn out. Its very bloody treasury was getting packed with ill-gained wealth.

Now the passion in this libidinous man was directed, not only to the corruption of young men, an odious and detestable thing, but also to the violation of the daughters of the first citizens.[2] For wherever he went, young girls would be torn from the embrace of their parents immediately and at his whim. He judged himself happy because of these things; he considered the felicity of his power to rest upon them, so long as nothing was denied his passion and evil desire.

I pass by Constantius,[3] because he was different from the rest, and he was worthy to hold command of the world alone.

---

1 Marcus Aurelius Valerius Maximianus; cf. Seston, *op. cit.*, pp. 60-67. The name *Herculius* was to justify his position. Diocletian had taken the name *Jovius*, son of Jupiter.
2 Here, Lactantius is not regarding the moral question in the comparison, but the social ranks involved.
3 C. Flavius Julius Constantius, the father of Constantine; cf. Seston, *op. cit.*, p. 242.

Chapter 9

But the other Maximian (Galerius),[1] whom Diocletian attached to himself as son-in-law,[2] was worse, not only than those other two whom our own times knew, but also worse than all the evil rulers there have ever been. A natural barbarism was inherent in this beast, a savagery alien to Roman blood. Nor was this strange, since his mother, a woman from the other side of the Danube, had fled into new Dacia by crossing the river when the Carpians were infesting the land. His bodily appearance was in keeping with his character: towering in stature and massive in corpulence, he was swollen and spread to a horrible magnitude. With voice and action and appearance, he struck fear and terror into all.

Even his father-in-law had a very great fear of him. This was its cause.[3] Narses, king of the Persians, under the inspiration of the example of his grandfather and ancestors, was eager to seize upon the Orient with great forces. Then Diocletian, as he was fearful and cast down in spirit at every upset, and fearing, at the same time, the lot of Valerian, did not dare to stand in his way, but he sent this man (his son-in-law) to Armenia, himself remaining in the Orient to observe the turn of events. The son-in-law, using the tricks which it is the custom for barbarians to use in conducting war with all their own peoples, attacked the enemy, impeded because of their number and burdened with packs, without difficulty. When King Narses had been put to flight, he returned with booty and huge spoils, adding haughtiness to himself and fear to Diocletian. After this victory, he was exalted to such heights

---

[1] C. Galerius Valerius Maximianus. He is usually called Galerius.
[2] In 293, he married Valeria, daughter of Diocletian, repudiating his first wife.
[3] Cf. Seston, *op. cit.*, pp. 165ff.

that he was now taking honor from the name of Caesar.[4] When
he had learned this from letters brought to him, he shouted in
a terrible voice and with a violent expression: 'How long will
it be "Caesar"?' Then he began to rant most insolently that
he wished to be seen and spoken of as sprung from Mars and
that he preferred to be as another Romulus and to soil the
reputation of his mother, Romula, with disgrace, in order
that he himself might seem sprung from the gods.

But I am postponing a discussion of his deeds so as not to
confuse the time order. For after he had accepted the title of
emperor, his father-in-law despoiled and out of the way, then
he began to rage wildly at last and to despoil all things.

Diocles—for thus he was called before his reign—although
he subverted the state with such plans and such accomplices,
and although for his crimes he did not gain anything like
what he merited, reigned, however, a long time and with great
felicity, for as long as he did not defile his hands with the
blood of the just.

Now I will reveal the cause which finally led him to instigate
a persecution.

Chapter 10

Once, while he was conducting affairs in parts of the Orient,
as he was from fear a searcher into the future, he was offering
a sacrifice of cattle and was seeking from their entrails what
things were to happen. Then, certain of his ministers who had
knowledge of the Lord, while they stood near him as he sac-

---

[4] It is obvious that it was inferred that Galerius was bringing added honor to the title. He had been appointed Diocletian's own Caesar in the East in 293 when he formed the tetrarchy, that is, two Augusti, one for East and one for West and a Caesar for each. The two Caesars were to succeed the Augusti. This is what actually happened. Diocletian and Maximian abdicated in 303, and Galerius and Constantius Chlorus (the Caesar of the West) succeeded as Augusti, appointing two new Caesars.

rificed, made the immortal sign on their foreheads.¹ When this was done, the demons took to flight and the sacred rites were disturbed. The augurs trembled; they did not perceive the customary signs in the entrails; and, as though the offerings had not already been made, they began to perform the rites again and again. But each time the slain victims showed nothing, until the master-augur, a Tages,² either because he suspected something or had seen the action, said that the sacred signs were not making any response for this reason, that some profane men were present at the divine rites. Then, in a rage, Diocletian ordered, not only those who were ministers of the sacred rites, but all who were in the palace to make sacrifice. He gave orders that any who might refuse were to be punished with clubbings. By means of these orders which were delivered through officers, he charged even the soldiers to be forced to the nefarious sacrifices. Those who would not obey were withdrawn from service. His raging fury went so far that it could not do anything more against the law and religion of God.

Then, after some time had passed,³ he came to Bithynia to spend the winter, and to the same place there came Maximian Caesar (Galerius) also inflamed with crime, so that he instigated the doting old man to conduct a persecution of the Christians because he had already made a start.

I have found out that the account which follows was a cause of that one's (i.e., Maximian's) fury.

---

1 Cf. *Inst.* 4.27.8 (vol. 49, this series).
2 This was the name of the mythical founder of Etruscan divination, liver inspecton (cf. Cicero, *De divinatione* 2.23). We need not think that Lactantius meant it as the chief augur's own name.
3 Perhaps in 302/303, or even earlier, because Diocletian abdicated in 303. In a passage of Eusebius studied by Moreau (cf. *op. cit.*, n. 22, p. 267), Galerius is definitely held to be the author of these measures referred to here.

Chapter 11

The mother of Galerius[1] was a worshiper of the gods of the mountains. Since she was a very superstitious woman, she offered sacrificial repasts almost every day and made donations of the meals to her countrymen. Christians kept away, and while she would be dining with her fellow-pagans, they would redouble fasts and prayers. Therefore, she conceived a hatred for them and, with womanly complaints, she prevailed upon her son, no less superstitious, to get rid of these men.

Therefore, secret councils were held during a whole winter, when no one was admitted, and all thought that the greatest affairs of state were being treated. For a long time, the old man, the Augustus, resisted his fury, showing how dangerous it was to have the whole world disturbed and the blood of many shed, that they were accustomed to die willingly,[2] and that it would be enough if he would keep only those of the palace household and his soldiers from the practice of that religion. However, he was not able to influence the wildness of the impetuous man. He decided, then, to get the opinion of his friends.[3] This was Diocletian's type of malice. When he had determined what was a good thing to do, he did it without counsel so that he himself might get the praise; when there was something evil, since he knew it would be criticized, he called many into his counsel so that whatever he himself should be found wanting in would be ascribed to the fault of others.

A few judges, therefore, and some military leaders who held superior rank were called in and questioned. Certain ones among them, from a personal hatred of Christians, believed that these were enemies of the gods and of state religion and, therefore, ought to be done away with. Those who thought

---

[1] Romula, the mother of Galerius.
[2] Cf. Tertullian, *Apol.* 46.14; 50.16; *Against Marcion* 5.10; Minucius Felix 37.1.
[3] His personal advisers, the *Consilium principis*. This group became known as the *consistorium* by the middle of the fourth century.

differently, either fearing the man or wishing to gratify his wishes because they knew what he wanted, voiced a pretended agreement with that same opinion. Not even in this way was the emperor swayed to give his assent, but he thought it best to consult the gods and sent an augur to Milesian Apollo. The response came that the God of the Christians was an enemy of the divine religion. Thus he was led away from his own decision; and, although he was not able to resist his friends, his Caesar, and Apollo, he did attempt to hold this moderation, that he ordered the affair to be conducted without bloodshed, although the Caesar wanted those who refused to sacrifice to be burned alive.[4]

Chapter 12

A favorable and propitious day was sought for carrying out the affair and the Terminalia feast days, which occur seven days before the Kalends of March,[1] were selected especially, so that a terminus, as it were, should be placed on this religion. 'That day was the first of death and it was first the cause of evils,'[2] those which befell themselves and the world.

When this day dawned—one of the old men being consul for the eighth time, the other for the seventh[3]—suddenly, while it was still not full daylight, the prefect came to the church with leaders and tribunes and officers of the treasury. They tore down the door and searched for a picture or image of God. When the Scriptures were found, they were burned.

---

[4] On the conduct of Galerius in this matter of persecution, cf. J. Moreau, 'Notes d'histoire romaine,' *Annales Universitatis Saraviensis* II (1953) 89-99.

[1] The feast of the *Termini* (rocks which marked the boundaries) and of the god *Terminus* occurred on the 23rd of February. Cf. Ovid, *Fasti* 2.639ff.; Prudentius, *Contra Symmachum* 2.1006ff.; and Augustine, *City of God* 7.7.
[2] Vergil, *Aeneid* 4.169-170.
[3] In 303, the two Augusti, Diocletian and Maximian, were consuls for the eighth and seventh time, respectively.

The chance for booty was given to all. There was pillaging, trepidation, running about all around.

The rulers themselves in their observatory-site (because the appointed church was visible as they looked up from the palace because of its high position) for a long time argued together, whether it would be necessary for fire to be applied. Diocletian won, having a cautious attitude, lest part of the city be destroyed when a great conflagration (such as the persecution would warrant) should be set. For many great houses encircled the church on all sides.

So the praetorians came in a drawn up battle line with axes and other implements; and, throwing these from all sides, they leveled that most outstanding temple to the ground in a few hours.

Chapter 13

The next day[1] the edict was published in which it was ordered that men of that religion should be deprived of all honor and dignity and be subjected to torments; and no matter from what rank or grade they came every action against them would hold weight; and they themselves would not be able to plead in a court against a charge of injury or adultery or theft; in short, they would not have freedom of speech. Although it was not right, still it was with great courage that a certain man[2] pulled down and tore up this edict, as he said deridingly that victories of the Goths and Sarmatians were proposed in it. Immediately, he was taken, and he was not only tortured, but he was actually cooked, according to the directions of a

---

[1] The promulgation date, February 24; cf. Eusebius, *History of the Church* 8.2.4.
[2] The *Syriac Martyrology* preserves the man's name, Euethios. Cf. H. Lietzmann, *Die drei ältesten Martyrologien*2 (Bonn 1911) 9, and *Acta sanctorum* September III, pp. 12-14.

particular recipe,³ and then finally burned up, having suffered with admirable patience.

Chapter 14

But the Caesar was not content with the laws of the edict. He prepared to set Diocletian off on another score. In order to drive him to the determination of the most cruel persecution, he set fire to the palace through the aid of secret agents.¹ And when part had been burned, the Christians were charged with being public enemies and, because ill-will was so high, the name of the Christians was being burned along with the palace. They were charged with having plotted with the eunuchs for the death of the princes, the two emperors having been almost burned alive in their own palaces.

Diocletian, however, who always wished to appear clever and intelligent, was able to discover nothing, but, inflamed with wrath, he began at once to put all his domestics to torture. He himself sat and had the innocent roasted at the fire. Likewise, all the judges and all those, in short, who were officials in the palace received the faculties and put them to torture. They vied with each other so as to be first to find out something.

Nothing was ever discovered though, for, of course, no one tortured the household of the Caesar. That one was present and kept pressing the matter, nor did he allow the anger of the ill-advised old man to settle. After fifteen days, he again contrived another fire. This one was discovered more quickly, but it did not become apparent who caused it. Then the Caesar, whose departure had been in readiness since the middle of winter, rushed out that very same day, claiming that he was taking flight so as not to be burned alive.

---
3 Some editors would choose the word *lentissime* here and have the manner of cooking by slow heat be an added note of torture.
1 No other author lays the charge of these fires to Galerius.

Chapter 15

Then the emperor raged, not only against those of his own household, but against all. In the first place, he compelled his daughter, Valeria, and her husband, and Prisca to be defiled by pagan sacrifice.[1] When those who had been the most powerful eunuchs were killed, those on whom the palace and he himself depended, the priests and deacons were seized, and condemned without any proof or confession. They were led away with all their families. There was no respect for sex or age. Men were seized and burned, not individually, because there was such a great number, but they were herded into devouring fires. The domestic servants of the palace were plunged into the sea, millstones tied to their necks.

The persecution was no less intense against the rest of the people. The judges went about through all the temples and forced everybody to sacrifice. The prisons were full.[2] Unheard of kinds of torment were conceived. In order that justice might not be rashly applied in favor of anyone, altars were set up in secretarial rooms and before the tribunal so that those coming to court should sacrifice first and then plead their cases; and, therefore, the approach to the judge was as though an entrance hall to the gods.

Letters had found their way even to Maximian and Constantius so that they would do the same things. Their opinion had not been looked for in such great matters. And, indeed, the old Maximian willingly carried out the instructions throughout all of Italy for he was not a very clement man. Constantius, so as not to seem to disapprove of the precepts of the previous rulers, allowed the church buildings, the meeting places, that is, the wall which could be restored, to be torn down; but the temple of God which is in men,[3] he left untouched.

---

1 This inference that Valeria and her husband were Christians is not corroborated by any strongly reliable source.
2 Cf. Eusebius, *op. cit.* 8.9.
3 Cf. *Inst.* 4.13.26; *De ira* 24.14.

Chapter 16

So the whole world was upset, and outside of the Gauls,[1] from the East even to the West, the three wildest beasts were raging. 'Not if I had a hundred tongues and a hundred mouths and a voice of iron, could I comprehend all the forms of their crimes, could I get through all the names of the punishments,'[2] which the judges throughout the provinces inflicted upon the just and the innocent. Anyway, why is there any need of relating those things, especially to you, very dear Donatus, who have experienced more than the rest the storm of raging persecution?

For, although you had fallen into the hands of Flaccinus,[3] the prefect, a violent murderer, and then when you had come before Hierocles,[4] the governor who had been a vicar, who was an author[5] and councilor for the carrying out of the persecution, you finally furnished to all an example of unconquered fortitude before Priscillian, his successor. Nine times subject to torments and various sufferings, you nine times overcame your adversary with your glorious confession; in nine battles, you unwarred the devil with his satellites; by nine victories, you triumphed over the world with its terrors. How pleasing was that spectacle to God when He beheld you as victor, not bringing under subjection to your chariot white horses or huge elephants, but, best of all, the very triumphant ones themselves![6]

---

1 The Gauls were the territories governed by Constantius.
2 Vergil, *Aeneid* 6.625-627.
3 This man has not been identified.
4 Identified by several scholars chiefly on epigraphical bases; cf. the summary given by Moreau, pp. 292-294.
5 He is no doubt the author referred to in the *Institutes* 5.2.12-13 (vol. 49, this series), the 'master' who wrote three books against the Christians called *Philaletheis*. (*Inst.* 5.3.23.) On the doctrine of Hierocles, cf. De Labriolle, *La réaction païenne*, new edition (Paris 1942) 306ff.
6 The chariot of a triumphal procession was drawn by four white horses (cf. Livy 5.23), and elephants were frequently part of a triumph, too.

This is true triumph, when the masters (of the world) are mastered. For they were conquered and subjected by your virtue, inasmuch as by despising their abominable order you spurned with stable faith and strength of mind all their trappings and the slight terrors of tyrannical power. The beatings accomplished nothing against you; the hooks availed nothing; the fire nothing; the sword nothing; the various kinds of torments did nothing. No power could wrest faith and devotion from you. This is being a disciple of God. This is what it means to be a soldier of Christ, one whom no enemy may attack, no wolf drive from the heavenly fold, no snare induce, no pain overcome, no suffering afflict. Finally, after those nine most glorious combats in which the devil was vanquished by you, he did not dare to engage with you any further, whom he tested in so many conflicts and found not able to be overcome. And although the victor's crown has been prepared for you, he has ceased to demand anything further of you, lest you should take it now. Though you may not receive this at present, however, it is being preserved for you completely in the kingdom of God because of your virtues and merits.

But let us get back to the outline of our discussion.

Chapter 17

After this crime had been perpetrated, Diocletian, although his good luck had already left him,[1] set out at once for Rome to celebrate there the day of the Vicennalia,[2] which was to be on the twelfth day before the Kalends of December (Nov. 20).

---

1 Cf. ch. 9, p. 148.
2 He celebrated it at the same time as the triumph over Narses. It was the occasion of an amnesty in honor of the twentieth anniversary of Diocletian's accession. The scholarship on the question based on the *Acts of the Martyrs* and epigraphical sources is summarized by Moreau, pp. 297-304.

When the solemn rites were celebrated, because he could not bear the freedom of the Roman people, impatient and sick in soul, he left the city as the Kalends of January (the first) were drawing near, when the consulship was being conferred on him for the ninth time.[3] He could not endure the thirteen days of waiting so that he might begin this consulship at Rome rather than at Ravenna, but, setting out in the dead of winter and struck by cold and storms, he contracted a sickness, slight but chronic; and, being disturbed and bothered throughout the journey, he had to be carried most of the way on a litter.

And so, when summer had gone, through a circuitous route along the bank of the Hister, he reached Nicomedia, but the sickness had now become severe. Although he saw that he was oppressed with it, he was carried on, nevertheless, in order to dedicate a circus which he had built. It was now a full year after the Vicennalia.

Then he was so overcome with weakness that the sparing of his life was asked from all the gods. Finally, on the Ides of December (the 13th), grief suddenly appeared in the palace; there was sadness and weeping on the part of the judges, trepidation and silence in the whole city. Now they were saying that he was not only dead, but buried as well, when suddenly, in the morning of the next day, the report was spread that he was living, and the expressions of the domestics and the judges changed with alacrity. Nor were there lacking those who suspected that his death was being concealed until the Caesar should come, lest some revolution be instigated, perhaps, by the soldiers. This suspicion had such weight that no one would have believed that he was alive, except that on the Kalends of March he appeared, scarcely recognizable, of course, since he had suffered under sickness for almost an entire year. He who had slept in death on the Ides of December had recovered life.

---

[3] The year 304. It was Maximian's eighth consulship.

But it was not an entire recovery, however, for he became demented, so that at certain times he would be insane and at others would seem clear.⁴

Chapter 18

Not many days later the Caesar arrived, not to congratulate his (adoptive) father, but to force him to yield his power. He had now but recently been in conflict with the old Maximian,¹ and he had alarmed him by injecting the fear of civil war.

So, at first, he met Diocletian gently and in a friendly manner, telling him that he was old now,² and not strong, and not capable of the management of the affairs of state, that he ought to rest after his labors. At the same time, he suggested to him the example of Nerva who had handed over the empire to Trajan.³ Diocletian, however, said that it was not fitting, if he should fall back into the shadows of a lowly life after having reached such great brilliance in his peak position. He said also that it was not at all safe, because during such a long rule he had gained the hatred of many people. He showed that Nerva, reigning only a year, had abdicated from the control of the state and returned to private life, in which he had grown old, because he was not able to bear the burden and care of such great concerns, either on account of his age or his lack of experience. But, he went on to say that if Galerius wished to have the name of Emperor, it would not bother him if they were all called Augusti.

---

4 Cf. Eusebius 8.13.11.

1 The pushing of the abdication is formally assigned to Galerius, and the subsequent action of the old Maximian who took back the purple twice (cf. 26.7 and 29.5) shows that he had been forced to abdicate.
2 When he died in 313, he was only 68.
3 Nerva had really not abdicated; he had associated Trajan with him as co-ruler.

That one, however, who had already in hope seized upon the whole world, since he saw that nothing, or not much more, besides the name was coming to him, answered that the original arrangement of Diocletian himself ought to be held to, so that there might be two greater ones in the state who would exercise supreme control, and then two lesser ones to be assistants. He argued that between the two concord could easily be preserved, but that it could be kept in no way among four equals. And if Diocletian should not want to yield to him, he would take matters into his own hands and see to it that he would no longer be a 'lesser' ruler and the 'last' of them all.[4] Already fifteen years had passed since he had been relegated to Illyricum, that is, to the banks of the Danube, to struggle with the barbarian peoples, while the others were ruling in more relaxed and quieter lands in a luxurious manner.

Upon hearing this, the sick old man, who had already received the letters of old Maximian (who had written all that that one would say) and who had learned that an army was being raised by him, said to him in a voice full of tears, 'Let it be, if this is what you want.'

It remained for Caesars to be chosen by the common deliberation of them all.

'What is the point of deliberation, since it must be necessary for those other two to agree to what we will have done?'

'Clearly it is so, for their sons must be the ones named.'

Now, Maximian had a son, Maxentius, son-in-law of this Maximian (Galerius), a man of perverse and evil mind, so proud and stubborn that he was wont to give deference to neither his father nor his father-in-law; and for this reason, he was hateful to both of them.

Constantius also had a son, Constantine, a most upright young man and very worthy of that high rank. He was loved

---

[4] He was 'lesser' as a Caesar and 'last' because even Constantius had precedence over him; cf. ch. 21.1.

by the soldiers and wanted by private citizens as well because of his distinguished and fine appearance, his military accomplishments, the probity of his morals, and his exceptional congeniality. He was then present at Diocletian's court, having been long since made a tribune of the first rank by him.

'What shall be done, then?' asked Galerius. 'The former,' he said, 'is not worthy. He who has despised us when he was but a private citizen, what will he do when he gains power?'

'But the latter is quite pleasing, and he will rule in such a way that he will be judged better and more clement than his father,' said Diocletian.

'Then it will come to be that I am not able to do what I wish. Men should be named,' added Galerius, 'who are to be at my disposal, those who fear me, who will do nothing except at my order.'[5]

'Whom shall we appoint, then?'

'Severus,'[6] he said.

'What! That excitable dancer, that drunkard, to whom night is as day, and day as night?'

'He is worthy,' he answered, 'because he faithfully exercised his command of the soldiers; and I have already sent him to Maximian to be invested by him.'

'All right. But whom will you make the other Caesar?'

'This man,' he said, indicating a certain young Daia,[7] a semi-barbarian, whom he had recently ordered to be called Maximin after his own name. For Diocletian, too, had formerly changed his name for him in part, on account of an omen, because Maximian (Galerius) displayed loyalty most scrupulously.

'Who is this whom you present to me?' asked Diocletian.

'A relative of mine, he said.

Then the other groaned and said: 'You do not give me

---
5 Such an appointment would have increased the power of the Flavians to the detriment of Galerius.
6 Flavius Valerius Severus (305-307).
7 Galerius Valerius Maximinus. He was a nephew of Galerius. He is usually called Maximin Daia.

THE DEATHS OF THE PERSECUTORS 161

capable men to whom the guardianship of the state can be entrusted.'

'I have approved of them,' he retorted.

'You seem to be on the verge of taking control of the empire,' capitulated Diocletian. 'I have labored enough, and I have seen to it that under my command the state should stay unharmed. If any harm comes to it, it will not be my fault.'

Chapter 19

When these matters had been determined, action was taken on the Kalends of May. All eyes were fixed upon Constantine. There was no doubt in anyone's mind. The soldiers who were present and the officers who had been chosen and summoned from the legions were rejoicing, intent upon this one man; they were desiring him and they were making known their wishes.

There was a lofty place about three miles outside the city. On its height, Maximian himself had assumed the purple, and there a column with an image of Jupiter had been erected. Everybody went there. An assembly of the soldiers was convoked. The old prince addressed them in tears, saying that he was old, that he was seeking rest after labors, that he was turning the power over to stronger rulers, and that he was replacing them with other Caesars. The expectation of everyone as to what appointments he would make was very high. Then suddenly, he names Severus and Maximinus the Caesars. All were struck dumb. Constantine was standing on the platform,[1] head held high. There was some general hesitation as to whether the name of Constantine had been changed. Suddenly, however, in the sight of all, Maximian made a gesture of turning away from Constantine and brought Daia forth from behind

---

[1] His presence on the tribunal with the court made it all the more certain to everyone that he would be named.

and placed him in a central position, having removed from him the garment of private citizen. Everyone wondered who this man was and where he came from. No one, however, dared to cry out against it, though all were disturbed by the unexpected strangeness of the situation.

Diocletian put on him his own purple which he removed from himself, and Diocletian became Diocles again. Thereupon, he stepped down from the platform. Then, the old king was conducted through the city and carried outside it in a carriage and sent back to his native place.

Daia, however, recently raised from the cattle and the forests, became at once a soldier of the guard, then a protector, and soon a tribune. The following day, as Caesar, he received the Orient to beat it down and trample underfoot, for he who knew neither military service nor state affairs was now a shepherd, not of sheep, but of soldiers.

Chapter 20

Maximian (Galerius), after he accomplished what he wished, the expulsion of the old Augusti, was now conducting himself as the sole lord of the whole world. He despised Constantius, even though it was necessary for him to be named first, because he was of a gentle nature and was impeded by poor health. He was hoping that Constantius, his co-Augustus, would die shortly, but if he did not, it seemed that he would divest the hated one easily. What would happen if he were forced by the other three incumbents to lay down his command?

Galerius himself had a friend, an old tent-mate and associate of early service, Licinius,[1] whose suggestions he followed in all his acts of ruling. He did not wish to make him a Caesar, so as not to thus name him an adoptive son, in order that

---

[1] Flavius Licinianus Licinius. He took the name Valerius when he came to power.

later on he might put him into the place of Constantius and call him Augustus and brother. Then, in truth, he himself would hold the principate and, reveling wildly throughout the world according to his own caprice, he would celebrate the twentieth anniversary affair and would himself put his enemy[2] out of the way, substituting for the Caesar his own son who was then nine years old.[3] Thus, when Licinius and Severus would hold the supreme command and when Maximin Daia and Candidianus would have the second name of Caesar, surrounded by an unattackable wall, he would spend a secure and tranquil old age.[4] His plans were tending in this direction. But God, whom he made his enemy, shattered all his contrivings.

Chapter 21

When he had secured the greatest power, therefore, he directed his mind toward the disruption of the world which he had opened out before himself. For after the defeat of the Persians (whose rite and practice it is to devote themselves as slaves to their kings and whose kings use their people as a slave-household), that nefarious man wished to introduce their custom into the Roman world. From the time of his victory, he praised it shamelessly. Because he could not practice it openly, he acted in such a way that he himself would take liberty away from men. First of all, he took the honors of public office. Not only decurions were tortured by him, but also the first men of cities, distinguished and very perfect

---

[2] Constantius Chlorus.
[3] Lactantius is our only source for the existence of this son, Candidianus, born of a concubine and adopted by Valeria; cf. chs. 35.3; 50.2-3.
[4] The arrangement of the tetrarchy gets somewhat upset here. Galerius and Constantius Chlorus were the Augusti with Severus and Maximinus (Daia) as Caesars. Perhaps his idea was just his own abdication, for Licinius was to replace Chlorus. Severus was to succeed him, and Candidianus was to fill the place of the promoted Severus.

men,[1] and, indeed, for quite unimportant and purely civil cases. If they seemed deserving of death, crosses were ready for them; if not, shackles were prepared. Mothers of families, free born and even noble girls were seized for the gynecaeum.[2] If someone were to be beaten, four stakes were fixed in an enclosure upon which no slave even was ever stretched.

Why should I relate his sport or his distractions? He had bears, very much like himself in fierceness and size, which he had selected throughout the whole time of his reign. As often as he wanted to be amused, he ordered each one of these, selected by name, to be brought forward. Men were thrown to them, not to be eaten, but to be swallowed down. When their limbs were strewn about, he laughed quite delightedly, nor did he ever dine except in the presence of human blood.

Fire was the punishment of those who did not have dignity. This is the type of death which he had at first directed against the Christians, when the laws were made, so that, after torture, the condemned might be burned with slow fires. After they had been bound, a light flame was applied first to the feet for so long a time until the flesh of the soles, contracted by the heat, would be pulled away from the bones. Then torches, lighted and immediately extinguished, were applied to the individual members of the body, so that no part of it was left untouched. During all of this, the face was sprinkled with cold water and the mouth was washed with a liquid, lest, the jaws becoming stiff with dryness, the breath would leave too quickly. This would take place finally, only after all the skin had been roasted away throughout a long day, when the force of the fire had penetrated to the inner organs. Then they made a pyre, and the already charred bodies were cremated.

---

1 Throughout this section, Lactantius uses the terms and titles of the ranks in this period of the Empire: *honores* (the privileged ones because of their offices); *decuriones* (jurors); *primores* (chief men in municipal senates); and *egregii* and *perfectissimi viri* (dignitaries of the equestrian order).

2 *Gynecaeum*, comparable to the *opus publicum* for men. In the *gynecaeum*, women and girls were forced to manufacture the imperial cloths and garments.

The bones, ground and reduced to powder, were tossed into the rivers and the sea.

Chapter 22

Those practices, therefore, which he had learned in torturing the Christians, from very habit he applied to all. With him no punishment was slight. There were no islands, no prisons, no metal mines; but fire, the cross, wild beasts were daily and ordinary occurrences. His domestic slaves and functionaries were punished by the lance. In the case of the death penalty, punishment by the sword was for very few cases, and this type was conferred as though a benefit upon those who, because of services or merits, had been granted this 'favorable' death.

But now those previous penalties were light in comparison with these: eloquence was extinguished; advocates were put out of the way; lawyers were exiled or killed; literature was regarded as a wicked profession, and those who were skilled in it were proscribed and execrated as enemies and an opposition party;[1] license for everything was assumed, because laws were disregarded; and military judges, devoid of all culture and humanity, were sent into the provinces without assessors.

Chapter 23

However, that was public calamity and the common grief of all once the census was taken up in the provinces and cities.[1] Because census agents were spread everywhere exacting everything, there was hostile disturbance and the likeness of horrible

---
[1] This tyrant suspected the intellectuals, but Constantius, Maximian, and Diocletian favored *belles-lettres*. That the attitude of rulers varied, cf. Pliny's *Panegyric on Trajan* 47. There is a general article on patronage in the *Oxford Classical Dictionary* 655, and a good introductory chapter in W. Y. Sellar's *Virgil*, pp. 1-8; 21-31.

[1] In 307, he had renewed Diocletian's census.

captivity. Fields were measured out piece by piece; vines and trees were counted; animals of every kind were marked down; men were counted individually; in the cities, urban and rustic population were united; all the market places were packed with families; each one was present with his children and his slaves. Torturings and beatings resounded;[2] sons were held up against their parents; the most faithful slaves were questioned and harassed against their masters, and even wives against husbands. If all things else failed, men were tortured to self-accusation, and when pain had overcome them, crimes which were not their own they had ascribed to them. No excuse was made for age or health. The sick and weak were brought out; the ages of individuals were reckoned, years being added to the young and taken away from the old. Everything was full of grief and sadness.

The things which those of old had done against conquered peoples by right of war, he dared to do against Romans and those subject to Romans, because his forefathers had been subjected to a census which Trajan victoriously imposed upon the constantly rebelling Dacians as a punishment. After this, men put down a price for their heads, gave a fee for life. And faith was not put in the same census-takers, but others were sent in their wake to find out more information, and the process was ever repeated. Though these did not find out anything, they added what they pleased, so that they might not seem to have been sent in vain. Meanwhile, the animals diminished in number and men died; nevertheless, taxes were exacted for the dead, so that it was not free of charge either to live or to die.[3]

There remained only the beggars from whom nothing could be exacted as a fee. Misery and hard luck had made them safe from every kind of injury. But, indeed, that 'reverent' man pitied them so that they should not want! He ordered them

---

[2] Tortures were applied to get complete accounts.
[3] Cf. Aristotle, *Rhetoric* 2.1383b: the proverbial 'to rob even a corpse of its winding sheet.'

all to be collected, carried off on ships, and dumped into the sea. Such a merciful man, to see to it that there would be no one in wretched circumstances under his rule! Thus, while he takes care that no one avoids the census through pretense of destitution, he kills a multitude of the truly destitute contrary to all human principles.

Chapter 24

Now, there drew near to him the judgment of God, and a period followed in which his affairs began to waver and fall to ruin.[1] He had not yet directed his attention to the overthrow and expulsion of Constantius, while he was engaged in those affairs which I described above. And he was waiting for that one's death, though he did not think that he would die so quickly.

When Constantius was suffering under serious illness, he had issued instructions that his son, Constantine, be sent back to him. He had now pleaded for him for long, but in vain. That one (i.e., Galerius), however, wished nothing less than this. He had often striven after the youth in insidious ways, for he dared nothing openly, lest he stir up against himself civil war and, what he feared especially, the hatred of the soldiers. Under pretense of exercise and games, he had put him in the way of wild beasts, but it was to no avail, because the hand of God was protecting the man. God liberated him from the hands of that Galerius at the very turning point. After the request had been asked of him very often, Galerius, since he could no longer refuse, gave the sign at the end of the day, but ordered that he was not to set out until the next day when he would receive the orders. This was because either he himself was going to retain him on some pretext, or he was going to send letters so that he would be held by Severus.

---
1 Cf. Vergil, *Aeneid* 2.169-171.

Since Constantine suspected this, after supper when the emperor was at rest, he hastened to set out, and taking all the state horses from the many stopping places, he rode away quickly.[2] The following day, after he had slept until mid-day according to his purpose, the emperor (Galerius) ordered Constantine to be summoned. He was told that Constantine had set out immediately after supper. He began to rage furiously. He called for the state horses so that he could have him brought back. He was told that the relay stations were robbed of their mounts. He held back his tears only with difficulty.

But Constantine, using incredible speed, had reached his father, now failing rapidly, who gave the command into his hands with the approval of his soldiers. And thus he received the repose of his days at his bed, as he had wished.

When he took control, Constantine Augustus did nothing until he returned the Christians to their religion and their God. This was his first sanction of the restoration of the holy religion.[3]

Chapter 25

A few days later, a laurel-wreathed image[1] of Constantine was brought to the vile beast. He deliberated long as to

---

[2] The sources on this departure of Constantine from the court of Galerius are divided. Some attribute it to honorable reasons only; first in this class are Lactantius, Eusebius in his so-called *Life of Constantine* (not at all historical, but panegyrical), and the anonymous Valesianus (a pagan writer whose fourth-century work gives a biography of Constantine). Others see in this departue only his personal ambition. The hostile tradition seems to have begun with the writings of his nephew, Julian the Apostate. For a biographical treatment of Constantine, cf. L. B. Holsapple, *Constantine the Great* (New York 1942).

[3] It is not likely that Constantine could effect anything so drastic as the revision of acts of Galerius at once; Lactantius summarizes in this sentence the Constantinian acts of the few years around 318-320, the time of his conversion. Cf. A. Piganiol, *L'Empéreur Constantin* (Paris 1932) 48; Holsapple, *op. cit.*, pp. 163ff.

[1] Images, thus sent by newly-accepted princes, were probably of wax or painted on some cloth or parchment.

whether he should take it. It was almost his intention to burn it along with the man who brought it, except that some friends turned him from this madness, warning him of the danger. All the soldiers, as they put it, would take up the cause of Constantine, since unknown men without their support had been made the Caesars, and they would rush to his side with the utmost eagerness if he should come ready for war.

So, very much against his will, Galerius accepted the image and sent him the purple, so that he might appear to have willingly taken him into his alliance. Now his plans had been upset, nor was he able to name another one from outside the tetrarchy as he had wished.[2] But he figured out this device, to name Severus as the Augustus because he was older, and Constantine, not emperor as he had been made; but he would order him to be called Caesar with Maximin Daia, so that he might throw him from second place into fourth.[3]

Chapter 26

Affairs now seemed to him to be arranged after a fashion, when suddenly another terror was brought upon him, the news that his own son-in-law, Maxentius, had been made emperor at Rome. The cause of this movement was the following. When he had decided to devour the whole world by instituting his census, he jumped even to this insanity, that he did not wish even the Roman people to be immune from this captivity.[1] Census-takers were then appointed and sent to take enrollment of the Roman people. At about the same

---

[2] Galerius' plan was not to change the number arrangement of Diocletian, but his choice of Licinius was outside of the plan of succession.
[3] Galerius, Severus, Maximin Daia (Caesar since May 1, 305), and Constantine. Cf. the chart on p. 134 of the Introduction in order to follow this shifting personnel of the tetrarchy.

---

[1] Rome had been heretofore exempted because of its 'sacred' status. Cf. *Codex Theod.* xi.20.3.

time, he had done away with the praetorian camp also. And so the few soldiers who had been left in Rome in camp, seizing the opportunity, killed some of the judges—not without the approval of the people, who were aroused—and invested Maxentius with the purple.

When this news was brought, Galerius was disturbed somewhat by the strangeness of the situation, but he was not overfrightened, however. He hated the man. And he could not make three Caesars. It seemed enough for him to have done that once, a thing which he did not wish to do. He summoned Severus, urged him to get back the command, and sent him with the army of Maximian to attack Maxentius. He sent him to Rome where those soldiers, taken up with the keenest enjoyments, desired not only that the city be safe, but that they might live there.

Maxentius was fully aware of the greatness of his crime. Although he could bring over to his side by right of inheritance the soldiers of his father, however, he thought that it would be possible that his father-in-law, Maximian (Galerius), fearing this very thing, would leave Severus in Illyricum and would come himself with his army to attack him. So he sought to what extent he might fortify himself against the impending danger. To his father, staying in Campania since he had resigned his command, he sent the purple and named him 'Augustus for the second time.' That one, eager for a revolution, and because he had laid down his power unwillingly, gladly snatched at the opportunity.

Meanwhile, Severus was coming and approached the walls of Rome with an army. At once, the soldiers desert, tearing down his standards, and turn themselves over to him against whom they had set out. What remained for the abandoned leader but flight? But Maximian, already having resumed command, came against him. At his approach, Severus fled to Ravenna and shut himself up there with a few soldiers. When he saw that he was going to be delivered to Maximian, he gave himself over, and returned the purple robe to the same one from whom he had received it. When he had done this, he asked for nothing other than an easy death. But, his veins having been cut, he was forced to die slowly.[2] (From this point on, Maximian Galerius persecuted even his own.)

Chapter 27

When Herculius[1] had learned about the violence of the other Maximian (Galerius), he began to think that that one had become inflamed with anger upon hearing of the death of Severus.[2] And he feared that, being roused to enmity, he would come with an army, perhaps joined by Maximin Daia and doubled forces, which he would be in no way able to resist. When the city was fortified and carefully equipped with all things, he set out into Gaul to win over Constantine to his side by the marriage of his younger daughter.[3] Meanwhile, having collected an army, Galerius invaded Italy. He came to Rome intending to wipe out the senate and slaughter the citizens, but he found everything closed up and fortified. There was no hope of breaking in; siege was difficult; there were not enough forces for surrounding the walls. For he had never actually seen Rome, and he had thought it would be not much larger than the cities with which he was familiar.[4]

Then, some of the legions detesting the deed, a father-in-law attacking his son-in-law, and Roman soldiers attacking Rome, changed their allegiance and left his command. Then,

---

2 The death of Severus did not take place immediately; he was captured, sent to Rome and imprisoned there. Cf. *Anon. Vales.* 4.10; Zosimus 2.10.2. Cf. the treatment of this question by H. Mattingly, 'The Imperial Recovery' in *Cambridge Ancient History,* Vol. 12, ch. 9, pp. 344ff. The sentence which follows in the text is considered as a mutilated marginal note and has been omitted by some editors.

---

1 Marcus Aurelius Valerius Maximian. Cf. ch. 8, n. 1, p. 146.
2 Actually, this did not take place until perhaps after his retreat from Rome.
3 Fausta. Cf. Holsapple, *op. cit.* 131.
4 Cf. J. A. Richmond, *The City Wall of Imperial Rome* (Oxford 1930).

too, the rest of the soldiers were wavering, for that one with broken pride and dejected spirits, and fearing the end of Severus, had cast himself at the feet of the soldiers, and begged them not to turn him over to the hands of the enemy, until he changed their minds by the great promises he made them. He gave the order to retreat and fearfully took flight in which he could be overtaken easily if anyone should follow with even a few men.

Since he feared this, he gave the soldiers the opportunity of scattering as far as possible and robbing and pillaging all things, so that if anyone wished to pursue, he would not have the provisions for it. That part of Italy where he led his destructful band was devastated. Everything was ravaged: women were attacked, girls violated, fathers and husbands tortured to turn over their daughters, their wives, their goods. As though they were prizes stolen from barbarians, they took away their cattle and beasts of burden.

In this way, Galerius returned to his own dominions, that one-time Roman emperor, now depopulator of Italy, because he had destroyed all things in his way as an enemy. Indeed, as that one had once received the name of emperor, he had now declared himself an enemy of the Roman name. For even his claim of title he wished changed, so that it might be known, not as the Roman, but as the Dacian Empire.

Chapter 28

After his flight when the other Maximian[1] had returned from Gaul, he held command together with his son,[2] but obedience was shown to the young man more than to the old, for, in truth, the son's power was prior to his father's and greater, since he had even conferred it upon his father. The old man took it ill that he was not able to do freely what

---
1 Maximian Herculius.
2 Maxentius.

he wished, and he envied his son with a puerile jealously. He plotted, therefore, to expel the youth to vindicate his own right. This seemed easy because he had the soldiers who had abandoned Severus. He convoked the people and the soldiers as though he were about to hold a *contio* on the present evil condition of the state. When he had said much about these matters, he turned his hand to his son, and, indicating him as the author of the evils, the chief of the calamities which the state was enduring, he tore the purple from his shoulders. That one, thus despoiled, threw himself down from the tribunal and was caught by the soldiers. Embarrassed and upset by their wrath and clamor, the impious old man was driven from the city also, as another Superbus.[3]

Chapter 29

Going back again against the Gauls, where he delayed for some time, he set out against Maximian (Galerius), the enemy of his son, as though to discuss with him about putting the state in order, but in reality it was to kill him under the guise of reconciliation and take his kingdom, since he had been shut off from his own wherever he had gone.

Diocles was present there. He had been summoned recently by his son-in-law, so that he might confer the imperium, a thing which he had not done before, upon that Licinius, a substitute for Severus. And so, it took place while both were present.[1] Thus, at one time, there were six rulers.[2]

Therefore, since his plans were checked, the old Maximian prepared a third flight also. He returned to Gaul, full of evil

---

[3] The reference is to the expulsion of Tarquin the Proud, the last of the Etruscan kings of early Rome, traditionally deposed in 509 B.C. by Brutus and Collatinus, son-in-law of the king.

[1] November 11, 308, though Jerome places the date as 307.
[2] The senior Augusti, Diocletian and Maximian (Herculius); the Augusti, Maximian Galerius and Licinius; and the Caesars, Maximin Daia and Constantine.

purpose and crime, to surround Constantine, the emperor, his son-in-law, and the son of his son-in-law, by a wicked design; and, in order to deceive him, he laid aside his royal garments.

The people of the Franks were in arms. He persuaded Constantine, who did not suspect anything, not to lead his entire army with him, that with a few soldiers he could conquer the barbarians. He intended, thereby, that he himself would have an army which he would seize, and that Constantine could be overcome on account of the scarcity of soldiers. The young man believed him as an experienced old man, and he obeyed him as his father-in-law, so he set out, leaving the greater part of his soldiers behind.[3]

That one waited a few days until he thought Constantine would have entered the lands of the barbarians, and then suddenly put on the purple, invaded the treasury, and made lavish gifts as was his custom. He fabricated about Constantine charges which at once fell back upon himself. Immediately, the things which were going on were announced to the emperor. With marvelous speed, he rushed back with his army. The impostor was overwhelmed without warning, not yet sufficiently prepared, and the soldiers went back to their emperor.

His father-in-law had seized Massilia and had watched at the gates. The emperor approached very near and addressed him who was standing on the wall. He was not sharp or hostile, but he asked what he wished of him, how he had failed him, why he was doing what was especially not befitting him. The other, however, kept hurling maledictions from the walls. Then suddenly, from behind him the gates were opened and the soldiers were let in. They dragged to the emperor the rebel emperor, an impious father, a treacherous father-in-law. He heard the crimes which he had done,

---

[3] This section is an attempt on the part of Lactantius to attribute only the most honorable motives to Constantine while he blackens those who oppose him.

took the royal garment from him, and, after having rebuked him, granted him his life.

Chapter 30

Thus having lost the honor of his role as an emperor and a father-in-law,¹ and impatient under the humiliation, Maximian again contrived treachery, because he had escaped punishment that one time. He called his daughter, Fausta, and urged her, now with prayers, and again, with flattery, to the betrayal of her husband. He promised her another husband, one more worthy. He asked her to allow the bedroom to be left open and not carefully watched. She promised that she would do this, and then went right off to tell her husband. A setting was arranged whereby the crime would be manifestly discovered. A certain worthless eunuch was substituted who would die for the emperor.

During the quiet of the night, Maximian got up; he saw that everything was favorable for his treachery. There were but a few guards, and they were, indeed, quite far away. However, he said to these that he had a dream which he wished to relate to his son (in-law). Armed, he drew near, killed the eunuch, then ran off boasting and admitting what he had done.

Suddenly, from another direction, Constantine appeared with a band of armed men. The corpse of the slain man was taken out from the bed. The murderer stood openly caught.² He gazed dumbfounded, as if 'he were a hard flint standing there or a Marpesian rock.'³ He cried out violently against

---

1 Apparently, such was the only punishment that Maximian received, but Lactantius is our only source for these two successive plots against Constantine by Maximian. Zosimus, Eutropius, and Orosius all refer to the interview with Fausta, but the accounts and versions are all confused as to her part in the affair.
2 Cf. *Inst.* 1.7.12 (vol. 49, this series); cf. also Plautus, *Aulularia* 469; *Bacchides* 318; *Trinummus* 895.
3 Vergil, *Aeneid* 6.471.

the charge of impiety and crime. Finally, there was given to him the right of choosing the type of his death, 'and from a high beam, he fastens the knot of an unlovely death.'⁴

So, that very great emperor of the Roman name who, after a long period of time, kept an anniversary of twenty years with mighty glory, ended a detestable life with a shameful and ignominious death. His proud neck was struck and pierced.

Chapter 31

From this time on, God, the Vindicator of religion and of His people, turned his gaze to the other Maximian,¹ the author of the terrible persecution, so that He might now show the force of His Majesty against him. Already the man was thinking about celebrating the Vicennalia.² He who had long since afflicted the provinces by making exactions of gold and silver in order to make payments which he had promised, now afflicted them again with another axe,³ one now called by the name of the Vicennalia.

Who could worthily relate with what annoyance on the part of the people this exaction was borne? The soldiers of all the divisions—I should rather say, executioners—came to each individual. To whom one should first make satisfaction was not clear; there was no excuse for those who did not possess wherewith to pay. Many tortures had to be endured, unless there were turned over immediately what there was not! There was no chance of respite, since they were hemmed in by many guards. At no time of the year was there even a slight rest. Often there was conflict on the part of the judges over the same citizens, or among the judges themselves, or

---

4 *Ibid.* 12.603.

1 Maximian Galerius.
2 This was the twentieth anniversary celebration. Cf. K. C. Guinagh, 'The Vicennalia in Lactantius,' *Classical Journal* 28 (1933) 149ff.
3 Cf. Seneca, *Epistulae* 88.38; Tertullian, *Apol.* 4.7; *De anima* 30, etc.

the soldiers. There was no area without an exactor, no vintage without its guard; nothing was left for food for the laborers. Although these things are intolerable, the knowledge that the food snatched from the mouths of men has been gained at great labor is in some way bearable, at least with the hope of a better future. But, why clothing of every kind? Why gold? Why silver? Is it not necessary that these things are acquired from the profit of the selling of fruits and produce? Why, these things then, most foolish tyrant, I ask you, when you take away all the fruits? Who, therefore, has not been dispossessed of his goods, so that the wealth which was under his control should be scraped together for a votive offering which he will never celebrate?

Chapter 32

When Licinius, therefore, was named emperor (i.e., Augustus), Maximin Daia became enraged and was most unwilling that he himself should be named a Caesar and hold a third place.[1] Galerius sent legates to him often, praying him to hear him, to consider his disposition, to yield to his age,[2] and to show respect to his gray hairs. But that one the more boldly raised his horns and argued from the right of precedence or priority, that he should be the superior, since it was he who assumed the purple. He despised the prayers and mandates of Galerius.

The beast was hurt and growled. For, although he had made that ignoble Caesar, for this reason, that he should be subservient to himself, that one, however, forgetting his so great benefit, was impiously repugning his will and his requests. Overcome by the stubborn rage of Maximin Daia, he did away with the name of Caesars altogether, and called himself and

---
1 Cf. ch. 29, n. 2.
2 Galerius had, after all, conferred the purple on Licinius as related in ch. 29.

Licinius 'Augusti' and Maximin and Constantine, the 'Sons of the Augusti.'³ Then, Maximin wrote, as though making an announcement in the Campus Martius in connection with a recent promulgation, as it were, that he had been named Augustus by the soldiery.⁴ Galerius received the news in grief and sadly ordered that all four be named emperors.

Chapter 33

It was in the eighteenth year that God struck him with an incurable disease. He developed a terrible cancer in the lower part of the genital organs, and it spread widely.¹ The surgeons operated on him and cared for him. But after the scar had already formed, the wound broke and, from the burst veins, he lost blood almost to the point of death. The blood flow was stopped only with difficulty. Fresh care and healing are applied once again. At last, the scar stage is again reached. And again, by a slight movement of the body, the wound opens. There is a greater loss of blood than before. He grows pale and weak from loss of blood and vitality. Then, even the flow of blood is checked. The wound begins not to respond to medicine. Each successive cancer spreads, and the more it is cut, the more widely it spreads; the more it is cared for, the more it increases. 'Masters in the art fail, Chiron, son of Phillyra and Melampus, Amythaon's son.'² Noble physicians

---

3 This was purely a formal concession, because the Caesars were already the 'Sons' of the Augusti, but it seemed to appease Maximin for the time being.
4 This announcement was to intimidate Galerius, but it was also indicative of the importance exercised by the army in actual fact. Galerius was forced to accept the inevitable. Cf. Eusebius, *History of the Church* 8.13.15.

1 Cf. Eusebius, *ibid.* 8.16.3. This 18th year of Galerius began on March 1, 310. The punishments described are very much like those which divine vengeance laid upon Herod. Cf. the account in Josephus, *Wars of the Jews* 1.656; *Antiquities of the Jews* 17.169.
2 Vergil, *Georgics* 3.549-550.

are brought from all sides; human skill avails nothing. Resort is made to idols. Apollo and Asclepius[3] are besought; a remedy is begged. Apollo gives a cure, but the evil becomes much worse.

Disintegration was not far off, and it had already seized all his lower parts. His organs were rotting from within, and the whole area of the buttocks was in decay. However, the hapless physicians did not cease to care for him and tend him, though without hope of overcoming the evil. With repercussions deep within, the dread disease attacked his inner organs. The foulness caused worms. The stench pervaded, not only the palace, but the whole city. Nor was this strange since the elimination of his bowels and urine had become no longer separate. He was eaten by the worms and his body dissolved into rottenness. With intolerable sufferings, 'he lifts to heaven hideous cries, like the bellowings of a wounded bull that has fled from the altar.'[4]

Hot cooked meats were placed near the infested portions so that the heat and aroma from them would draw the worms. When these odors were released, an inestimable swarm burst forth, and yet the fecund decay of the wasting organs had generated a much greater supply. Then, due to the spreading of the disease, the parts of the body had lost their proper appearance. The upper portion as far as the wound had dried up; he was wretchedly thin; the pale skin had sunk deep between his bones. The lower portion, without any shape of feet, had blown up like bags and separated.

And these things went on for an entire year, when, finally overcome by his evils, he was forced to acknowledge God.[5] During the intervals of a new, compelling pain, he exclaimed that he would restore the temple of God and make satisfaction

---
[3] The gods of medicine and healing.
[4] Vergil, *Aeneid* 2.222-223. Cf. 2 Mach. 9.9ff.; 13.28; Josephus, *Antiquities of the Jews* 17.169.
[5] Cf. Eusebius, *History of the Church* 8.17.1; *Vita Constantini* 1.57.3.

for his crimes.⁶ Already dying, he sent forth an edict. The general tenor and style of this edict we give in the following chapter.⁷

Chapter 34

Among the other things¹ which we are continually arranging for the good and utility of the state, indeed, up to now, we had been intending to correct all things according to the old laws and public discipline of the Romans. And we strove to provide for this, that even the Christians, who had abandoned the religious beliefs² of their forefathers, should return to good dispositions. For some reason, it seems such a great determination had invaded those same Christians, and such a great foolishness had taken possession of them, that they would not follow those institutions of the ancients³—which perhaps the ancestors of those very same Christians had established at first—but they were making laws for themselves according to their own will and as they pleased. And all this in such a way that they observed these laws and gathered together by them peoples spread throughout different regions. Finally, when our order of this nature had been published, that they

---

6 Cf. *Inst.* 5.13, p. 359 (vol. 49, this series). In spite of all the details of description in this chapter, Lactantius is more sober than the others who have given the account: Eusebius, Rufinus, and Orosius.
7 This edict, 'The Palinode of Galerius,' is extant in a Greek version in Eusebius, *History of the Church* 8.17.3-10. Cf. the study by J. R. Knipfing, 'The Edict of Galerius (311 A.D.) Re-considered,' *Revue Belge de Philogie et d'Histoire* I (1922) 695ff.

1 Here, we have a summary of the vast program of reform set up by Diocletian to be a guiding chart, so to speak, for the tetrarchy. The text presents the material as a direct quotation. The legal nature of the document, therefore, may explain some of the abstruseness and cumbersomeness of its style.
2 The word is *secta* which must be considered as a whole system of life, a manner of acting. Cf. A. Blaise, *Dictionnaire Latin-français des Auteurs Chrétiens, s.v. secta,* p. 747.
3 In the *Inst.* 5.19, 376f. (vol. 49, this series), Lactantius discusses this very point with effective irony. The persecutors who acted in the name of their gods could but refer to the judgments of their ancestors.

should return to the customs of the ancients, many were led by the danger to comply; many even were overthrown by it. And when very many persevered in their determination, and when we saw that those same ones were neither offering due religious worship to the gods nor reverencing the God of the Christians,[4] by the consideration of our most gentle clemency, and regarding the everlasting custom whereby we are wont to grant pardon to all men, we have believed that our most ready indulgence should be extended to these also. Therefore, they may once more be Christians[5] and build their meeting places, so that they may not do anything contrary to discipline. Moreover, in another letter, we intend to make known to magistrates what they are to observe.[6]

Whence, in the light of this indulgence on our part, these Christians ought to pray to their God for our health and for the safety of the state and their own,[7] so that, considered from all sides, the state may flourish, and that they may be able to live secure and unhampered in their own places.

Chapter 35

This edict was set forth at Nicomedia on the last day of April, himself and Maximin being consuls again for the eighth time. Then, when the prisons were opened,[1] you were freed from custody, dearest Donatus, with the other confessors, the

---

4 This is not the reproach of atheism against the Christians. It is merely the statement of the condition, almost intolerable, of the Christians who refused to worship the state gods and who were denied the practice of their true religion.
5 The liberty that was theirs before the Edict of 303 is implied.
6 This edict was published at Nicomedia on April 30, 311. His death occurred before the publication of the second letter which we can believe he fully intended.
7 The Christians did pray for the state. Origen had said that a Christian's prayers were his service, his 'militia' to the state. Cf. also Arnobius 4.36. On this tradition, of Jewish origin, cf. M. Goguel, *La Naissance du Christianisme* (Paris 1946) 600.

---

1 Cf. Eusebius, *History of the Church* 9.1.7.

prison having been as a home to you for six years![2] However, even after the passing of this edict, he did not receive pardon for his crime from God; but after a few days, when he had commended his wife and son to Licinius and turned them over to his keeping, and since all the parts of his whole body were now disintegrating, he was consumed with the dread decay.[3] And this was learned at Nicomedia in the middle of the same month,[4] where the Twentieth Anniversary celebration was to be held the following first of March.

Chapter 36

When this news was heard, Maximin hurried,[1] turning his course from the East, to seize the provinces and claim for himself everything as far as the straits of Chalcedon, because Licinius was being delayed. And he entered Bithynia where he won favor for himself by being present and held a census with the great joy of all. There was rivalry and almost war between the two commanders. With armed men, they were holding the opposite banks. But a friendly peace was arranged on certain conditions and, in the strait itself, a treaty was made and hands were joined.

Maximin returned [to Nicomedia] in security and became in his actions such as he had been in Syria and in Egypt. First of all, he took away the indulgence shown to Christians by the general edict (of Galerius) through suborning embassies of cities to ask that it be not permitted to Christians to construct meeting places within their territories. He did this so

---

2 Donatus had been imprisoned upon the publication of the fourth edict. Cf. N. H. Baynes, 'Two Notes on the Great Persecution,' *Classical Quarterly* 18 (1924) 189ff.
3 On the death of Galerius, cf. Eusebius, *History of the Church* 8, app. 1; Jerome, *Chronica* a.2325; Orosius 7.28.12.
4 Between the 20th and 30th of May.

1 Maximin, at Tarsus or Antioch, must have learned of the death about the end of the month.

that he might seem to be forced and impelled by persuasion in the doing of that which he was going to do of his own accord.[2] Agreeing with these embassies, by the way, he appointed high priests of a new fashion, one for each city, selected from the foremost citizens. These would daily offer sacrifices to all of their gods and would give very close attention to the ministry of the old priesthoods, so that the Christians would neither build their assembly places nor would they come together either publicly or privately. The new officials would seize them and compel them under force of their authority to attend their sacrifices, or they would bring them before the judges. This was slight, except that he also superimposed on the provinces single officials, pontifices, as it were, men of a higher grade of dignity, and he ordered both groups of priests to be clothed in white vestments when they came forth.[3] He was preparing to do that which he had long since been doing in parts of the East. For although he was professing clemency, it was only for the sake of appearance. He forbade the servants of God to be killed, but he ordered them weakened. And so from the confessors of the faith eyes were dug out, hands cut off, legs maimed, noses or ears mutilated and removed.

Chapter 37

While he was contriving these things, he was deterred by letters from Constantine.[1] So he dissimulated. If any [Chris-

---
[2] Cf. Eusebius, *History of the Church* 9.2-4. Very probably, these requests were more spontaneous than either Eusebius or Lactantius would have us believe. Still, it is certain that Maximin fostered and abetted any such initial requests. Cf. N. H. Baynes, 'The Great Persecution,' and 'Constantine,' chs. 19 and 20, in the *Cambridge Ancient History*, Vol. 12, pp. 646ff. and 678ff.
[3] These vestments of white linen were characteristic of the Egyptian clergy.
[1] These 'letters of Constantine' can be precisely determined. They are identified with the 'law' established by Constantine and Licinius after the victory of the Milvian Bridge. Lactantius has been too previous in his mention of the letters and their restraining power, and he has attributed their merit to Constantine alone.

tians] had fallen into his hands, however, (during that period), they were secretly thrown into the sea. His own custom also of sacrificing each day in the palace he did not stop. He had first come upon this fancy: that all the animals on which he fed should not be prepared by the cooks, but should be immolated at the altars by the priests, and that nothing whatsoever should be placed on his table unless it had been offered as a libation or in sacrifice or drenched in wine, so that whoever had been invited to dine would go out from there defiled and impure.

In other things also, he was like his master. For if Diocles or Maximin had left anything at all untouched, this one scraped it off, taking everything without any shame. Therefore, the barns of private owners were closed; warehouses were boarded up; debts were contracted for years to come. On one side, there was famine, though fields were productive; on the other, charity was unheard of. Herds of beasts and cattle were taken from the fields for the daily sacrifices. He had so spoiled his own household by this fare that they spurned grain. And he poured that out in waste any place at all, without choice, without measure, while he fitted out all his satellites (and there was a great number of them) with precious garments and golden jewelry; to his herdsmen and secretaries he gave silver; and foreigners he honored with every kind of bounty. Because he took away the property of living men, or gave it as a gift to his own, as each one of them had been after what did not belong to him, I do not know whether I should think that any thanks ought to be given to him, because, in the manner of kind-hearted robbers, he took off bloodless spoils.[2]

Chapter 38

But, oh, that truly capital crime, and a desire of working corruption exceeding that of all those who have existed so far!

---

[2] Lactantius ascribes to Maximin the same characteristic traits of a tyrant that had been those of his master, Galerius.

I know not what to say except that it was blind and unbridled, and yet the matter cannot be expressed in these words because of its unworthiness. The magnitude of the crime has overcome the function of the tongue.

Eunuchs and seducers carefully investigated all things. Wherever a very lovely face was discovered, fathers and husbands had to give way. The clothing was torn off noble matrons and virgins, and they were inspected minutely lest any part of their bodies be not completely fitting for the royal chamber. And if one of them had depreciated in any way, she was killed in water, as though modesty were an offense against majesty under that adulterer. Some husbands, too, who could not bear the pain when wives whom they cherished as most precious because of their virtue and loyalty were defiled, killed themselves.[1]

Under this monster, there was no observance of shame, except when marked deformity held off a lustful barbarian woman. At length, too, he had now brought in this custom: no one was to marry without his permission, so that he himself might be the foretaster or tester for every marriage. He gave noble women who had been impaired to his own slaves to be their wives.

His counts also imitated, under the lead of such a prince, his outrages,[2] and they violated the bed chambers of their hosts with impunity. For who would file suit for damages? Each one took the daughters of the middle class as he pleased. Those of the higher class who could not be taken were sought as benefits; nor could anyone refuse when the emperor had subsigned the request, or he would have to face destruction or have some barbarian as son-in-law. For there was hardly an attendant at his side unless he was of the type of those who, driven from their own Gothic lands at the time of the Twenty-

---

[1] Eusebius, *History of the Church* 8.14.14, makes allusion to the women who preferred death to dishonor, but Lactantius is the only one who mentions the husbands' acts of suicide. Cf. also *Inst.* 6.23, pp. 457ff. (vol. 49, this series).
[2] Cf. Eusebius, *History of the Church* 8.14.11; also the *Inst.* 5.6, p. 341.

Year Celebration, had given themselves over to Maximian (Galerius), the evil of the human race, so that, fleeing the servitude of the barbarians, they might lord it over the Romans. Surrounded by these satellites and protectors, he held the East as his plaything.

Chapter 39

Finally, when he had given this license to his lusts, so that he thought that whatever he desired was right, he could not even refrain from the Augusta whom he had recently called 'mother.'[1] After the death of Maximian, Valeria had come to him because she thought that she would be safer in his territory, especially since he had a wife. But the wicked animal was immediately inflamed with lust.[2] The woman was still dressed in black, the time of mouring not yet over. He sent legates to her requesting marriage and stating his intention to cast out his wife if she acceded to his request.

She gave answer in the only way she could. First, that she could not engage in nuptials in funeral attire, the ashes of her husband, his father, being still warm. Then, that he was acting wickedly if he were to repudiate a wife loyal to him, and that he would certainly do the same thing to herself also. Finally, she said that it was wrong for a woman of that name and station, without any precedent or example, to have a second husband.

What she had dared to say was announced to him. His desire turned to wrath and fury. Immediately, he proscribed the woman, seized her property, took away her counts, killed her attendants with tortures, and relegated Valeria herself with her mother into exile. He sent her to no fixed place, either, but tossed her mockingly now here, now there. And he condemned her intimate women friends, charging them with adultery.

---
1 Valeria, the wife of Galerius who was 'father' to Maximin, the Caesar.
2 Cf. Vergil, *Aeneid* 8.623.

Chapter 40

There was a very fine woman who already had grandchildren, and this woman Valeria loved as another mother. He suspected that she had refused him under that friend's advice. He commissioned the governor of Bithynia to kill her in a shameful way.

Then, there were associated with her two other women, equally noble. One of these had left a daughter at Rome as a Vestal Virgin.[1] This woman was a close friend of Valeria, but the friendship was practiced stealthily. The other was the wife of a senator, but she was not too close to the Augusta. But each was killed on account of the great beauty of her person and because of her virtue. The women were seized suddenly, not for trial, but for outrage. Nor did any accuser stand forth. A certain Jew was found, guilty of other crimes, who, influenced by the hope of impunity, gave false witness against the guiltless women. The judge, just and careful,[2] led him forth outside the city lest he be stoned to death.

This was the tragedy of Nicaea. Torments were inflicted on the Jew. He said what he had been ordered to say. The women were constrained by the torturers lest they contradict. The innocent were ordered to be led out. There was weeping and mourning, not only on the part of each husband of a well-meriting wife who was present, but of all those whom the indignity and unheard of nature of the case had brought out. But not even by the attack of the people were those unfortunate souls wrested from the hands of the executioners, for summoned and equipped in military fashion clubmen and arrowmen pursued them.[3] Thus they were led to punishment

---

[1] An added bit of evidence of the nobility of those whom Maximin was attacking.
[2] The irony is closely imitative of Cicero; cf., for example, the case against Verres.
[3] The text is quite corrupt in this section, but it is evident that Lactantius is stressing the details of the military equipment that was necessary on this occasion.

in the midst of wedges of armed men. And they would have lain unburied, since their domestics had taken to flight, unless the pity of friends, secretly exercised, had buried them. The promised impunity was not granted to the adulterer, either. But when he was fastened to a gibbet, he revealed the whole mystery and, with his last breath, he declared to all who saw him that innocent women had been killed.

Chapter 41

The Augusta, however, who had been relegated to certain desert regions of Syria, made her father, Diocletian, aware of her misfortune through secret messengers. He sent messengers and asked Maximin to send his daughter back to him. He availed nothing. He besought him again and again. She was not sent back. Finally, he selected a certain relative, an able military man, to bring him warning of his benefactions. He, too, brought back word of his powerless prayers and unfulfilled embassy.

Chapter 42

At the same time, statues of the elder Maximian were being torn down by the order of Constantine, and his images, wherever he was depicted, were removed.[1] And since generally the

---

1 The *damnatio memoriae* took place, according to Lactantius, quite a long time after the death of Maximian. The initiative came perhaps from the Senate wishing to efface all traces of the Herculian dynasty of Maximian and Maxentius after Constantine's decisive victory over the latter. Much of our information on this matter has been verified by the work of numismatists. Cf. J. Maurice, *Numismatique Constantienne*, 3 vols. (Paris 1908-1912); *Constantin le Grand. L'origine de la Civilisation Chrétienne* (Paris 1919). The fact that Lactantius places the order on the overturning of statues before the victory of the Milvian Bridge should not cause question. The *De mortibus* is not a chronologically accurate account. Cf. the articles by W. Ensslin in Pauly-Wissowa, *RE*, on Maximianus I and Maximianus 2, Vol. 14.2, cols. 2486-2528.

two old men (Diocletian and Maximian) had been pictured together, the images of both were being taken down at the same time. So Diocletian, when he saw, while he was still living, what had never befallen any other emperor, afflicted with double grief, decided that he should die. He threw himself about this way and that, his mind distracted with grief, and he took neither food nor rest. Sighing and groaning much, with frequent tears, he gave vent to throwing about his body, now on a bed, now on the bare ground. Thus, he who had been a most fortunate emperor for twenty years was now cast down by God to a lowly life, and trampled upon by injuries and brought to a hatred of life; he was finally consumed by hunger and anguish.[2]

Chapter 43

There was now one survivor of the adversaries of God, Maximin. His end and fall I will relate herewith. While he felt envy toward Licinius, because he had been preferred to himself by Maximian (though he had recently pledged friendship with the latter), however, when he heard that Constantine's sister[1] was betrothed to Licinius, he believed that that connection was uniting the two emperors against himself. He secretly sent legates to the city to ask for the alliance and friendship of Maxentius. He couched his request in familiar terms. The legates were received graciously. The friendship was formed. Pictures of the two were set up together.

Maxentius gladly grasped at this aid, divine, as it were, for

---
[2] This version of Lactantius combines the two most ancient traditions on the death of Diocletian, that of natural death (Eusebius and others) and that of suicide by poison (*Epitome de Caesaribus* 39) or by hanging (Suidas). According to Lactantius, the death of Diocletian precedes that of Maximin, but another tradition, represented by Zosimus, John of Antioch, and the Chronographers, indicates the date of his death as 316.

[1] Constantia, the half-sister of Constantine, daughter of Constantius Chlorus and Theodora.

he had declared war on Constantine, as though he were going to vindicate the death of his father. From this, the suspicion had arisen[2] that the old man had feigned the fatal discord with his son, so as to make way for himself for getting rid of the others and to claim for himself and his son the empire of the whole world when those others had been removed. But that was false.[3] He had this purpose, that after his son and the others had been removed, he would restore himself and Diocletian to power.

Chapter 44

Civil warfare had already been stirred up between them.[1] And although Maxentius kept himself at Rome, because he had received a warning that he would perish if he went outside the gates of the city, war was being waged, however, by capable leaders. Maxentius had the greater strength, because he had received his father's army from Severus and he had recently drawn out one of his own from the Moors and the Gaetulians.

The struggle went on, and the Maxentian forces were gaining until after Constantine, with strengthened courage and prepared for both outcomes,[2] moved all his troops closer to the city and settled at the region of the Milvian Bridge.[3] The day was approaching on which Maxentius had taken command, that is, the sixth day before the November Kalends, and the fifth anniversary celebration was being ended. Constantine

---

2 There was a tradition to the effect that the quarrel was feigned. Cf. Eutropius 10.3.1-2; Orosius 7.28.9; and John of Antioch, frg. 169 (Müller).
3 Cf. ch. 29.1. Lactantius strives to blacken the reputation of Maximian and thereby excuse and exalt Constantine the more.

---

1 The campaigns must have begun in 311. Cf. W. Seston, 'Recherches sur la chronologie du regne de Constantine le Grand,' Revue des Études Anciennes 39 (1937) 211ff.
2 Cf. Vergil, Aeneid 2.61.
3 This part of Lactantius' account is the source of much later writing on Constantine, legendary even more than factual. Cf. N. H. Baynes' treatment in the Cambridge Ancient History, Vol. 12, pp. 681-683; Holsapple, Constantine the Great, pp. 149-193.

was warned in quiet to mark the celestial sign of God on his shields and thus to engage in battle.[4] He did as he was ordered. He inscribed the name of Christ on the shields, using the initial letter X, crossed by the letter I with its top portion bent.[5] Armed with this sign, the army took the sword.[6] It proceeded against the enemy without any commander and crossed the bridge. The lines clashed on equal fronts; the battle raged on both sides with the greatest violence: 'Flight was unheard of for the one and the other.'[7]

There was a sedition in the city, and the leader was charged with being a deserter of the public safety, and when he was seen—for he was holding a circus in honor of his anniversary—the people with one accord suddenly shouted that Constantine could not be conquered. Upset by this shout, he left, and, calling certain senators, ordered them to consult the Sibylline Books. In them, it was discovered that on that day the enemy of the Romans was to perish. He was led on to hope of victory by this oracle, and set out and came to the line of battle.

The bridge was cut down behind him.[8] When he was seen, the fighting grew more intense, and the hand of God was over the battle line. The Maxentian line was routed, and he himself turned to flee and hastened toward the bridge which had

---

[4] Cf. ch. 46.3. Perhaps the recitation of the battle prayer was influenced by that of Judas Maccabaeus (2 Mach. 15.12-17).
[5] Throughout the writings of Lactantius, it is evident that to him the words *Caeleste signum* signify 'the sign of the cross' (*Inst.* 4.26, 27; *De mort.* 10.2). The words used alone, however, cannot signify the monogram of Christ, but the use of the verb *notare*, 'to mark or express an idea by means of an abbreviation,' helps to give us this notion. There is vast literature on the exact sign that Constantine used. It is excellently summarized in Moreau's *Commentary*, pp. 433ff. The monogrammatic cross of definitely cruciform style, ☧ ⳨, did not appear until the middle of the fourth century. The form then was probably the simplest of the classical monograms for Christ, ⳩, or ✝.
[6] Cf. Eusebius, *History of the Church* 9.11; *Vita Constantini* 1.29.
[7] Vergil, *Aeneid* 10.757.
[8] Lactantius is the only source for this detail. It is not known whether this was Maxentius' snare for Constantine. If so, he fell into the trap himself.

been demolished. Overwhelmed by the rush of those fleeing, he was drowned in the Tiber.⁹

When this most bitter of wars was over and Constantine was received as emperor with the great rejoicing of the Senate and the Roman people, he learned of the perfidy of Maximin; he seized letters and came upon the statues and images.¹⁰ The Senate decreed to Constantine, by reason of his virtue, the title of first name [i.e., the Senior Augustus]. Maximin was claiming this for himself. When news of the victory of the liberated city had been brought to Maximin, he received it no differently than if he himself had been conquered. Then, when he learned of the decree of the Senate, he so chafed with anger and hurt that he openly expressed his enmity and uttered imprecations mixed with jokes against the 'Great Emperor.'¹¹

Chapter 45

When affairs had been arranged in the city, Constantine went the next winter to Milan. Licinius came there to receive his bride.¹ When Maximin understood that they were engaged in solemn nuptials, he moved his army from Syria and, with the winter raging as fiercely as possible and his delay doubled, he rushed into Bithynia with weakened troops. For, because of the great storms and snow and mud and cold and labor, the beasts of every kind were lost. The lamentable loss of these animals along the way was already announcing what would be the prospect of the war that was coming, a like destruction for the soldiers.

---

9 Cf. Eusebius, *History of the Church* 9.9.7; *Vita Constantini* 1.38; *Epitome de Caesaribus* 40.7, Zonaras 13.1.12. The body was recovered and the head brought to Rome and then to Africa to assure the people there of the death of their emperor.
10 It must be remembered that Lactantius was writing this account during the years 318-320, several years after the events described.
11 'Maximus Augustus' was Constantine's title from his entry to Rome.

---

1 The stay of Constantine and Licinius at Milan was from January to March. Cf. the words of the Edict in ch. 48.

He did not delay within his own territory, but, crossing the strait at once, he approached the gates of Byzantium in arms. Praesidiary soldiers were there, stationed by Licinius in case of an event of this kind. He tried to bribe these, at first, with gifts and promises and, later, to frighten them by the force of an attack, but neither violence nor promise had any effect. Eleven days had been spent now,[2] during which there was time for sending messengers and letters to the emperor, when the soldiers, despairing not from lack of faith, but from scarcity of numbers, gave themselves over. From here, he moved on to Heraclea, and there, being detained for the same reason, he lost several days' time.

Now Licinius, having quickened his march, had come to Adrianople with a few troops, when that other,[3] delaying awhile and receiving Perinth in surrender, advanced eighteen miles to a stopping place.[4] He was able to go no farther, for the second place[5] was being held by Licinius, and it was the same number of miles distant. That one had collected as many soldiers as he could from the nearest places and was continuing on the way toward Maximin, rather to delay him than with the intention of a struggle or the hope of victory, because Maximin had an army of seventy thousand armed men, whereas he himself had collected scarcely thirty thousand. For his soldiers had been scattered throughout different regions, and the scarcity of the time did not allow them all to get together.[6]

Chapter 46

As the armies were drawing very near now, it was evident that the battle would be very soon. Then, Maximin made a

---

[2] This precise detail shows the extent of Lactantius' information on this campaign; the other sources deal with generalities (Eusebius 9.10.2; *Epitome de Caesaribus* 40.8, etc.).
[3] Maximin.
[4] This was Tzurulum (Corbu).
[5] Drusipara.
[6] These details of the position and preparedness of Licinius emphasize the miraculous nature of the victory.

vow of this sort to Jupiter,[1] namely, that if he gained the victory, he would wipe out the Christian name and completely destroy it. Then, the next night an angel of the Lord stood before Licinius in his sleep and warned him to rise very quickly and pray to the most high God with all his army.[2] Victory would be his if he did this. After these words, when he thought it best to rise, and since he who warned him still stood by, he then showed him how and with what words he should make his prayer.[3] Then, since sleep was gone, he ordered a notary summoned, and dictated these words just as he had heard them:

> O God most high, we pray Thee: O holy God, we entreat Thee. We commend all justice to Thee; we entrust our safety to Thee. We entrust our command to Thee. Through Thee we live; through Thee we rise up victorious and happy. O most high, holy God, hear our prayers. We stretch forth our arms to Thee. Hear us, O holy and most high God.[4]

Several copies of this prayer were made and were distributed to the officers and tribunes so that each would teach it to the soldiers. The courage of all was increased, since they believed that the victory was announced to them from heaven.

The commander decided on the first of May[5] for the battle, which was the eighth anniversary of Maximin's reception of the title, so that he would be most strongly conquered on his own anniversary, as the other (Maxentius) was conquered at

---

[1] Maximin poses for one last time as the official enemy of the Christian religion.
[2] This angel of Licinius is a feature of the complete legend of the conversion of Constantine. The warnings of God have reached mortals during their sleep, however. Cf. Job 32.15,16.
[3] This is the Christian version of the origin of the prayer.
[4] Cf. the summary of the research on this prayer given by Moreau, pp. 451ff. Cf. also Holsapple, pp. 212ff. There is no doubt of Licinius' confirmed paganism and his readiness to revert to Christian persecution a little later. The story of the soldiers' recitation of the prayer is a dramatic one, but the words were so happily vague that each officer and soldier might identify (and must have done so) the words 'most high and holy God' with whatever deity he recognized as supreme.
[5] Cf. ch. 19.

Rome. Maximin wanted to go forth very early. He arranged his line the day before in the morning so that he might celebrate the next day as a victor. It was announced that Maximin had moved into camp. The soldiers seized their arms and advanced against him. There was a plain lying between, sterile and bare, which they called Ergenus.[6] Now each battle line was in view. The forces of Licinius put aside their shields, unfastened their helmets, stretched their hands to heaven, and said the prayer for their commander, the officers leading them. The line doomed to perish heard the murmur of the praying men. When the prayer was said three times, they put their helmets on and took up their shields, now filled with courage. The commanders advanced for a talk together. Maximin could not be drawn to peace, for he despised Licinius and expected that he would be deserted by his soldiers, because he was stingy with them in the matter of granting bonuses, whereas he himself was prodigal. And he had instigated the war with this intention, that, gaining the army of Licinius without a struggle, he would continue against Constantine at once with doubled forces.

Chapter 47

Therefore, they draw nearer; the trumpets blare; the standards advance. The Licinian forces make an attack and push against their adversaries. They, however, frightened exceedingly, could neither free their swords nor hurl spears. Maximin was going around the line and appealed to the soldiers of Licinius now with prayers, now with bribes. In no place was he listened to. An attack was made against him and he retreated to his own men. His line was slaughtered with impunity, and so great a number of legions, such a force of

---
[6] This name has been supplied by H. Gregoire, 'Deux champs de bataille: Campus Ergenus et Campus Ardiensis,' *Byzantion* 12 (1938) 585-586. The manuscript and editors before Moreau give *Serenus* here.

soldiers was mowed down by a few. No one was mindful of name,[1] no one of valor, no one of early ancestors. It was as if they had come to a vowed death, not battle. Thus did the most high God subject them to a slaying at the hands of their enemies. A tremendous multitude had already been laid low.

Maximin saw now that the outcome was other than he thought it would be. So he cast off the purple and putting on the clothing of a slave took to flight by crossing the channel.[2] Of his army, one part was prostrate; the other part surrendered or was hurled into flight. The deserter-commander had taken away the shame from deserting. He had made his flight on the first of May, that is, the one night and the one day, and he arrived at Nicomedia the next night, since it was about a hundred sixty miles away from the place of the battle. Seizing his children and wife and a few counts from the palace, he made for the Orient. In Cappadocia, he stopped and gathered together soldiers from the flight and from the East. And thus he resumed his royal robes.

Chapter 48

Licinius, however, after he had taken and distributed part of that army, led his army across into Bithynia a few days after the battle. Entering Nicomedia, he rendered thanks to God by whose help he had conquered, and on the thirteenth day of June, Constantine and himself being consuls for the third time,[1] he ordered a letter published about the 'restora-

---

1 Cf. Horace, *Odes* III.5.10.
2 Cf. Eusebius, *History of the Church* 9.10.4; *Vita Constantini* 1.58.3.

1 It was Maximin who had taken the consulship with Constantine, but the substitution by Licinius dates probably from his taking over of Maximin's estates.

tion of the Church.'² The letter was to be put before the *praeses* and was of this nature:³

When I, Constantine Augustus, and I also, Licinius Augustus, had met together under happy circumstances at Milan,⁴ and were giving consideration to all matters which pertained to the public good and security, we decided that these things, among others, which we saw would be for the advantage of many men, should be ordained first of all, namely, by which means reverence of the divinity was held. We believed that we should give both to Christians and to all men the freedom to follow religion, whichever one each one chose, so that whatever sort of divinity there is in heavenly regions may be gracious and propitious to us and to all who live under our government.⁵

And, therefore, we have determined⁶ that this purpose should be undertaken with sound and most upright reason, that we think the opportunity should be denied to no one whatsoever who has given his attention to the observance of the Christians or to that religion which he feels to be most suited to himself, so that the highest deity, whose religion we foster with free minds may be able to show to us in all affairs his customary favor and benevolence. Wherefore, it was fitting that your devotedness know that this was our pleasure, that all those conditions with reference to the Christians, which were contained in our former letters and sent to your office, now being completely removed, everything which seemed severe and opposed to our clemency may be annulled; and now all who have the wish to observe the religion of the Christians may hasten to do so without any worry or molestation. We believed that these things should be most fully made known to Your Solicitude, so that you might know that

---
2 The term is purposefully ambiguous.
3 This document appears in Eusebius also; cf. *History of the Church* 10.5.2-14.
4 Perhaps only the marriage (ch. 45) is referred to.
5 This phrase seems to register doubt as to what gods exist or may exist. Perhaps it is revealing of Constantine's agnosticism at this period.
6 It is not technically correct to speak of an *Edict* of Milan. These points are no more than decisions or determinations reached by the two heads of state. Cf. the excellent commentary for this portion of the text in Moreau, pp. 457-464. Cf. also Holsapple, pp. 178-193; A. Alföldi, *The Conversion of Constantine and Pagan Rome*, pp. 25ff.

we had given to those same Christians free and untrammeled opportunity to practice their religion. Since you see that this has been granted by us to these same Christians, your devotedness understands also that to others as well the freedom and full liberty has been granted, in accordance with the peace of our times, to exercise free choice in worshipping as each one has seen fit. This has been done by us so that nothing may seem to be taken away from anyone's honor or from any religion whatsoever. And in addition we have decreed that this should be decided concerning the Christians. If those same places, in which they had been formerly accustomed to assemble, and about which in the letters formerly sent to your devotedness a different order had been given; if some are seen to have purchased them before this, either from the treasury or from some other person, they shall restore the same to the Christians without money payment or any seeking of a price, all frustration and ambiguity being put away. Those who have received them as a gift shall likewise restore them to these same Christians as quickly as possible. Also, if those who have bought these places or those who have received them as a gift seek anything of our benevolence, let them apply to the vicar so that provision may be made for them through our clemency. All these things are to be taken care of for the body of the Christians[7] by your direction and without delay.

And since those same Christians are known to have possessed not only those places in which they were accustomed to assemble, but also others which belonged not to individual men but to the corporate society, that is, their churches, you will order that all these, according to the law which we have stated above, should be restored to these same Christians, that is, to their society and congregation, without any hesitation or quarrel, the above-mentioned reasonableness being preserved, that those who restore them without price shall, as we said, look for indemnity from our bounty. In all these provisions for the benefit of the aforementioned body of Christians, you will apply your most efficacious concern, so that our command may be very quickly fulfilled, and that in this also

---

7 Reference is made to the collective or corporate ownership by the Christians of cemeteries, churches, and other movable and immovable goods.

provision may be made through our bounty for the public peace.
To this extent it will happen, therefore, that the divine favor toward us, as has been stated above, which we have experienced in such great matters, will continue through all time, that our successive acts will prosper with public blessings. And that the formula of our graciousness and of this sanction may reach the attention of all, it will be expected that this be written and proclaimed by you and that you publish it and bring it to the knowledge of all, so that it may not be possible that this provision of our generosity be hidden from anyone.
He urged by this written proclamation and also by the spoken word that the meeting places be returned to their early status. Thus, from the overthrow of the Church until its restoration, there was a period of ten years and four months, more or less.[8]

Chapter 49

In his flight, the tyrant avoided Licinius who was pursuing with his army, and again he sought the narrow passes of the Taurus Mountains. By building fortifications and towers, he attempted to block the way and, then, because the victors were breaking their way through and tearing down all barriers, he fled at length to Tarsus. There, already being pressed on both land and sea, and since he had no hope of refuge, in anguish of mind and fear, he fled to death as though to a remedy against the evils which God had heaped upon him.[1] But first, he gorged himself with food and wallowed in wine, just as they are wont to who think that they do this

---

8 Cf. ch. 12, p. 151. It was exactly 10 years, 3 months, and 10 days from Feb. 23, 303, to June 13, 313.

1 Lactantius alone gives this suicidal inference; the other authorities attribute the death of Maximin to natural causes. Eusebius, however, also adds the horrible details which Lactantius gives *(History of the Church* 9.10.14; *Vita Constantini* 1.58ff.). In all, Eusebius gives three different versions of the death: *History of the Church* 9.10.6; 9.10.13ff.; 9.10.15. Later tradition combined the contradictory elements.

for the last time, and, in such a state, he drained the cup of poison. This was vomited from the overloaded stomach, and so its potency had no avail because of his present condition. Then, there was a change to a condition of evil languor, like that of pestilence, so that he experienced torture for as long as his breathing continued.

Now the poison had begun to take effect in him. Since his inner organs were raging because of its power, he was carried outside of himself by an insupportable pain, even to madness of mind, so much so that for four days, afflicted with an insanity, he tore at the dry ground with his hands and devoured it as though hungry. After many severe tortures, then, when he beat his head against the walls, his eyes sprang from their sockets. Then, at last, deprived of sight, he began to see God making judgment of him through white-robed ministers.[2] He cried out, therefore, as they who are being tortured are accustomed to, and said that not he but others had committed his crimes. Then, driven to it by the torments, as it were, he confessed Christ, next, imploring and beseeching Him to have pity on him. Thus, amid groans which he gave forth as if he were being burned, he gave forth his guilty spirit in a detestable type of death.[3]

Chapter 50

In this manner, God conquered overwhelmingly all the persecutors of His Name, so that neither their offspring nor any of their stock remained. For when Licinius had gained supreme control, he ordered Valeria to be killed, first of all,

---

[2] This is a feature of such apologetic writing. Cf. the death of Galerius, ch. 33. The idea of the white-robed ministers is a commonplace; cf. Apoc. 3; Prudentius, *Peristephanon* 1.67.

[3] The death occurred probably at the end of August or the beginning of September, 313. On the 13th, the news had already reached Egypt. Cf. A. E. R. Boak, 'Early Byzantine Papyri,' *Études de Papyrologie* 3 (1936) 31.

THE DEATHS OF THE PERSECUTORS   201

whom not even the angry Maximin had dared to kill after her flight, when he saw that he himself would have to die, and also Candidianus whom Valeria, sterile as she was, had adopted when he was born of one of the concubines. However, when the woman learned that he had conquered, she had changed her clothing and mingled with his court in order to look out for the fortune of Candidianus. Because he had gone to Nicomedia and seemed to be held in honor, he was killed, though he feared no such fate. When she heard of his end, she immediately took to flight.

He killed also Severianus, son of Severus,[1] already grown up, who had followed Maximin fleeing from the line of battle as though he had designs on taking the purple after that one's death. He got rid of him by subjecting him to a capital sentence. All of those, long since fearing Licinius as evil,[2] had preferred to be with Maximin, except Valeria. That which she had refused to give to Licinius when he wished it, her inheritance through her own right of all the property of Maximian, she had denied as well to Maximin. He killed the eight-year-old son of Maximin, his oldest child, and the seven-year-old daughter who had been betrothed to Candidianus.[3] But first, their mother was thrown headlong into the Orontes; there she had often caused chaste women to be drowned. Thus, all the impious, by a true and just judgment of God, received the same sufferings which they had inflicted.[4]

---

1 Though Severus had played no part in the persecutions, his son was punished. This is one of the opportunities Lactantius uses to cast aspersions on Licinius.
2 Another attack on Licinius. Lactantius uses the word *malum*, chosen perhaps because of its vagueness.
3 An alliance arranged by Maximin, probably in hopes of continuing the policy of the tetrarchy.
4 This is strongly apologetical material. Cf. Luke 23.41; also Jerome, *Commentary on Zacharias* 3.14 for similar statement of the theme.

Chapter 51

Valeria, too, who had been wandering for fifteen months[1] through various provinces, helped by popular devotion, was, at last, recognized at Thessalonica. She was arrested along with her mother,[2] and the two paid the penalty. They were led to punishment in the sight of a mighty throng and as recipients of its pity for such great misfortune. When they were beheaded, their bodies were thrown into the sea. Such was the shameful manner of their end.[3]

Chapter 52

I have been of the opinion that all these things should be put in writing truthfully—for I am speaking to one who knows the case—just as they happened, lest the memory of such great events should fade; and, in case anyone should wish to write a history, that he might not corrupt the true account by being silent about the sins of those men or about the judgment of God upon them.[1] We ought to give thanks to the eternal loving-kindness of God who has looked down upon the earth, because He has deigned to renew His people and to gather them together again, when they had been partly destroyed by rapacious wolves and partly dispersed. And He has seen fit to extirpate the evil beasts who had trodden upon the pastures of the sheep of the Divine Shepherd and had ravaged their folds.

---

1 This detail furnishes a *terminus post quem* for the composition of the *De mortibus*, or at least for its definitive redaction, if this chapter and the next are considered additional material.
2 Prisca, the widow of Diocletian.
3 Lactantius is the only one who furnishes details of the death of Valeria and Prisca. The implication is that there was a feigned trial, perhaps in line with the classic charge of adultery; cf. ch. 39. This section helps to blacken the character of Licinius still further.

1 These words provide us with a statement of Lactantius' purpose; they state the intention as well as the limitations of the work.

Where are now those magnificent family names of the Jovii and Herculii,[2] famed through the nations, which were first assumed boastfully by Diocletian and Maximian, and which afterwards flourished when they had been passed on to their successors? Truly has the Lord destroyed them and wiped them out from the earth.

Let us celebrate with exultation, then, the triumph of God.[3] Let us flock to the victory of the Lord with praises. Let us celebrate it with praying day and night. Let us celebrate it so that the peace given to His people after ten years He may establish forever. And do you, especially, Donatus, my dear, who deserves to be heard by God, entreat the Lord that He may mercifully and graciously preserve His mercy to His servants. Pray Him to ward off all the snares and attacks of the devil from His people, so that the Church may flourish and be guarded by perpetual peace.

---

2 This is exaggeration because Licinius was still using the name *Jovius*. Coins struck in 314 bear the title. Again in 317, Constantine had an inscription made using the term IOVI CONSERVATORI, even though he may have renounced by that time all but lip service to the ideas for which the term stood. The joy of Lactantius is well able to be understood, however. He had lived through the horrors of a religious persecution.

3 Cf. *Inst.* 7.27 (vol. 49, this series); Eusebius, *History of the Church* 10.4.72.

THE PHOENIX

(DE AVE PHOENICE)

INTRODUCTION

THE BEAUTIFUL POEM, *The Phoenix*, which has been ascribed to Lactantius is the composition of a cultured man of letters for cultured readers. The legend of the phoenix, a brilliantly colored bird of the East, unique, with a life-span of a thousand years (other tremendous numbers are given, too), which reappears at long intervals, seemingly after having arisen from its own ashes, strongly attracted ancient writers.[1] The myth appears in old Sanskrit poetry, in Egyptian religious literature, and in many Greek and Roman writers from the time of Herodotus.[2]

That an early Christian writer like Lactantius should have made such great use of this strange tale for a symbolic discussion of paradise and the resurrection may seem at first rather strange. Actually, it is quite normal. The Fathers were not wiser in science than the naturalists of their day who, as the editor of *The Ante-Nicene Fathers* claims, 'taught them the history of the phoenix and other fables.'[3] The Greek *Physiologus*,[4] for example, a collection of uncertain authorship and

---

[1] A complete article covering the various beliefs in connection with the wonder bird and also its treatment by the Greek and Latin writers is found in W. H. Röscher, *Ausführliches Lexikon der Griechischen und Römischen Mythologie* (Leipzig 1897-1909) III, 3450-3472. Cf. also the article by Leclercq in *Dictionnaire d'Archéologie Chrétienne et Liturgie*, 14.1 (Paris 1939) 682-692, where there is greater emphasis on the Christian adaptations of the legend, especially in the plastic arts. An article written as a result of research in connection with the present translation is 'Phoenix Redivivus,' *Phoenix* 14.4 (Winter 1960) 187-206.

[2] There is a still earlier trace in Greek literature, a fragment of Hesiod (frg. 163, Loeb edition, p. 7), which treats of the bird's longevity.

[3] A. Roberts and J. Donaldson, *Ante-Nicene Fathers*, Vol. 1 (New York 1899) viii.

[4] Cf. the study by F. Sbordone, *Physiologus* (Milan 1936) which presents also the recensions of the different periods.

place of production of some fifty fabulous anecdotes, mostly animal accounts, was well known to Christian writers of the fourth century when the work was translated into Latin. It was undoubtedly known to some of them in its Greek form. Lactantius was certainly of the Greek tradition. We have only to recall his abundant use of the Sibylline verses and the Greek of the Hermes Trismegistus as sources for his major work to feel quite sure that the tales of the *Physiologus* were familiar to him.

These tales were strongly moralizing and symbolical and, in the recensions which have come down to us, the subject matter is closely interwoven with traditional Christian commentary on Sacred Scripture. The phoenix is used, for example, in connection with interpretations of John 10.18,[5] and Matthew 26.61,[6] in addition to the reading of Psalm 91.13 where 'as the phoenix' is given in place of 'as the eagle.'

We might venture the suggestion, however, that for the Fathers the inspiration to use the phoenix story came from sounder sources. There might even be Old Testament authority for its use. We read in Job 29.18: 'In my own nest I shall grow old; I shall multiply years like the phoenix.' This translation, that of the new Confraternity edition,[7] based, no doubt, heavily on Hebraic tradition, is appreciably the appropriate one here. As far as can be determined, however, such a reading in Latin was not available to Lactantius.[8] What the Septuagint or any Greek text might have offered can throw no light on the problem, because the Greek word *phoinix* means 'palm tree' as well as the bird, 'phoenix.' The more common Latin equivalent, *palma,* certainly acquired textual

---

[5] Cf. Sbordone, pp. 199-201.
[6] *Ibid.,* pp. 289-290.
[7] *The Holy Bible,* Vol. 3: Job to Sirach (Paterson, N. J. 1955) 53.
[8] A reading of the positive microfilm files of the not as yet printed pages of the *Vetus Latina,* property of the Beuron Archabbey and available through the facilities of the Institute of Oriental Research at the Catholic University of America Library reveals no extant Old Latin reading of *phoenix* in place of the Vulgate *palma* except an allusion to its very fable-like appearance in certain Hebrew texts, a comment of Gregory the Great in his *Moralia* 19.

precedence and authority in this verse of Job, perhaps by analogy with other passages where the word *palma* is the more appropriate, e.g., Psalm 91.13.

Still the tradition must have remained, and it was venerable. Perhaps such interpretations as were the results of the exegesis of the rabbinical schools were more known than the actual text of Sacred Scripture. This must have been the case with the application of the tale of the phoenix. Reference is found in the Talmud, the Midrash-Rabbah on Genesis,[9] to the naïve explanation of the privileged lot of this wonder bird. It was thought that Eve tempted all the animals of Paradise, and not just Adam, to eat of the forbidden fruit. All save the phoenix yielded. Thus, the long life and marvelous history of the bird were interpreted as a reward.

Interesting though this lore may be, we need not feel that it was the sole basis for patristic excursuses. The Fathers did accept the mistaken scientific notions of their times, but they had a natural feeling for the aptness of their illustrations. The phoenix, the palm, and sand[10] all connote great strength and an uncountable number. The bird, particularly, is in addition a most poetic symbol. Therefore, it lends notes of mystery and mysticism to the Christian doctrine of the resurrection of the flesh which is being presented.

The extant poem, *The Phoenix,* in elegiac couplets is ascribed to Lactantius. It is known from Jerome's account[11] that our author wrote a *Hodoiporikon,* an account of a journey from Africa to Nicomedia, and it has been suggested that he worked into this narrative the legend of the oriental bird with a Christian coloring. Such an exercise does not seem at all unlike Lactantius who attained his distinction among early Christian authors for the purity of his classical style and the

---

9 Cf. H. Freedman, and M. Simon, *Midrash-Rabbah,* Vol. 1 (London 1931) 151-2; H. Freedman, Sanhedrin II, *The Babylonian Talmud* (London 1935) 746ff.
10 Hebrew and Syriac bibles have the word for sand in the verse of Job which we are considering, as does the new edition of the Authorized King James Version.
11 *De viris illustribus* 80.

strong use of the subject matter and allusions of his pagan models. Some have thought, too, that after the disappearance of the earlier work of Lactantius, Christian copyists attached his name to this elegiac poem which is held to be too strongly pagan in flavor to be the work of the African apologist. Others who have accepted the Lactantian authorship of the work[12] prefer to consider it as belonging to his pre-Christian period. Similarities of thought, language, and style between this poem and the genuine writings of Lactantius, however, seem to favor our placing it in the period of his Christian writing.[13]

The first to use the fable in order to illustrate points of Catholic doctrine was Clement of Rome.[14] Tertullian elaborated on the tale and seized upon the idea of the phoenix as a proof of the resurrection of the body.[15] Perhaps the most touching application of the theme in Christian writing is that of Saint Ambrose in the funeral oration for his brother,[16] and the same writer dwells upon its deeper religious meaning in his *Hexaemeron*.[17] Saint Gregory of Tours, in his sixth-century work *De cursu stellarum*, places the phoenix as the third of the seven wonders of the world. He actually mentions Lactantius as the author of the poem, *De ave phoenice*.[18] Saint Isidore of Seville in the seventh century discussed the bird in his *Etymologies*, Book XII, *On Birds*.[19] From then on, the theme was taken up and it has permeated early medieval

---

12 Pichon and Brandt were of this opinion.
13 Certainly the chiliastic references (lines 59-62), the eulogy on chastity (lines 163-165) and the Christian note of this world as the 'place where death holds sway' (line 64) point to the Christian period of Lactantius, and the use of details of pagan mythology without any attempt to 'christianize' (Deucalion 11; Phoebus 33 and 58; Venus 64, for example) is very much like Lactantius in the *Institutes;* cf. 2.9; 5.1; 5.5 (vol. 49, this series).
14 Cf. *Epistle to the Corinthians* 1.25.
15 Cf. *De resurrectione carnis* 13.
16 Cf. *De excessu fratris Satyri* 2.59.
17 Cf. *Hexaemeron* 5.23.79-80.
18 *De cursu stellarum* 12: Tertium est quod de phoenice Lactantius refert.
19 There is also a reference in Isidore's *Origines* 14.3.3.

and the later literature of Europe, and the bird has been a favorite subject for early and later Christian art as well.[20]

The elegaic poem by Lactantius is the first appearance of the myth in the dignity of a complete poem. It is written in beautiful elegaic couplets in the manner of Ovid. It is very probably the model for the *Idyllium, Phoenix,* the 110 hexameters of the Roman poet, Claudian, which was written in 395,[21] and it most certainly served as the basis for the early Anglo-Saxon *Phoenix* in alliterative accentual verse, perhaps written by the Northumbrian Cynewulf.[22]

Special editions and studies to be consulted are the following:

Bianco, B. *Il carme 'De ave Phoenice' di Lattanzio Firmiano,* Chieri, 1931.

Brett, Sister Mary Catherine. *Lactanti De Ave Phoenice: An Introduction, Translation, and Commentary* (unpublished Master's thesis), Catholic University of America, Washington, D. C., 1930.

Duff, J. Wright, and Arnold M. Duff. *Minor Latin Poets,* Loeb Classical Library, Cambridge, Mass., 1935, pp. 643-665.

Fitzpatrick, M. C. *Lactanti De ave Phoenice, With Introduction, Text, Translation, and Commentary* (Diss. Univ. of Penn.), Philadelphia, 1933.

Leroy, M. 'Le chant du Phénix,' *L'Antiquité Classique* 1 (1932) 213-237.

---

20 Cf. articles cited in n. 1.
21 Cf. the Loeb edition of Claudian, Vol. 2, pp. 222-231.
22 Cf. the edition in *Everyman's Library, Anglo-Saxon Poetry,* selected and translated by R. K. Gordon (London and New York 1950). The Anglo-Saxon *Phoenix* is contained in *The Exeter Book* which was edited with translation, notes, and introduction by I. Gollancz in 1895.

THE PHOENIX

HERE IS A SPOT in the Near East, pleasant, secluded, where the mighty gate of the everlasting pole lies open, not, however, near to the sun's risings in summer or in winter, but where he pours the days from the heavens in the spring.¹

There a plain spreads open tracts, and no mound rises, nor does any hollow valley² gape; but beyond are mountains, whose ridges are considered lofty, by twice six cubits does that place tower.

Here is the grove of the sun, and a wood planted with many a tree, verdant with the splendor of perpetual leafage.³

When the pole became ablaze with Phaethontean fires, that place was untouched by the flames; and, when the flood had immersed the world in its waves, it mounted above the waters of Deucalion.⁴

Not to this place come any enfeebling diseases, no weak old age; neither cruel death nor poignant fear is present, nor wicked crime, nor raging desire of wealth, nor wrath, nor fury burning with the love of slaughter; bitter grief is away from here, and need covered with rags, and sleepless cares, and violent hunger.⁵

There is no tempest there, nor does the rough force of the

---

1 Cf. Gregory of Tours, *De cursu stellarum* 12; also Ennius, quoted in the *Institutes* 1.18; and Venantius Fortunatus, *Carmina* 3.9.2.
2 Cf. *cavae valles* in Vergil, *Georgics* 2.391.
3 Cf. Ovid, *Metamorphoses* 1.565; Gregory of Tours, *loc. cit.*
4 For the story of Phaethon's driving of the car of his father, Apollo, cf. Ovid, *Metamorphoses* 2.1-332. Deucalion and Pyrrha were saved in an ark during the flood. Their story is often compared with that of Noe.
5 Cf. Vergil, *Aeneid* 6.274-276, the probable source of these personifications; also the Pseudo-Cyprian, *De resurrectione mortis* 246-247.

wind rage; the hoar-frost does not cover the ground with cold dew; no cloud covers the plains with its fleece-wrap; nor does any turbid moisture of water fall from the lofty sky.[6]

But in the center of the place, there is a fountain[7] which they call by the name of 'Living'; it is clear, gentle, and rich with sweet waters,[8] which, bursting forth once during the course of each month, does with its spray twelve times irrigate the entire grove.

Here a kind of tree rising with lofty boughs bears tender fruit that is not ready to fall upon the ground.

This grove, these woods, are haunted by a unique bird, the Phoenix. She is unique, inasmuch as she lives renewed by her own death.[9]

Phoebus she obeys, and to him she yields her homage, a remarkable satellite; her parent Nature has given her this office to fulfill.

When at her early rising the saffron Aurora grows red, as soon as she puts the stars to flight with her rosy light, three times, four times that bird dips her body into the holy waters; three times, four times she sips water from the living spray.[10]

She rises then and settles upon the highest point of the high tree which alone looks down upon all the grove, and turning toward the fresh rising of the nascent Phoebus, she awaits his rays and the rising beam.[11]

And when the Sun has forced back the portals of the gleaming gate and the fine mist of the first light has flashed, she begins to pour forth melodious strains of sacred song and to greet the new day with wondrous voice which neither the notes of the nightingale nor musical pipes can match with

---

[6] Cf. Vergil, *Georgics* 1.397; Lucan 4.124; Ennius, *Annales* 1.108.
[7] Cf. Gregory of Tours, *loc. cit.*
[8] Cf. Pseudo-Cyprian, *De pascha* 27f. The epithet 'living' as applied to water is strongly biblical; cf., for example, Gen. 16.14; 24.62; Apoc. 22.1.
[9] Cf. Ovid, *Amores* 2.6.54. The Latin adjective is *unica*, the only one of its kind, peerless. In most accounts, the phoenix is a male bird, but Lactantius evidently follows Ovid *(unica avis)* here.
[10] Cf. Gregory of Tours, *loc. cit.*
[11] Cf. Vergil, *Aeneid* 4.130: *iubar exoriens.*

Cyrrhaean measures;[12] nor is the dying swan[13] thought to be able to imitate it, nor the sonorous strings of the Cyllenean lyre.[14]

After Phoebus has led his horses out upon the expanse of Olympus and has revealed the whole circle,[15] moving all the time, she with a thrice-repeated flapping of her wings applauds him, and after she thrice venerates her fire-bearing lord,[16] she is silent.

And the same bird also distinguishes the swift hours by indescribable notes by day and by night; she is an over-seer of the grove and woods, a priestess to be venerated, and the sole sharer, O Phoebus, of thy secrets.

Then after she has passed through a thousand years of life,[17] and long ages have rendered her burdensome, in order to repair the age lapsed by declining periods, she flees the familiar, sweet couch of the bower.

And when in her eagerness to be reborn she has left the sacred spot, then she seeks this world where death holds sway.

The long-lived bird directs her swift flight into Syria, to which antiquity itself gave the name of the Phoenix,[18] and

---

12 Cirra was an ancient town of Phocis near Delphi where Apollo was worshiped.
13 The word is *olor*, a poetic term for *cycnus* (swan), sacred to Apollo.
14 The allusion is to Mercury and his temple on Mt. Cyllene in Arcadia where he was born of Maia.
15 Possibly the whole world is meant; cf. Vergil, *Aeneid* 4.118.
16 The word is *head*, but it refers to the sun; cf. Ovid, *Metam.* 2.59.
17 Tacitus *(Annales* 6.28) assigns five hundred years for the life span of the phoenix, but he also mentions 1461 years (365¼ x 4); Martial gives *decem saecula (Ep.* 5.7.2); and Pliny *(Nat. Hist.* 29.1) states 1000 years, as do Claudian, 27, and Ausonius, *Epist.* 20.9.
18 Having the palm tree and the country of Phoenicia both derive their names from that of the bird is good poetic license. Actually, it would seem that the first form was the name of the country; there followed *Phoenices* for the people. The word, *phoinix,* was used for the dye or the crimson color because it was first used by the people of that region. The same word in Greek means palm tree (cf. the note in the introduction to this work), and it is possible that etymologically there is connection with some old root meaning 'strength' or 'length of life' for which both the tree and the bird are symbols, particularly in Near Eastern lands. Lactantius' is the first literary account to connect Phoenicia with the bird. Pliny (13.4) connected the tree with the bird.

through pathless deserts she seeks secret groves where a remote wood lies hidden through the glades.

Then she selects a lofty palm with its summit in the heavens (the tree, too, has the Greek name, Phoenix, from the bird), and into this tree no harmful living creature can break through, nor any slimy serpent, nor any plundering bird.

Aeolus then encloses the winds in hanging caverns,[19] lest they mar the bright air with their blowings, or lest a cloud gathered by the south wind should move aside the rays of the sun and be of harm to the bird.

Then she builds for herself either a nest or a sepulchre; for she dies that she may live; in fact, she produces herself.[20]

Here she brings juices and odors from the thick wood, those which the Assyrian gathers, which the opulent Arab culls, which either the Pygmean tribes or those of India pluck, or which the Sabaean land produces from its tender bosom.[21]

In this place she piles up cinnamon, and the scent of the far-penetrating amomum, and balsam with mixed leafage; nor is there missing the twig of the mild cassia or that of aromatic acanthus, nor the tears and pungent drop of the frankincense.[22]

To these she adds tender ears of young spikenard, and thy strength, Panacea, allied with myrrh.[23]

Forthwith on the prepared nest she lays her body, which is subject to change soon, and on the life-giving bier she places her withered members; next, with her mouth she scatters the juices round and about her members, entering upon death prepared by her own services.

---

19 Cf. Ovid, *Metam.* 13.810f.; 14.224; Cicero, *Tusculans* 1.16.37; Vergil, *Aeneid* 1.52. Aeolus is the god of the winds, ruler of the islands between Sicily and Italy where he kept the winds shut up in caverns.
20 Cf. Gregory of Tours, *loc. cit.;* Claudian, *Phoenix* 44, 77; Ovid, *Metam.* 15.397.
21 The allusions are to spices of Africa and Asia. The Pygmies were legendary dwarfs of Africa; the other places referred to are Asian.
22 Cf. Pseudo-Cyprian, *De resurrectione mortis* 216-217; Vergil, *Georgics* 4.123; Ovid, *Metam.* 15.394.
23 Cf. Ovid, *ibid.* 398. *Panchaia,* the usual form, is a fabled island east of Arabia, famous for precious stones and myrrh. Cf. Vergil, *Georgics* 2.139; Pliny, *Natural History* 10.4.

Then amid the varied odors she commends her spirit, and she does not fear the trust involved in so great a laying-down.[24]

In the meantime, her body, destroyed by a producing death, grows warm, and the heat itself gives birth to a flame, and from the aetherial light afar off it conceives fire; it blazes, and, when scorched, it dissolves into ashes.[25]

These ashes, collected into a pile, as it were, nature[26] stirs up, and it has effect like to that of seed.

Hence an animal is said to arise, first without limbs, and it is said to be the milky color of a worm. It grows, but for a certain measure of time it sleeps and gathers itself into the shape of a smooth egg.[27]

And, just as field caterpillars, when they are held by a thread to the rocks, are wont to change to butterflies,[28] thence the shape which it was before is formed again, and the phoenix sprouts forth when the shell has broken.

There is no food in our world granted to her, nor has anyone the charge of feeding the yet unfledged bird. She sips the fine ambrosial dews from heavenly nectar which has fallen from the star-bearing pole.

She takes these; with these the bird is nourished in the midst of the odors until she puts forth her mature form. But when she begins to flourish in primeval youth, she flies forth, ready now to return to her native home.

Before this, however, whatever remains of her own body, and the bones or ashes and the shells, she puts into a balsam ointment and a mixture of myrrh and dissolved frankincense, and fashions it into a round form with task-performing mouth.[29]

---

24 This couplet sets a Christian note. Cf. Luke 23.46 (cf. Ambrose, *De Spiritu Sancto* 2.7.56); 2 Tim. 1.12; Ps. 53.141; Lactantius, *Inst.* 4.19; Claudian, *Phoenix* 94.
25 Cf. Gregory of Tours, *loc. cit.;* Pseudo-Cyprian, *De Sodoma* 138.
26 There is textual difficulty here. *Natura* is adopted in the Brandt text; the Loeb text has *umore*, the emendation of Ritschl; and there are others as well. For the present translation, Brandt's reading is followed.
27 Cf. Gregory of Tours, *loc. cit.*
28 Cf. Ovid, *Metam.* 15.372-374.
29 Cf. Claudian, *Phoenix* 72.

Carrying this in her talons she hastens to the city of the Sun;[30] she brings it into the sacred temple and places it upon the altar.

She shows herself to be admired, and she presents herself to be venerated: so great is the beauty of the bird; such great honor attends her.

First of all, her color is like that of the tender pomegranate seeds (which they have) because the skin covers them under the sway of Cancer,[31] a color such as is in the leaves which the wild poppy bears when Flora spreads her cloak on the glowing soil.[32]

Her shoulders and beautiful breast shine with this covering; with this garb her head, with this her neck and the ridge of her back gleam. Her tail is drawn out, marked by metallic yellow, on the spots of which a scarlet mixture blushes.

From above Iris marks the feathers of her wings just as she is accustomed to paint her colors upon a cloud from her place in the sky. The bird gleams, marked with a shining mixture of emerald, and her gemmed beak glitters open with its clear horn.[33]

Large are her eyes (you would think them twin hyacinths), from the middle of which a bright flame gleams. Fitted to the shining head is a radiated crest, lofty, recalling the glory of Phoebus' own head.[34]

Scales cover her legs marked with metallic yellow, but her claws are painted the color of rosy beauty.

Her appearance seems to be a cross between the figure of a peacock and the gaudy bird of Phasis.[35] Her greatness the

---

[30] The usual form of the legend gives Heliopolis as the destination; cf. Pliny 10.4.
[31] Cf. Vergil, *Eclogues* 10.68; Ovid, *Metam.* 10.736f.; *Fasti* 4.607f.
[32] Flora is the goddess of flowers; cf. Ovid, *Fasti* 5.195-196.
[33] Cf. Gregory of Tours, *loc. cit.*
[34] This is a poetic use of *refero* meaning 'to recall' or 'to resemble.' Cf. Vergil, *Aeneid* 4.329; 12.348; Horace, *Carmina* 3.5.28.
[35] The bird of Phasis, a river in Colchis, is a pheasant; cf. Ovid, *Metam.* 6.652ff.

winged creature which is sprung from the land of the Arabians can scarcely match, whether that be beast or bird.[36]
However, she is not slow, as are the birds who by reason of their great bodies have sluggish movements from their heavy weight, but she is light and quick, full of regal beauty; such does she keep herself ever in the regard of men.

Egypt comes hither for the marvels of such a sight, and the ovating crowd salutes the rare bird. Straightway they carve out her form on holy marbles[37] and mark the event and the day with a new title.

Every kind of flying creature draws itself together in meeting, nor is there any remembrance of prey nor any fear. Thronged by a chorus of birds she flies through the heights, and the crowd which attends her is happy in its sacred function.

But after they reach the regions of pure ether, the crowd soon turns back; then she is concealed in her own proper habitat. Ah, thou bird of happy lot and purpose, to whom God Himself has granted the power of being born from herself!

Happy indeed is that bird, whether male or female or neither; she fosters no pacts with Venus.[38] Death for her is Venus; her sole pleasure is in death. In order that she may be born, she desires first to die.[39]

She is offspring to herself. She is her own father and also her heir. She is nurse of herself and ever a nurseling for herself.[40]

---

36 The reference is to the ostrich, which might be considered either a land animal or bird. This is the only instance discovered for the use of the word *magnities,* a synonym for *magnitudo.*
37 The phoenix has ever been inspiration for plastic artists, both pagan and Christian. Cf. articles in Röscher and DACL, cited in the introduction.
38 Cf. Ovid, *Metam.* 4.378-379. The feminine gender has been arbitrarily chosen for this translation.
39 Cf. Ambrose, *Expositio in Psalmos* 118.19B.
40 Cf. Claudian, *Phoenix* 24; 101.

She is herself indeed, but still not the same, and neither is the same herself, for she has acquired life eternal by the good of death.[41]

---
[41] Cf. Ovid, *Metam*. 15.170f.; also Tertullian, *De resurrectione carnis* 13.

APPENDIX

APPENDIX

Works Attributed to
Lactantius

a. On the Motions of the Soul—*De motibus animi*

The *Codex Ambrosianus* (formerly *Bobiensis*) of Milan, F 60 Sup. (8th or 9th century) contains a fragment which bears the marginal inscription: *Lactantius de motibus animi*. The fragment consists of but a few lines, the form and content of which suggest Lactantian authorship. It is likely that the author had a complete treatise on the subject, a complement to his *De opificio Dei*. The fragment follows.

The Fragment *On the Motions of the Soul of* Lactantius

Hope, fear, love, hate, joy, sadness, pleasure, desire, anger, compassion, zeal, admiration. These motions or affections of the soul have existed from the beginning of the creation of man by God. They are implanted in human nature for its full well-being and utility, so that, through their ordered and rational control, man might be able to exercise them in performing manfully the good acts of virtue, through which he might justly merit to receive everlasting life from God. For when these motions of the soul are restrained within their proper limits, that is, posited in good proportion, they prepare the good acts of virtue during the present life, and they prepare for the everlasting rewards of the future. When they flow beyond their measure, however, and swerve off into a bad proportion, vices and iniquitous acts arise, and these bring forth eternal punishments.

b. On the Passion of the Lord—*De passione Domini*

The poem, *De passione Domini,* On the Passion of the Lord, is no longer attributed to Lactantius; but, although the *De resurrectione* and *De pascha* are assigned to Venantius Fortunatus on the testimony of the oldest manuscripts, as yet no definite authorship has been assigned for the *De passione Domini.* It is very probably the work of a later writer, perhaps one of the Renaissance writers in Italy, even. Manitius,[1] however, holds for an early author. Because it has not been excluded from the Lactantian corpus by Brandt,[2] it has seemed best to include it among the present translations. Although it bears no resemblance to the genuine writings of Lactantius, the poem does express some profound religious sentiments.

---

1 M. Manitius, *Geschichte der christliche-lateinische Poesie,* p. 50.
2 Cf. *Prolegomena* to Part II, CSEL, Vol. 27, pp. xxii ff.

APPENDIX

Poem—at times attributed to Lactantius

On the Passion of the Lord

Whoever you are who come here and advance upon the threshold of the inner temple, stop but a little, and look upon Me, an innocent sufferer for your offense. Lay Me up in your mind; keep Me in your heart.[1]

I am He who, pitying the bitter misfortunes of men, came hither as the mediator of the peace that was promised and the complete atonement of the blame of all men.[2]

Here the brightest light from on high has been rendered to earth; here is a loving representation of salvation; here I am for you the rest, the right way, the true redemption, the ensign[3] of God, and the memorable mark of destiny.[4]

For your sake and for your life, I entered the womb of the Virgin, I was made man, and I suffered a horrible death; and rest I found not any place upon the earth, but everywhere threats and everywhere labors.

First of all, a rude hut in the land of Juda was a dwelling for Me at My birth, and for My Mother close to Me; here dry grass, spread in a narrow manger, gave to Me amid the slumbering beasts My first bed.

I passed My first years in the lands of the Pharaos, an exile from Herod's realm; and the remaining years, after My return

---

1 Cf. Venantius Fortunatus, *Carmina* 1.2.1; 10.5.1; also Philomusus, *Epitaphium Christi* 1.
2 Cf. Philomusus, *ibid.* 27-28; Prudentius, *Psychomachia* 1.
3 Cf. Prudentius, *Apotheosis* 448; Paulinus Petricordiae, *Vita S. Martini* 2.238; 248; 4.599; 5.154.
4 This is very probably to be interpreted in the Christian sense of predestination, although the Latin word *fatum* is used.

to Judea, I passed always in the company of fasting, even in that of extreme poverty itself and the lowliest conditions, ever directing by salubrious counsels the intentions of men to a pursuit of loving goodness, joining to this healthful teaching many manifest miracles.

Wherefore, impious Jerusalem, stirred up by mad cares,[5] and the bitter hatreds of envy, and blinded with rage,[6] dared to visit upon Me, though innocent, a bloody death by deadly torments upon a terrible cross.

And as I Myself wish to go through these things in greater detail, and if it pleases you to go through all My groanings with Me and to feel My pains, bring together before your mind the plots or the treacheries, and the wicked price of My innocent blood, and the pretended kiss of my disciple-friend, and the insults and contentions of the raging mob.

Besides, take the blows and the tongues made swift for accusation; fashion with your mind the witnesses, and the unspeakable judgment of blind Pilate, and the huge cross pressing into My shoulders and My wearied back, and My heavy steps to a wretched death.

Now behold Me, now indeed deserted, but having gone through the extremes of punishment, and lifted far from My beloved Mother; gaze upon Me from head to foot; behold My hair matted with blood;[7] My blood-stained neck under this very hair; and My head drained (of blood) by cruel thorns; and a stream of blood pouring down on all sides over My divine face.

Look upon My eyes, compressed and deprived of light, My smitten cheeks; behold My parched tongue poisoned with gall, and My countenance pale with death.

See My hands fastened with nails, and My arms extended, and also the great wound of My side; see the bloody flow from that wound and My feet that are dug, and My bloody legs.

---

5 Cf. Vergil, *Aeneid* 5.779.
6 Cf. *ibid.* 2.244; Philomusus 33.
7 Cf. Vergil, *Aeneid* 2.277; Cantalicius, *Contemplatio ad crucifixum* 7-8.

Bend your knee and with weeping adore the venerable wood[8] of the cross, and seeking the earth, drenched with innocent blood, pour out upon it tears flowing from a humble countenance, and bear Me and My counsels always in a devoted heart.

Follow the path of My life; consider both the torments that have been related and the severe death; and, recalling the innumerable pains of My body and soul, learn to endure hardships; and be vigilant for your own salvation.

These remembrances, whenever you shall be pleased to dwell upon them (if by any chance the faith that is genuine,[9] if the piety and grace worthy of My labors should arise in your mind), will be stimuli of real virtue; and they will be shields against the snares of the enemy, by which having been made keen in every contest you will be safe, and as victor you will bear the palm.

If these remembrances turn away your senses in love with a perishable world from the fleeting shadow of earthly beauty, they will bring it about that you will not venture, captivated by empty hope,[10] to confide in the perishable things of unstable fortune, or to hope in the passing years of this life.

Truly when you thus see these faltering things of earth, and when, through love of a better fatherland, you are deprived of the wealth of the world and the enjoyment of things, the devotions and prayers of the saints who have gone before[11] will extol you by holy customs and the hope of a blessed life, and will refresh you amid grievous pains with heavenly dew, and will feed you with the sweetness[12] of the promised good, until such time as the great grace of God calls your shining

---

8 Cf. Orientius, *De Trinitate* 49.
9 Cf. Vergil, *Aeneid* 3.434.
10 Cf. *ibid.* 11.49.
11 The author uses the word *priorum*, i.e., those who have gone before; it is an interesting view on the consoling doctrine of the communion of saints.
12 Cf. Sedulius, *Carmen Paschale* 1.150.

soul[13] back to regions above, your body being left behind after the last sufferings.[14]

Then freed from all labor, then happy in beholding the angelic choirs and the happy ranks of the saints, then in the delightful court of eternal peace your soul will reign with Me, happy forever.[15]

---

13 Cf. Vergil, *Aeneid* 9.349.
14 The Latin is *ultima fata*, the last fates.
15 Cf. Vergil, *Georgics* 4.90; Philomusus 49-50.

INDICES

GENERAL INDEX

Academicians, 87, 91.
Academy, 45.
Adam, 209.
Aeolus, 216.
affections, 63, 67, 72, 88, 96, 223; in God, 96-97, 98, 99.
Africa, 146, 209.
Alfoldi, A., 127, 128n., 144n., 197n.
anger, 60, 65, 68, 72, 74, 100-104, 108, 109, 113, 114, 153, 154, 168, 171, 173, 177, 186, 213, 226; absence of in God, 61, 64-65, 67, 68, 69, 101, 113; definition of, 102; incompatible with kindness, 64.
Antichrist, 140.
Apollo, 179, 213n.; of Miletus, 113, 151.
Aristoxenus, 48.
Armenia, 147.
Asclepius, 179.
Assyria, 135.
Athenians, 75.

Aristides, 106.
atoms, 77-79, 80, 81, 83.
augury, 148, 149, 150-151, 184.
Augusti, 133, 158, 162, 170, 178, 192.
Aurelian, 132, 143.
Aurora, 214.
Autun, 130.
avarice, 144, 146.

Babylon, 135.
Baynes, N. H., 129n., 135n., 182n., 183n., 190n.
beasts, condition of, 11-12; natural defenses, 8-9, 12; strength of, 12.
Bianco, B., 211.
birds, nature of, care of young, 11-12.
Bithynia, 3, 125, 149, 182, 192, 196.
Blaise, A., 7n., 30n., 35n., 92n., 180n.
Boak, A. E. R., 144n., 200n.
body, 6, 7, 10, 16, 35, 52, 83,

231

95, 105, 116, 228; the parts, 19, 23, 24, 26, 33, 34; arrangement of parts, 8, 18, 23, 26, 27, 30, 38; beauty of, 9, 10, 19, 23, 26, 31, 33-34, 42-43; composition of, 14; formation of parts, 18-19, 26-27, 30, 33, 36, 42, 107; functions of parts, 8, 18, 19, 21, 27, 31, 32, 34, 35-36, 43-44; inner organs, 23, 31, 35, 38, 39, 41, 200; purpose of parts, 21-22, 24, 36, 39, 43; utility of parts, 9, 19, 21, 23, 31, 34, 35; a vessel, 7, 17; weakness of, 13, 15.
bones, structure of, 19, 24, 25-28, 31.
Bosphorus, 128.
Brandt, S., x, 4, 122, 125, 210 n., 217n., 224.
breath, 36-37, 45.
Brett, Sister M. Catherine, 211.
bulk, of animals, 13.
Byzantium, 193.

Caenofrurium, 143.
Caesar, Tiberius, 138.
Caesarea, 128.
Caesars, 148, 151, 153, 158, 159, 160, 161, 163, 169, 170, 177.
Campania, 170.
Campus Martius, 178.
cancer, 178-179.
Candidianus, 163, 201.
Cantalicius, 226n.
Cappadocia, 196.

Carinus, 133.
Carpians, 141, 147.
Catulus, Quintus, 111.
census, 165-167, 169, 182.
Chalcedon, 182.
Christ, 200; death of, 226-227; monogram of, 191; passion of, 226-227; resurrection of, 139, 207.
Christensen, A., 142n.
Christianity, ix, 127; apology for, ix; efficacy of, ix.
Christians, 149, 150, 151, 153, 164, 165, 168, 181, 182, 183, 184, 194, 197, 198.
Church, 137-139, 140-141, 199, 203.
Cimon, 106.
Clymene, 7n.
coition, 40, 79.
conception, 39-41.
Constantia, 189n.
Constantine, 119, 125, 126, 127-131, 132, 133, 134, 137 n., 159, 160, 168-171, 173n., 174, 175, 178, 183, 188, 189-192, 195, 196, 197, 203n.
contio, 173.
Coppleston, F., 77n., 84n.
Crispus, 126.
Curio, 111.
Cynewulf, 211.

Dacia, 141, 147.
Dacians, 166.
Danube, 147, 159.
death, 14, 15-16, 48, 53, 96, 99, 110, 157, 164, 165, 167, 171, 176, 190, 196, 199, 200,

INDEX 233

213, 219, 220, 225; consequence of sickness, 14; dissolution of nature, 14; untimely, 14-17.
Deaths of Persecutors, authenticity, 122-125; date, 125-127; historical significance, 127-135; value of, 131-133.
Decius, 141.
DeLabriolle, P., 155n.
Delian League, 106n.
Demetrianus, 5, 55.
demons, 125, 135, 140, 149.
Deucalion, 213.
devil, 140, 155, 203.
Diagoras, 76, 84.
Diocles, 133, 147, 162, 173, 184, 202n.
Diocletian, 121, 122, 125-127, 132-134, 137n., 144, 145n., 147, 149, 150, 153, 156, 158, 159-162, 169n., 173n., 180n., 188, 189, 190, 203.
discipleship, meaning of, 156.
Divine Nature, 61, 68, 96.
Divine Plan, 21, 22, 31, 47, 75.
Divine Providence, 7, 10, 11, 14, 16, 17, 20-21, 22, 28, 59, 63, 66-67, 75, 76, 80, 82-85, 91, 93, 99, 131, 135; vindication of, 3.
Domitian, 140.
Donatus, 61, 110, 123, 137, 155, 181, 182n., 203.
Duff, J. W., and A. M. Duff, 211.

ears, 21-23, 26, 28, 31.
edict, 152-153; of Galerius, 180-181, 182; of Milan, 126, 132, 197n.; of prices, 145; of Sardica, 137n.
Egypt, 182, 219.
Egyptians, 87.
elements, of world, 95.
Elias, 140n.
eloquence, 56.
Empedocles, 51.
emperor, 178.
Ensslin, W., 188n.
Epicureanism, 79.
Epicureans, 59, 64n.
Epimetheus, 7n.
Ergenus, 195.
error, 62-63, 69, 70, 71.
Erythraea, 111.
Eve, 209.
evil, 65, 92, 101, 102, 104-106, 145, 150, 199; foreign to God, 65.
eyes, 8, 21-23, 26-27, 28, 29, 30, 31.

faith, 137, 156, 166, 227.
Fausta, 130, 171n., 175.
fear, 74, 84, 88, 89, 96, 113, 114, 116, 147-148, 199, 201, 213, 219.
feet, 18, 21, 23, 24, 29, 31.
fertility (reproduction), 9.
fetus, 39-40.
fire, as punishment, 152, 153, 164, 165, 217.
Fitzpatrick, M. C., 211.
Flaccinus, 155.
Flora, 218.
Franks, 174.
Freedman, H., 209n.

Gaetulians, 190.
Galerius, 121, 122, 125, 126, 129, 132, 133, 134, 147, 148 n., 149, 150, 153n., 159, 160, 162, 167, 168, 169, 170-173, 176, 177, 178, 182, 186.
Gallienus, 142n.
Gaul, 126, 130, 171, 172.
Gauls, 155, 173.
Gilson, E., 49n.
God, anger in, 96, 97, 98, 102, 105-114, 116, 120, 122, 125, 135, 143; Artificer, 3, 7, 8, 13, 15, 17, 30, 31, 33, 35, 42, 44, 45, 62, 83, 85, 89, 94, 107; denial of existence, 66-67, 76; enemies of, 138; existence of 59, 75; impassibility of, 59, 66, 110; Intelligence, 8, 27; judgment of, 107, 121, 167, 201, 202; kindness of, 64, 65, 67, 69, 70, 96; knowledge of, 73, 107, 115; law of, 105-106; Light of the Mind, 62; Messenger of, 63, 64; name of, 200; oneness of, 85-88; power of, 63, 65, 73, 98, 106, 109, 115, 138, 143, 191; Sense and Reason, 8, 87; sign of, 191; triumph of, 203; Vindicator of religion, 176.
Goguel, M., 104n., 181n.
Gollancz, I., 211n.
good, 65, 92, 104, 105, 150; highest, 93; opposition to evil, 69, 91-92, 93, 95.
Gordon, R. K., 211n.

Goths, 152.
Gregoire, H., 195n.
Guinagh, K. C., 176n.

hands, 13, 18-19, 31, 33-34.
head, 18, 23-24, 28, 31, 33.
Hebrews, 59.
Henoch, 140n.
Herculii, 203.
Herod, 225.
Higgins, M. G., 142n.
Hister, 157.
Holsapple, L. B., 133n., 168n., 171n., 190n., 194n., 197n.
honors, of public office, 152, 163, 165.

Iapetus, 7n.
ignorance, 61.
Illyricum, 159, 170.
impious, 138, 201.
India, 216.
information, letters of, 154, 159.
informers, 154, 159, 166, 185, 186.
insanity, 142, 143, 169.
Italy, 154, 171, 172; devastation of, 172.

Jerusalem, 226.
Jews, 138.
John of Antioch, 189n., 190n.
Jovii, 203.
Juda, 225.
Judas, 139.
Judea, 226.
Jupiter, 161, 194, 203.
justice, 63, 72-73, 74, 88, 94-95,

97, 104, 105, 115, 116, 139, 141, 154; Divine, 121, 125, 135.
kindness, in God, 64, 65, 67, 69, 70, 96.
Knipfing, J. R., 180n.
knowledge, 61, 72, 99, 177; lack of, 62; of God, 148.

Laubmann, G., x.
law, 102, 107, 145, 165; just, 99; necessity for, 95.
Leclercq, 207n.
Leroy, M., 211.
Leucippus, 77, 82, 84.
Licinius, 125-127, 131, 132, 134, 137n., 162, 163, 169n., 173, 177, 178, 182, 183n., 189, 192-197, 199-201, 203n.; proclamation of, 197-199.
Lietzmann, H., 152n.
life-principle, meaning of, 35, 36, 44, 49-51, 105; production of, 53-55.
Lucius Caelius (Caecilius) Firmianus, see Lactantius.
lust, 185, 186, 187.

man, eternal and immortal, 9; frailty of, 10-11, 12-17; image of God, 91; name of, 83; nature of, 73, 83, 223; origin of, 111; reason for creation, 94; upright position of, 25, 34, 71, 94, 107-108.
Manitius, M., 224.
Marcus Tullius, see Cicero.

Mars, 148.
Massilia, 174.
Mathias, 139.
Mattingly, H., 130n., 171n.
Maurice, J., 130n., 131n., 188 n.
Maxentius, 125, 132, 133, 134, 159, 169, 170, 172n., 189, 190, 194.
Maximian, 130, 133, 134, 154, 158, 159-161, 170, 173, 175, 186, 188, 189, 201, 203.
Maximin, 125, 127, 134, 178, 181, 182, 183n., 184, 188, 189, 192, 193, 194, 195, 196, 201; Maximin Daia, 125, 133, 134, 160-163, 169, 171, 173n., 177; Maximin Herculius, 127, 146, 171, 172, 173n.; Maximin the Thracian, 132.
Maximinus, 161.
Melos, 76.
Micka, E. F., 60.
Midrash-Rabbah, 209.
Milan, 192, 197, 223.
Miltiades, 106n.
Milvian Bridge, 183n., 190.
mind, 6, 22, 25-29, 46, 49, 52-53, 61, 62, 63, 71, 82, 83, 103, 104, 108, 116, 227; location of, 46, 47, 48.
Moesia, 141.
Moissac, 122.
Moors, 190.
Moreau, J., x, 122n., 124n., 132, 137n., 138n., 140n., 143 n., 149n., 151n., 155n., 156 n., 194n., 197n.

236 INDEX

mouth, 20, 23, 31, 36, 37.
mutilations, 183.

Narses, 147, 156n.
naturalists, 207.
nature, 10, 12, 15, 37, 82, 83, 92, 214.
Nazarius, 130.
neck, 23, 24, 33.
Nero, 122, 132, 139, 140.
Nerva, 158.
Nicaea, 187; Council of, 128.
Nicomedia, 125, 126, 132, 134, 145, 157, 181, 182, 196, 201, 209.
nose, 23, 30, 31, 37, 45.
Numerian, 133.
numismatics, 130-131.

Octavius, 111.
old age, 15, 16, 213.
Olympius, 215.
Optatian, 130.
Orient, 147, 148, 162, 196.
Orientius, 227n.
Orontes, 201.

panegyrics, 126, 130.
Paradise, 207, 209.
pardon, 100, 106, 182.
Parker, H. M. D., 144n.
passions, base, 146.
patience, 100, 104, 107, 108, 153.
Paul, Saint, 139.
Paulinus Petricordiae, 225n.
peace, 119, 137, 182, 195, 203; eternal, 228; of Milan, 121.
Pease, A. S., 4.

Perinth, 193.
Peripatetics, 75, 88, 100.
persecution, 3, 119, 122, 131-132, 134-135, 137-139, 141, 142, 148, 149, 152-155, 176, 194, 200.
persecutors, 138, 200.
Persians, 142, 147, 163.
Peter, Saint, 139.
Phaethon, 213n.
Pharaos, 225.
Phasis, 218.
philosophers, 3, 5, 8, 10, 27, 44, 46, 50, 56, 61, 62, 63, 64, 70-71, 75, 77, 84, 88, 93, 101, 106, 113, 114.
Phoebus, 214, 215, 218.
phoenix, 207-209, 214-217; appearance of, 218-219; beauty of, 218-219; symbolism of, 209, 210.
Pichon, R., 122, 210n.
Pilate, 226.
pillaging, 172, 176-177.
pleasure, 116.
prayer, 194, 195.
pride, 6.
principate, 163.
Prisca, 126, 154, 202n.
Priscillian, 155.
Prometheus, 7.
prophets, 110, 140.
Protagoras, 75.
providence, human, 72.
prudence, 6, 12, 94, 103.
punishment, 67, 99, 100-104, 107-109, 112, 114, 138, 139, 142, 143, 149, 164, 165, 175, 189, 202, 224.

INDEX 237

Pyrrha, 213n.
Pythagoras, 84, 85, 87.

Rand, E. K., 128n.
Rapisardi, E., 60.
ratio, a system or construction plan, 6, 38, 42.
Ravenna, 157, 170.
reason, 4, 8, 9, 11, 12, 16, 17, 24, 33, 45, 47, 64, 70, 71, 73, 81, 83, 85, 88, 92, 100, 110, 115; highest endowment of man, 3, 12-13; vindication of, ix.
religion, 59, 62, 71-75, 84-86, 88, 94, 141, 150, 151, 152, 168; destruction of, 59, 74, 87, 151; false, 63, 74, 87, 151.
Renaissance, 244.
rhetoric, 121.
Richmond, J. A., 171n.
Ritschl, 217n.
Romans, 112, 143, 166, 186, 191.
Rome, 130, 139, 145, 156, 157, 169, 170, 171, 190.
Romula, 147, 150n.
Romulus, 147.
Roscher, W. H., 207n., 219n.
Rosetti, L., 4.

Sacred Scripture, 151, 208, 209.
salvation, 65.
Sapor, 142.
Sarmatians, 152.
Sbordone, F., 207n., 208n.
Seeck, O., 126n.

Sellar, W. Y., 165n.
senses, 8, 29, 33, 45-46, 62, 104, 227; sharpness of, 44; truth of, 29.
Septuagint, 208.
Seston, W., 144n., 146n., 147n., 190n.
Seven Sages, 87.
Severianus, 201.
Severus, 133, 134, 160, 161, 163, 169, 170, 171, 173, 190, 201.
sex, diversity of, 25, 40-41; purpose of, 104.
sexual desire, 104.
Sibyl, Cumaean, 112.
sickness, of man, 14-17, 37, 157, 167, 213.
Simon, M., 209n.
sinews, 22.
sleep, nature of, 52-53, 99.
society, 17, 89, 115.
Socrates, 62, 75, 84, 87.
soul, 6, 7, 10, 16, 17, 47-48, 49, 51, 83, 95, 105, 116, 228; powers of, 71.
Spain, 146.
speech, 9, 13, 72; freedom of, 152.
spices, 216, 217.
spine, 18, 24, 43.
Stade, K., 134n.
statues and images, 168-169, 188-189, 192.
Stoics, 59, 64n., 67, 70n., 75, 88, 91, 92, 100, 104.
Strato, 76.
suffering, of man, 14, 16, 17.
Superbus, 173.

238   INDEX

superstition, 150.
Syria, 182, 188, 192, 215.

Tages, 149.
Talmud, 209.
Tarsus, 199.
Taurus Mountains, 199.
teeth, 23, 32-33.
Terminalia, 107n.
Theodora, 189n.
Theodorus, 76, 84.
Theologoi, 86.
Theophrastus, 47n.
Thessalonica, 202.
Thrace, 143.
Tiber, 192.
tongue, 13, 23, 32, 33, 37.
torment, 152-156, 163, 165, 166, 176, 186, 187, 200.
Trajan, 158, 166.
treachery, 175.
Treves, 130.
truth, 61-65, 69, 70, 74-76, 88, 91; ignorance of, 66, 71, 77.
two, fittingness of the number, 31.

Valeria, 126, 147n., 154, 186, 200, 201, 202.
Valerian, 142, 143, 147.

veins, 23, 28.
vengeance, 97, 100, 101; divine, 119-125, 138, 139-140, 141, 142, 178-179, 199-201.
Venus, 219.
Vestal Virgins, 187.
Vicennalia, 156, 157, 176.
virtue, 156; in God, 107.
voice, 32, 37, 44-45, 72.

walking, power of, 17-19.
wealth, 116.
Waszink, J. H., 35n.
wisdom, human, 5, 9, 12, 16, 17, 33, 62, 70, 71, 73, 74, 83, 91, 92, 93, 103, 110.
Workmanship of God, value of, 3-4.
world, destruction of, 140; governance of, 66, 83, 89, 99, 105, 131; origin of, 10, 16, 76-77, 80, 81, 87; plan of, 78, 80, 82; purpose of, 89-90, 91.
worship, 63, 73, 88, 112, 115.

Xenocrates, 48.

Zeno, 130, 171n., 175n., 189n.

INDEX OF CITATIONS

I. INDEX OF PAGAN AUTHORS

Ammianus Marcellinus, 129.
Anonymous, the of Valois, 129, 168n., 171n.
Antisthenes, 87.
Apollodorus, 111.
Archytas, 103, 104.
Aristonicus, 111.
Aristotle, 3, 39, 40n., 41n., 85, 88, 101, 166n.
Ausonius, 215n.

Chrysippus, 82.
Cicero, 3, 7, 10, 18, 25n., 26n., 32n., 41n., 46n., 48n., 50n., 56, 61n., 62n., 66, 71, 73n., 74, 75n., 76n., 77n., 82n., 84, 86, 87, 88n., 89n., 91n., 93n., 94, 99n., 100, 101n., 102, 103n., 110n., 121, 131, 216n.

Democritus, 82, 84.

Ennius, 86, 213n., 214n.

Epicurus, 10, 20, 21, 22, 28, 65-66, 67n., 73, 74, 75, 81n., 82, 84, 92, 93-96, 98-99.
Euhemerus, 86.
Eumenius, 130.

Fenestella, 111.

Hermes Trismegistus, 87, 208.
Herodotus, 207.
Hesiod, 207n.
Horace, 52n., 196n.

Josephus, 178n., 179n.
Julian, 129, 168n.

Livy, 155n.
Lucan, 214n.
Lucretius, 10n., 11, 14n., 20, 21n., 27-28, 32, 52n., 54, 73, 77, 78, 79, 133.

Marcus Aurelius, 132.

240 INDEX

Martial, 215n.

Ovid, 107, 112, 151n., 211, 213n., 214n., 215n., 216n., 217n., 218n., 219n., 220n.

Plato, 13, 45n., 48, 62, 75, 84, 87, 103.
Plautus, 175n.
Pliny, 165n., 215n., 216n., 218 n.
Plutarch, 13n., 18n., 91n.
Posidonius, 66, 101.
Porphyry, 113n.
Probus, 50n.

Seneca, 14n., 68n., 101, 103n., 176n.

Sibylline Oracles, 111, 112, 113, 140.

Tacitus, 121, 129, 215n.
Terence, 107n.

Valerius Maximus, 103n.
Varro, 3, 4, 18, 24n., 26, 30, 32, 39, 41, 43, 45n., 49n., 50, 111.
Vergil, 6, 26, 50n., 53, 72, 86, 90, 151, 155, 167n., 175, 176, 178, 179, 186n., 190n., 191, 213n., 214n., 215n., 216n., 219n., 226n., 227n., 228n.
Victor, Sextus Aurelius, 130.

Xenephon, 87.

II. INDEX OF CHRISTIAN AUTHORS

Ambrose, Saint, 210, 217n., 219n.
Aquinas, Saint Thomas, 55n., 92n.
Arnobius, 51n., 59, 181n.
Augustine, Saint, 4, 24n., 26n., 45n., 49n., 60, 139n., 151n.

Claudian, 211, 215n., 216n., 219n.
Clement of Rome, 210.
Cyprian, Saint, 41n., 69n.

Eusebius, 128, 129, 130, 131, 149n., 152n., 154n., 158n.,

168n., 178n., 179n., 180n., 181n., 182n., 183n., 185n., 190n., 191n., 192n., 196n., 197n., 199n., 203n.
Eutropius, 129, 175n.

Gregory of Tours, 210, 213n., 214n., 216n., 217n., 219n.

Isidore of Seville, 12n., 18n., 22n., 24n., 25n., 26n., 27n., 28n., 30n., 32n., 33n., 34n., 36n., 38n., 39n., 40n., 41n., 42n., 44n., 50n., 51n., 78n., 83n., 210.

INDEX 241

Jerome, Saint, 53n., 122, 123, 173n., 182n., 201n., 209.

Lactantius, ix, x, 3, 4, 5n., 7n., 9n., 14n., 25n., 35n., 48n., 49n., 52n., 53n., 59, 60, 63n., 92n., 94n., 113n., 115n., 119, 121, 122, 123, 124-134, 144n., 145n., 146n., 163n., 164n., 168n., 174n., 175n., 180n., 183n., 184n., 185n., 187n., 188n., 189n., 190n., 191n., 193n., 199n., 201n., 202n., 203n., 207-211, 217 n., 223, 224.

Minucius Felix, 9n., 75n., 76 n., 86n., 87n., 93n., 150n.

Origen, 181n.
Orosius, 175n., 180n., 190n.

Philomusus, 225n., 226n., 229 n.
Prudentius, 151n., 200n., 225 n.
Pseudo-Cyprian, 213n., 214n., 216n., 217n.

Rufinus, 53n., 180n.

Sedulius, 227n.
Sulpicius Severus, 139n.

Tertullian, 35n., 139n., 140n., 150n., 176n., 210n., 220n.

Venantius Fortunatus, 213n., 225n.
Victorinus Petavius, 140n.

Zosimus, 130, 171n., 175n., 189n.

III. INDEX OF HOLY SCRIPTURE

(Old Testament)

Job, 208-209.
Psalms, 109n., 208, 209.

Isaia, 120-121.
2 Machabees, 179n.

(New Testament)

Matthew, 95n., 208.
Mark, 139n.
Luke, 139n., 201n., 217n.
John, 135, 139n., 208.

Acts, 139n.
Ephesians, 109n.
Apocalypse, 200n., 214n.

THE FATHERS OF THE CHURCH SERIES

(A series of approximately 100 volumes when completed)

VOL. 1: THE APOSTOLIC FATHERS (1947)
    LETTER OF ST. CLEMENT OF ROME TO THE CORINTHIANS (trans. by Glimm)
    THE SO-CALLED SECOND LETTER (trans. by Glimm)
    LETTERS OF ST. IGNATIUS OF ANTIOCH (trans. by Walsh)
    LETTER OF ST. POLYCARP TO THE PHILIPPIANS (trans. by Glimm)
    MARTYRDOM OF ST. POLYCARP (trans. by Glimm)
    DIDACHE (trans. by Glimm)
    LETTER OF BARNABAS (trans. by Glimm)
    SHEPHERD OF HERMAS (1st printing only; trans. by Marique)
    LETTER TO DIOGNETUS (trans. by Walsh)
    FRAGMENTS OF PAPIAS (1st printing only; trans. by Marique)

VOL. 2: ST. AUGUSTINE (1947)
    CHRISTIAN INSTRUCTION (trans. by Gavigan)
    ADMONITION AND GRACE (trans. by Murray)
    THE CHRISTIAN COMBAT (trans. by Russell)
    FAITH, HOPE, AND CHARITY (trans. by Peebles)

VOL. 3: SALVIAN, THE PRESBYTER (1947)
    GOVERNANCE OF GOD (trans. by O'Sullivan)
    LETTERS (trans. by O'Sullivan)
    FOUR BOOKS OF TIMOTHY TO THE CHURCH (trans. by O'Sullivan)

VOL. 4: ST. AUGUSTINE (1947)
    IMMORTALITY OF THE SOUL (trans. by Schopp)
    MAGNITUDE OF THE SOUL (trans. by McMahon)
    ON MUSIC (trans. by Taliaferro)

ADVANTAGE OF BELIEVING (trans. by Sr. Luanne Meagher)
ON FAITH IN THINGS UNSEEN (trans. by Deferrari and Sr. Mary Francis McDonald)

VOL. 5: ST. AUGUSTINE (1948)
THE HAPPY LIFE (trans. by Schopp)
ANSWER TO SKEPTICS (trans. by Kavanagh)
DIVINE PROVIDENCE AND THE PROBLEM OF EVIL (trans. by Russell)
SOLILOQUES (trans. by Gilligan)

VOL. 6: ST. JUSTIN MARTYR (1948)
FIRST AND SECOND APOLOGY (trans. by Falls)
DIALOGUE WITH TRYPHO (trans. by Falls)
EXHORTATION AND DISCOURSE TO THE GREEKS (trans. by Falls)
THE MONARCHY (trans. by Falls)

VOL. 7: NICETA OF REMESIANA (1949)
WRITINGS (trans. by Walsh and Monohan)
SULPICIUS SEVERUS
WRITINGS (trans. by Peebles)
VINCENT OF LERINS
COMMONITORIES (trans. by Morris)
PROSPER OF AQUITANE
GRACE AND FREE WILL (trans. by O'Donnell)

VOL. 8: ST. AUGUSTINE (1950)
CITY OF GOD, Bks. I-VII (trans. by Walsh, Zema; introduction by Gilson)

VOL. 9: ST. BASIL (1950)
ASCETICAL WORKS (trans. by Sr. M. Monica Wagner)

VOL. 10: TERTULLIAN (1950)
APOLOGETICAL WORKS (vol. I), (trans. by Arbesmann, Sr. Emily Joseph Daly, Quain)
MINUCIUS FELIX
OCTAVIUS (trans. by Arbesmann)

VOL. 11: ST. AUGUSTINE (1951)
COMMENTARY ON THE LORD'S SERMON ON THE MOUNT WITH SEVENTEEN RELATED SERMONS (trans. by Kavanagh)

VOL. 12: ST. AUGUSTINE (1951)
LETTERS 1-82 (vol. 1), (trans. by Sr. Wilfrid Parsons)
VOL. 13: ST. BASIL (1951)
LETTERS 1-185 (vol. 1), (trans. by Deferrari and Sr. Agnes Clare Way)
VOL. 14: ST. AUGUSTINE (1952)
CITY OF GOD, Bks. VIII-XVI (trans. by Walsh and Mtr. Grace Monahan)
VOL. 15: EARLY CHRISTIAN BIOGRAPHIES (1952)
LIFE OF ST. CYPRIAN BY PONTIUS (trans. by Deferrari and Sr. Mary Magdeleine Mueller)
LIFE OF ST AMBROSE, BISHOP OF MILAN, BY PAULINUS (trans. by Lacy)
LIFE OF ST. AUGUSTINE BY POSSIDIUS (trans. by Deferrari and Sr. Mary Magdeleine Mueller)
LIFE OF ST. ANTHONY BY ST. ATHANASIUS (trans. by Sr. Mary Emily Keenan)
LIFE OF ST. PAUL, THE FIRST HERMIT; LIFE OF ST. HILARION; LIFE OF MALCHUS, THE CAPTIVE MONK (trans. by Sr. Marie Liguori Ewald)
LIFE OF EPIPHANIUS BY ENNODIUS (trans. by Sr. Genevieve Marie Cook)
A SERMON ON THE LIFE OF ST. HONORATUS BY ST. HILARY (trans. by Deferrari)
VOL. 16: ST. AUGUSTINE (1952) —Treatises on Various Subjects:
THE CHRISTIAN LIFE, LYING, THE WORK OF MONKS, THE USEFULNESS OF FASTING (trans. by Sr. M. Sarah Muldowney)
AGAINST LYING (trans. by Jaffee)
CONTINENCE (trans. by Sr. Mary Francis McDonald)
PATIENCE (trans. by Sr. Luanne Meagher)
THE EXCELLENCE OF WIDOWHOOD (trans. by Sr. M. Clement Eagan)
THE EIGHT QUESTIONS OF DULCITIUS (trans. by Mary DeFerrari)
VOL. 17: ST. PETER CHRYSOLOGUS (1953)
SELECTED SERMONS (trans. by Ganss)
ST. VALERIAN
HOMILIES (trans. by Ganss)

VOL. 18: ST. AUGUSTINE (1953)
 LETTERS 83-130 (vol. 2), (trans. by Sr. Wilfrid Parsons)

VOL. 19: EUSEBIUS PAMPHILI (1953)
 ECCLESIASTICAL HISTORY, Bks. 1-5 (trans. by Deferrari)

VOL. 20: ST. AUGUSTINE (1953)
 LETTERS 131-164 (vol. 3), (trans. by Sr. Wilfrid Parsons)

VOL. 21: ST. AUGUSTINE (1953)
 CONFESSIONS (trans. by Bourke)

VOL. 22: ST. GREGORY OF NAZIANZEN and ST. AMBROSE (1953)
 FUNERAL ORATIONS (trans. by McCauley, Sullivan, McGuire, Deferrari)

VOL. 23: CLEMENT OF ALEXANDRIA (1954)
 CHRIST, THE EDUCATOR (trans. by Wood)

VOL. 24: ST. AUGUSTINE (1954)
 CITY OF GOD, Bks. XVII-XXII (trans. by Walsh and Honan)

VOL. 25: ST. HILARY OF POITIERS (1954)
 THE TRINITY (trans. by McKenna)

VOL. 26: ST. AMBROSE (1954)
 LETTERS 1-91 (trans. by Sr. M. Melchior Beyenka)

VOL. 27: ST. AUGUSTINE (1955) —Treatises on Marriage and Other Subjects:
 THE GOOD OF MARRIAGE (trans. by Wilcox)
 ADULTEROUS MARRIAGES (trans. by Huegelmeyer)
 HOLY VIRGINITY (trans. by McQuade)
 FAITH AND WORKS, THE CREED, IN ANSWER TO THE JEWS (trans. by Sr. Marie Liguori Ewald)
 FAITH AND THE CREED (trans. by Russell)
 THE CARE TO BE TAKEN FOR THE DEAD (trans. by Lacy)
 THE DIVINATION OF DEMONS (trans. by Brown)

VOL. 28: ST. BASIL (1955)
 LETTERS 186-368 (vol. 2), (trans. by Sr. Agnes Clare Way)

VOL. 29: EUSEBIUS PAMPHILI (1955)
ECCLESIASTICAL HISTORY, Bks. 6-10 (trans. by Deferrari)

VOL. 30: ST. AUGUSTINE (1955)
LETTERS 165-203 (vol. 4), (trans. by Sr. Wilfrid Parsons)

VOL. 31: ST. CAESARIUS OF ARLES (1956)
SERMONS 1-80 (vol. 1), (trans. by Sr. Mary Magdeleine Mueller)

VOL. 32: ST. AUGUSTINE (1956)
LETTERS 204-270 (vol. 5), (trans. by Sr. Wilfrid Parsons)

VOL. 33: ST. JOHN CHRYSOSTOM (1957)
HOMILIES 1-47 (vol. 1), (trans. by Sr. Thomas Aquinas Goggin)

VOL. 34: ST. LEO THE GREAT (1957)
LETTERS (trans. by Hunt)

VOL. 35: ST. AUGUSTINE (1957)
AGAINST JULIAN (trans. by Schumacher)

VOL. 36: ST. CYPRIAN (1958)
TREATISES (trans. by Deferrari, Sr. Angela Elizabeth Keenan, Mahoney, Sr. George Edward Conway)

VOL. 37: ST. JOHN OF DAMASCUS (1958)
FOUNT OF KNOWLEDGE, ON HERESIES, THE ORTHODOX FAITH (trans. by Chase)

VOL. 38: ST. AUGUSTINE (1959)
SERMONS ON THE LITURGICAL SEASONS (trans. by Sr. M. Sarah Muldowney)

VOL. 39: ST. GREGORY THE GREAT (1959)
DIALOGUES (trans. by Zimmerman)

VOL. 40: TERTULLIAN (1959)
DISCIPLINARY, MORAL, AND ASCETICAL WORKS (trans. by Arbesmann, Quain, Sr. Emily Joseph Daly)

VOL. 41: ST. JOHN CHRYSOSTOM (1960)
HOMILIES 48-88 (vol. 2), (trans. by Sr. Thomas Aquinas Goggin)

VOL. 42: ST. AMBROSE (1961)
HEXAMERON, PARADISE, AND CAIN AND ABEL (trans. by Savage)

VOL. 43: PRUDENTIUS (1962)
POEMS (vol. 1), (trans. by Sr. M. Clement Eagan)

VOL. 44: ST. AMBROSE (1963)
THEOLOGICAL AND DOGMATIC WORKS (trans. by Deferrari)

VOL. 45: ST. AUGUSTINE (1963)
THE TRINITY (trans. by McKenna)

VOL. 46: ST. BASIL (1963)
EXEGETIC HOMILIES (trans. by Sr. Agnes Clare Way)

VOL. 47: ST. CAESARIUS OF ARLES (1964)
SERMONS 81-186 (vol. 2), (trans. by Sr. Mary Magdeleine Mueller)

VOL. 48: ST. JEROME (1964)
HOMILIES 1-59 (vol. 1), (trans. by Sr. Marie Liguori Ewald)

VOL. 49: LACTANTIUS (1964)
THE DIVINE INSTITUTES, Bks. I-VII (trans. by Sr. Mary Francis McDonald)

VOL. 50: OROSIUS (1964)
SEVEN BOOKS AGAINST THE PAGANS (trans. by Deferrari)

VOL. 51: ST. CYPRIAN (1965)
LETTERS (trans. by Sr. Rose Bernard Donna)

VOL. 52: PRUDENTIUS (1965)
POEMS (vol. 2), (trans. by Sr. M. Clement Eagan)

VOL. 53: ST. JEROME (1965)
DOGMATIC AND POLEMICAL WORKS (trans. by John N. Hritzu)

VOL. 54: LACTANTIUS (1965)
THE MINOR WORKS (trans. by Sr. Mary Francis McDonald)

www.ingramcontent.com/pod-product-compliance
Lightning Source LLC
Chambersburg PA
CBHW032032290426
44110CB00012B/766